Wildlife of Australia

Iain Campbell and Sam Woods

PRINCETON UNIVERSITY PRESS

PRINCETON AND OXFORD

PRINCETON  POCKET GUIDES

Wildlife of Australia, by Iain Campbell and Sam Woods

Wildlife of East Africa, by Martin B. Withers and David Hosking

Wildlife of the Galápagos, by Julian Fitter, Daniel Fitter, and David Hosking

Wildlife of Southern Africa, by Martin B. Withers and David Hosking

Coral Reef Fishes: Indo-Pacific and Caribbean, Revised Edition, by Ewald Lieske and Robert Myers

A Field Guide to the Birds of New Zealand, by Julian Fitter

The Kingdon Pocket Guide to African Mammals, by Jonathan Kingdon

Mammals of China, edited by Andrew T. Smith and Yan Xie

Reptiles and Amphibians of East Africa, by Stephen Spawls, Kim M. Howell, and Robert C. Drewes

Copyright © 2013 by Princeton University Press
Published by Princeton University Press, 41 William Street, Princeton, New Jersey 08540
In the United Kingdom: Princeton University Press, 6 Oxford Street, Woodstock, Oxfordshire OX20 1TW

nathist.princeton.edu

Library of Congress Cataloging-in-Publication Data

Campbell, Iain, 1969–.
  Wildlife of Australia / Iain Campbell and Sam Woods.
    pages cm. — (Princeton pocket guides)
  Includes bibliographical references and index.
  ISBN 978-0-691-15353-7 (pbk. : alk. paper)
  1. Vertebrates—Australia—Identification. I. Woods, Sam, 1971– II. Title.

  QL606.58.A8C36 2013
  590.994—dc23   2012035655

British Library Cataloging-in-Publication Data is available

This book has been composed in Minion Pro

Printed on acid-free paper. ∞

Printed in Thailand

10 9 8 7 6 5 4 3 2 1

CONTENTS

PREFACE AND ACKNOWLEDGMENTS

The aim of this book is to give people visiting the most popular tourist areas of Australia a chance at identifying the animals they are most likely to see. Species have been selected drawing on Iain's extensive experience throughout the continent growing up in Australia, and spending long hours in the bush, and Sam's many trips Down Under over the past six years. Special emphasis has been given to species that are readily found in widely visited areas such as Kakadu National Park, Ayers Rock, the Great Barrier Reef, the Atherton Tablelands, Lamington National Park, the Blue Mountains, the Dandenong Ranges, southwestern Western Australia, and Tasmania. For more detailed information on these species, please refer to the more comprehensive guides listed in the bibliography. Decisions on species inclusion within the guide were based not on species abundance but on the likelihood of seeing the species. For example, Little Kingfisher, although generally considered a scarce Australian bird, has been included, as it is regularly encountered in Kakadu National Park.

The authors owe thanks to many people who helped in many ways in the production of this book. They would especially like to thank the following people: Nick Athanas, Keith Barnes, Glen Inghram, Nick Leseberg, Alan McBride, Tony Palliser, and Brett Taylor for their invaluable advice and continuing support during the production process. Iain also would like to thank Sue Post and Michael Jeffords for their infinite tolerance and fun while obtaining many of the photos in this guide, and Donna Reggett for logistical support in Australia. Iain and Sam would also like to extend thanks to all at Tropical Birding Tours who aided in various ways during the production. Lastly, Iain would like to extend gratitude to his wife, Cristina, and his children, Gabriel and Amy, for their patience and understanding during the long nights of working on this project.

VEGETATION ASSO

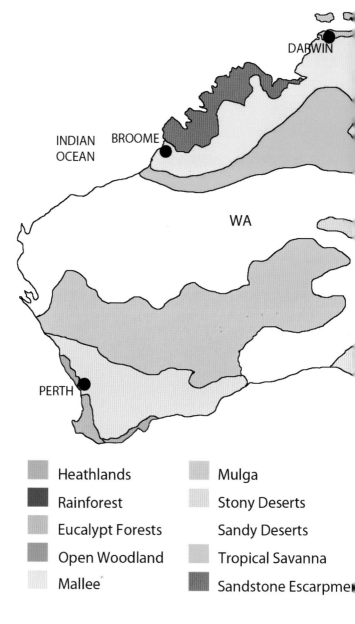

DARWIN

INDIAN
OCEAN

BROOME

WA

PERTH

	Heathlands		Mulga
	Rainforest		Stony Deserts
	Eucalypt Forests		Sandy Deserts
	Open Woodland		Tropical Savanna
	Mallee		Sandstone Escarpme

ONS OF AUSTRALIA

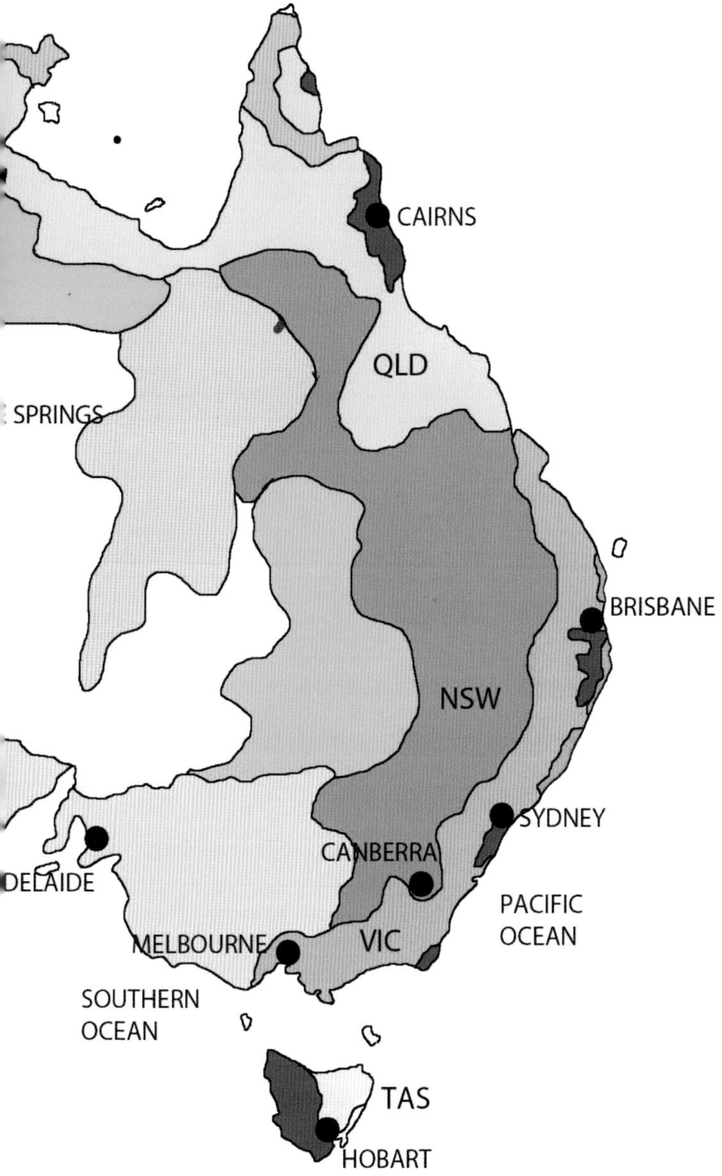
CAIRNS
QLD
SPRINGS
BRISBANE
NSW
SYDNEY
CANBERRA
DELAIDE
PACIFIC
OCEAN
MELBOURNE
VIC
SOUTHERN
OCEAN
TAS
HOBART

HABITATS

A. Sandy Cays and Barrier Reefs

Australia has two large barrier reef systems, one of which is located along the northwest Australian coastline, which is inaccessible and rarely visited. The other, the Great Barrier Reef, extends from east of Cape York Peninsula in ne. QLD, south to Gladstone in c. QLD. Parts of this massive reef system are very accessible and therefore are some of the most popular tourist attractions in the country. In a very few localities within this large system the coral sands have become concentrated to form small sparsely vegetated sandy cays, or islands. These remote cays are incredibly important for seabird colonies, as they provide safe areas free from land predators. In 2011 one of these well-visited islands, 4-acre Michaelmas Cay, near Cairns, held 160,000 breeding seabirds. More than thirty seabird species have been recorded there, with Sooty Terns and Brown Noddies providing the greatest number of nesting birds in the colony. Other species regularly seen around there include Great Crested, Lesser Crested, Little, Bridled, and Black-naped Terns; Great Frigatebirds; and Brown Boobies.

B. Mangrove

An intertidal wooded habitat concentrated on the north and northeast coastlines of Australia. More than twenty species of mangrove occur in the Cape York Peninsula (in the far northeast), and only a handful of species extend as far as NSW near the southern limit of the habitat. Forest formation varies from monotypic clusters to tall forests with multiple, well-developed stories (i.e., canopy, midstory, and understory), all of which have a muddy substrate with conspicuous lenticels (emergent roots). Good mangrove systems can be found around Darwin, Brisbane, and Cairns, which have boardwalks that allow access to birds such as Australian Yellow White-eye, Collared Kingfisher, Mangrove Honeyeater, Large-billed Gerygone, and Little Kingfisher. In general, mangroves are well protected, owing to their inaccessibility, except in eastern Australia, where there has been extensive clearing for tourist development (e.g., Surfer's Paradise and the Gold Coast, QLD).

C. Coastlines

Most of western, southern, and southeastern Australia (including TAS) is dominated by rocky coastlines and clean sandy beaches. The beaches tend to be dominated by shorebirds such as Pied Oystercatcher and Whimbrel, and in habituated parts of Australia are very prone to human disturbance. This has had an adverse effect on sensitive birds such as Hooded Plover. Rocky coastlines are less prone to human disturbance and therefore provide refuge for species such as fur seals, nesting Sooty Oystercatchers, and colonies of Black-faced Cormorants. Rocky headlands are also good places to look for pelagic species such as whales, albatrosses, and shearwaters.

A. Alpine Heath

Alpine heath occurs along the mountain ridges, above the tree line, from Lamington National Park (QLD) south to, and including, TAS. This habitat generally comprises waist- to head-high dense shrubs, with occasional scattered trees. Good examples are found at Barren Grounds (NSW), Snowy Mountains (NSW), and Cradle Mountain National Park and Mount Wellington on Tasmania. Although alpine heath is generally low in species diversity, and few species are restricted to this habitat, some of them are more abundant or conspicuous there, such as Beautiful Firetail, Flame Robin, Striated Heathwren, and Yellow-tailed Black-Cockatoo. Some rarer species are found only in this habitat, such as the scarce and secretive Eastern Bristlebird, and Corroboree Frog.

B. Coastal Heath

A widespread habitat that extends from north of Perth all the way around the south coast to c. QLD that grows on sand-dominated soils. The most extensive examples can be found where there is a strong Mediterranean climate, such as s. NSW, TAS, and southernmost WA. In general appearance and structure, coastal heath is similar to alpine heath, but the former is much more diverse in terms of both plant and animal life. Although the climate is often wet in these areas, the plants show adaptations to avoid desiccation in these windy environments. Banksias are common, but in *shrub form*, such as *Banksia eriquofolia* and *Banksia serrate*, which are very important for nectarivorous birds like honeyeaters. Reptiles that can be expected in this habitat include Red-bellied Black-Snake, Death Adders, Short-beaked Echidna, Red-necked Wallaby, and Rufous-bellied Pademelon. Typical birds from this habitat include Swamp Harrier, New Holland Honeyeater, White-cheeked Honeyeater, Little Wattlebird, and Red-eared Firetail (in WA only).

C. Coastal Scrub

Essentially a denser, more forestlike form of coastal heath. It generally forms in microenvironments *within* coastal heaths, where there is greater protection from wind, and in local areas with higher clay content in the soil. Coastal scrub is dominated by banksias in *tree form* such as *Banksia intergefolia*. Inside these small enclaves of microhabitat it genuinely feels lush and rainforest-like, as reflected in the bird and animal community. Eastern Yellow Robin, Lewin's Honeyeater, Spangled Drongo, Blue-tongued Skink, and Brown Snakes are found there, all of which are less abundant in the surrounding heath.

A. Tropical Rainforest

Tropical rainforest is confined to a small coastal area of Cape York Peninsula and a more extensive area known as the Wet Tropics in the Cairns region of ne. QLD. It is characterized by a large variety of evergreen trees that form a thick canopy and a relatively open understory, owing to poor light penetration. It appears much like the picture postcard images of rainforest in the tropics of the world, such as that found in New Guinea, Borneo, and the Amazon. The animal life is highly specialized, often found only in this habitat, and shows a greater affinity with the island of New Guinea to the north than it does with the drier regions through the rest of Australia. Indeed, some bird species are even migratory between Australia and New Guinea, such as Buff-breasted Paradise-Kingfisher, Chestnut-breasted Cuckoo, Channel-billed Cuckoo, and Red-bellied Pitta. Other spectacular resident birds and families that are representative of New Guinea forests include the mighty Southern Cassowary, Noisy Pitta, and Spotted Catbird. Mammals are represented by some very distinct species, such as Striped Possum, Lumholtz's Tree Kangaroo, Musky Rat-Kangaroo, Red-legged Pademelon, Spectacled Flying Fox, and the possumlike cuscus. Reptiles and amphibians are also well represented by Jungguy Tree Frog, velvet geckos, and Boyd's Forest Dragon. Good examples of this habitat include the Daintree/Cape Tribulation area of QLD.

B. Montane Rainforest

Also known as subtropical rainforest, it occurs in the high mountains of the Atherton Tablelands (ne. QLD) and continues in isolated pockets southward into c. NSW. In the south of this range it occurs at lower elevations than in the warmer north, being found right down to the coast around n. NSW (e.g., the Big Scrub). This habitat has undergone extensive clearing for timber production, cane farming, and dairy farming, and only very small pockets now remain. Good examples of this habitat can be found around the Atherton Tablelands in Curtain Fig, Mount Lewis, Mount Hypipamee National Park, and Lake Barrine; and in s. QLD at Lamington National Park. Lowland remnants occur around the Mount Warning/ Murwillumbah in n. NSW. Some of the animals represented in this habitat include Victoria's Riflebird, Australian Logrunner, Chowchilla, Regent Bowerbird, Green Catbird, Great Barred Frog, Lesueur's Frog, Mountain Brushtail Possum, and Red-legged Pademelon.

C. Tropical Palm Forest

A microhabitat within rainforests, including both tropical and montane rainforests. Although the microhabitat looks highly distinctive in terms of plant life, the animal life is very similar to that found in the surrounding rainforests. In n. QLD it can be a good place to find Striped Possum, Northern Brown Bandicoot, Orange-footed Scrubfowl, Papuan Frogmouth, and Carpet Python. In s. QLD and n. NSW, such as on Mount Tamborine, tropical palm forests can be good places to search for Albert's Lyrebird and Marbled Frogmouth. Probably the most accessible patch of this kind of forest can be found within the Centenary Lakes complex within Cairns.

A., B., and C. Wet Eucalypt Forests

Eucalypt forests are also known as sclerophyl forests. They are found from coastal e. QLD to VIC, all over TAS, and in sw. WA. Although very variable, these forests share the characteristic of being dominated by several tall eucalypt canopy species and having an understory of many other plant families. Viewed from a distance the forest looks very different from rainforest, but the distinction can be gradual, with rainforest within the gullies and eucalypt on the ridges. Up close the understory plant composition can be similar to that of rainforests, with some of the same species represented—and therefore similar animals as well—but the canopy is much more open, because it comprises straighter, slimmer-trunked trees that bear smaller leaves, which leads to a more extensive, denser understory than in the well-shaded rainforests. Therefore, in some areas (e.g., Mount Lewis, QLD) the distinction between wet eucalypt forest and rainforest is gradual and inconspicuous. Furthermore, so-called rainforests of Tasmania (photo A), are in fact largely wet eucalypt forests with some rainforest species represented in the understory and canopy. In the Blue Mountains of NSW (photo B) and the jarrah forests of sw. WA (photo C) the distinction is far clearer, with massive stands of monotypic eucalypt canopy trees, little midstory, and a thick understory. Birds typical of these highly variable environments include Superb Lyrebird, Scarlet Robin, Superb Fairywren, Eastern Spinebill, Yellow Wattlebird, and Black-headed Honeyeater. The classic wet eucalypt forest animal is the Koala, with others such as Platypus, Common Wombat, Common Ringtail Possum, and Red-necked Wallaby also occurring, in addition to the distinctive Pink-tongued Skink.

A. Karri Forest

Karri is a very distinctive type of wet eucalypt forest that is confined to extreme southwestern WA. Karri trees are a truly massive eucalypt species and are the largest of all Australian trees. Karri is also one of the tallest hardwood trees on Earth. This kind of forest is literally dominated by this one large tree species, making it a very striking habitat, characterized by the karris' enormous trunks, with few branches present except at the very highest levels, no midstory, and a sparse understory dominated by wattle trees (acacia). On the ground the prevalent cover is provided by ferns. Karri forest is generally depauperate in terms of animal species, although some western bird specialties can be found there, like Western Spinebill, Western Yellow Robin, and Western Thornbill, as well as more widespread species such as White-cheeked Honeyeater. These forests are centered on Pemberton in sw. WA.

B. Open Eucalypt Forest

These forests are found bordering wet habitats (including wet eucalypt forest, rainforest, and heaths) inland from the coast in a broad arc covering eastern and southern Australia, but are absent from the exceptionally dry areas of the south around the Great Australia Bight. (i.e., all of eastern Australia around to Adelaide, and then again from Esperance around to Perth). Any drive between Brisbane and Melbourne will be spent mostly in this habitat. A very open wooded habitat, with scattered trees, usually dominated by just a few slim-trunked eucalypt trees. It also generally has an extensive grassy understory. This is the habitat generally pictured when tourists think of the classic Aussie bush scene. It has been extensively cleared for sheep farming. This is a very diverse habitat with many animals, including Koala, Euro, Whiptail Wallaby, Peron's Tree Frog, Eastern Brown Snake, and Eastern Striped Skink, to name but a few. Birds found there include Spotted Pardalote, Glossy Black Cockatoo, Scarlet Honeyeater, Crested Shrike-Tit, Gray Butcherbird, and the familiar Noisy Miner.

C. Monsoon Forest

Dense forests found only on the coastal extremities of northern Australia that grow in areas with pronounced dry and wet seasons, and shed their leaves during the dry season. They occur in four distinct localities: most often along dry creek beds in dry terrains (Howard Springs, NT); along sandstone escarpments (Nourlangie Rock, Kakadau NP); in low-lying areas along the coast (East Point, Darwin), and around the Gulf of Carpentaria and the Cape York Peninsula within shallow, almost indiscernible, broad depressions. Monsoon forests are characterized by a thick canopy, although they are generally shorter overall than tropical rainforests, and have a shady, vine-dominated, open understory with a deep and extensive layer of leaf litter. Birds typical of this restricted habitat include the gorgeous Rainbow Pitta, Buff-sided Robin, and the striking but localized Black-banded Fruit-Dove (found only around escarpments). In the Cape York Peninsula, where these areas are found in depressions, the species composition reflects that found in the surrounding rainforest, such as Magnificent Riflebird, Fawn-breasted Bowerbird, Yellow-billed Kingfisher, and Green-backed Honeyeater. All these species are rare and local and restricted to Cape York Peninsula.

A. Tropical Wetland

These are large expanses of water, often containing mats of floating vegetation—sometimes bordered by reeds in shallow areas, and pandanus where there are steeper banks—found in the humid tropical regions of northern and northeastern Australia. Lilies are a major component, so this habitat is important for Comb-crested Jacanas, often referred to as "Lily-trotters," as well as Magpie-Geese and Green Pygmy-Geese. Massive congregations of Magpie-Geese can occur in such areas, numbering in the tens of thousands. Close inspection of pandanus can reveal Northern Water Dragon. pandanus also provides an important nesting habitat for Crimson Finch. Many of these wetland areas are temporal (e.g., Marmuluk in Kakadu NP), containing water only in the December to April wet season, while others are permanent, like Mareeba Wetlands in QLD and Yellow Waters Billabong in Kakadu National Park, which has water year-round. Artificial wetlands like Fogg Dam in the NT provide a similar habitat. These are very important for waterbirds especially, and in some areas (e.g., Yellow Waters) they provide great opportunities for exploring by boat, where kingfishers, cranes, herons, egrets, whistling-ducks, and dotterels can be seen congregating in significant numbers and feeding alongside spectacular wildlife such as Australia's most feared predator, the Estuarine Crocodile.

B. Temperate Billabong

These permanent oxbow lakes in temperate Australia lack the floating vegetation of their tropical counterparts and therefore often hold a mix of species different from that found in tropical wetlands. Waterbirds are often the most visible wildlife in these areas, where congregations of ibis, ducks, rails, herons, and shorebirds occur. The composition of these groups may be quite different from that found in tropical wetlands, however. For example, few whistling-ducks are seen, although temperate duck species such as Blue-billed, and Musk Ducks, and Australian Shoveler can be found along with others such as Red-necked Avocet and Yellow-billed Spoonbill. In inland Australia the borders of these wetlands are dominated by Red River Gums, and it is this tree that forms a crucial habitat for hole-nesting birds in the region such as Superb Parrot, the yellow form of Crimson Rosella, Regent Parrot, Pink Cockatoo, and White-browed and Masked Woodswallows. Barking Owls and Southern Boobooks also often are found at their highest concentrations in these areas with abundant nesting sites. Because such areas are important water sources for animals, a variety of wallabies and other mammals may be seen around dawn and dusk in such areas.

C. Inland Dry River

Inland dry rivers can also comprise a significant component of Red River Gums and therefore can be similar to temperate billabongs (see preceding section); however, they rarely contain water. Some flow for short periods only every few years. Thus these habitats are of little importance for waterbirds and as local sources of water for animals, although they retain their importance for hole-nesting bird species. They occur throughout inland Australia.

A. Open Woodland

A mixed woodland that usually comprises acacias, cypress pines, and eucalypts, although generally with no dominant canopy species. It is often disheveled looking with trees of varying heights and a great variety of tree species and tree forms—some multistemmed, others single-trunked. The canopy is not closed, and there is a significant development of the midstory. Although there is little understory, usually there is a substantial cover of grasses on the ground, with minimal leaf litter. As this habitat is so varied, it takes many different forms, and many different names are applied to it. The most common form is known as Brigalow, found in c. NSW up to c.s. QLD. This habitat is diverse in terms of animal life, with birds such as Western Gerygone, Varied Sittella, and Yellow-rumped Thornbill, as well as reptiles like Eastern Bearded Dragon and Burn's Dragon. Mammals are represented by Eastern Gray Kangaroo, and Feral Pigs are a prominent pest there.

B. Mallee

Mallee is a localized type of scrublike woodland dominated by a few mallee species of eucalypts and forms a distinctive structure. It is a dangerously uniform habitat, in which it is remarkably easy to get lost, comprising medium-height (3–6 m/10–20 ft high), multi-stemmed eucalypts that grow out from the base in a coppice-like fashion. Although appearing impenetrable from the edges, mallee is quite open when within it and easy to walk in, as there is limited understory, and the ground is flat and open, with a scattering of tinder-dry leaf litter that is neither deep or extensive. Mallee is found around the southern coast of Australia but also substantially inland in areas with a Mediterranean climate, with little rain in the winter (April to August) and almost no rain through summer. Mallee occurs in flat, very sandy, soils. In terms of plant life it is depauperate, as few other species are able to grow in this stressed sandy and dry environment. Much of the wildlife that occurs is specialized to this habitat. Notable bird species include Malleefowl, Chestnut Quail-Thrush, Red-lored Whistler, Purple-gaped Honeyeater, Black-eared Miner, and Shy Heathwren. Many reptile species are found only there, and although Shingleback can be found in other habitats, it is often abundant in mallee. Mallee has become severely fragmented from the pressures of wheat farming, although large tracts still exist in VIC (e.g., Little Desert NP) and SA (e.g., Gluepot Reserve).

C. Mulga

Mulga is an acacia-dominated equivalent of the mallee. Thus mulga is less uniform in appearance than mallee, often considerably taller, and with a more developed eye-level midstory, making it appear much less penetrable when walking within it. The higher diversity of plant life compared with that in mallee is reflected in the animal life, too, and those species that do occur there are usually far less specialized relative to their mallee counterparts. However, there is some overlap between these habitats in terms of species. The following inhabit both: Pink Cockatoo, Hooded Robin, Black Honeyeater, and Red-capped Robin. Some birds that are peculiar to mulga or more abundant there include Budgerigar, Splendid Fairywren, Mulga Parrot, Chestnut-breasted Quail-Thrush, and Pied Honeyeater. Other animals that inhabit mulga include Long-nosed Dragon, Central Bearded Dragon, and Red Kangaroo. Mulga occurs in far western NSW, sw. QLD, and much of inland WA, generally north of the corresponding mallee areas.

A., B., and C. Stony Deserts

Stony deserts are the most barren areas in Australia. These are found in n. SA, w. QLD, and s. NT. They are characterized by sparse and very low level vegetation, either centered around upland areas inland (e.g., West MacDonnell Ranges, NT; Mount Isa, QLD; and Flinders Ranges, SA) or on broad colluvial plains (e.g., Birdsville Track, in QLD and SA). The upland stony deserts (photos A and C) tend to be spinifex-dominated. These spiky, coarse grasses can be difficult to walk through but provide a very specialized habitat for a range of wildlife (photo A), including birds such as Spinifexbird, Spinifex Pigeon, Painted Firetail, Rufous-crowned Emuwren, and Dusky Grasswren, and animals like Black-flanked Rock Wallaby. The colluvial stony deserts are characterized by a layer of small pebbles and cobbles that have been varnished with silica, which gives them a shiny, smooth texture and that form an almost impenetrable layer to the fine red sands below. These barren-looking areas are known as Gibber Plains and support remarkably little wildlife (photo B). Animals that do occur there are extremely specialized and include birds such as Gibberbird, Chestnut-breasted Whiteface, and Inland Dotterel, all of which are very sparsely distributed species, highly nomadic, and very hard to find within this habitat. Unless one is specifically searching for animals, these regions often appear absolutely devoid of life.

A. and B. Sandy Deserts

A massive habitat in terms of land area, stretching from the west Australian coast right across the center of the continent into far western NSW. Australian sandy deserts are not the same as sandy deserts within North Africa (e.g., the Sahara) and the Middle East (e.g., the Saudi deserts), with their characteristic crescent-shaped and constantly moving sand dunes, which are located perpendicular to the prevailing winds. The Australian deserts comprise longitudinal dunes, located parallel to the prevailing winds, that are much more sedentary and stretch for many tens of kilometers. It is this sedentary nature of the Australian dune system that results in a very different looking habitat (photo A), with *spinifex* grasses growing on the sandy ridges, and acacia groves in the swales between the dunes. This permanent vegetation allows for a much richer flora and fauna assemblage than do the sandy deserts elsewhere in the world. The underlying characteristic of these deserts is that they hold many irruptive and nomadic species that respond dramatically to water levels, which in themselves vary tremendously from year to year or even decade to decade. In one year some areas may be barren, while in another years or years this same area can be flush with plant life and boast abundant animal life following a pronounced period of rains. Whereas some species of animals in this environment are sedentary, such as Eyrean Grasswren, others, such as the Princess Parrot, are extremely irruptive and nomadic. Animals exhibit these characteristics as well. For example, truly massive numbers (in the thousands) of Red Kangaroos congregate in years of abundant resources. A great example of this habitat type can be seen around Uluru (Ayers Rock), NT (photo B). One of the reptilian oddities of this habitat is the unique Thorny Devil.

C. Tropical Savanna

These grasslands are restricted to the humid tropical north of Australia, occurring most extensively in n. WA, the Top End of the NT, and the Cape York Peninsula south to c. QLD. This habitat is characterized by very sparse tree cover with an extensive, thick ground layer of grasses, which are naturally seasonally burnt. This creates a new flush of grasses after each burn. The effects of this phenomenon can be seen directly during a burn when flocks of Black Kites in particular gather to scavenge on any dead animals and prey on any others fleeing the flames. Notably, this industrious bird has also been observed taking embers from a burn and dropping them in an unaffected area. Other birds, like finches, that feed on grasses can also be affected by a burn, moving into an area of flush new grass growth to feed on the seeds. These include Gouldian, Masked, and Long-tailed Finches, and Pictorella Mannikins. Partridge Pigeons are also affected by the burn cycle and frequently forage within recently burnt areas (page 25, photo A). Tropical savannas are also affected by human-caused fires, and in areas where such fires are considerably more frequent than the natural burn cycle, this can adversely affect the species present. These are gradational habitats: at one end of the range are very few trees with little canopy cover, and mainly grasslands, whereas the wetter extreme can be universal canopy cover, which is sometimes called *tetradonta woodlands*. However, these variations in vegetational structure and the dominant tree type seem to have less influence on the fauna found within, which is remarkably similar at both extremes (e.g., many birds found in the Broome area of WA extend right across through the NT and into the drier sections of the Cape York Peninsula).

B. and C. Sandstone Escarpments

These rich red–stained rocks form dramatic formations that are restricted to tropical northern Australia, from the Kimberleys in n.WA to the Top End of the NT. There are other sandstone escarpments in northern Australia that could arguably be placed in this habitat category; however, we have excluded them and have placed them instead in stony deserts and sandy deserts, as the faunal assemblage most reflects those other habitat types rather than these escarpments, which have a distinctive character of their own. The Arnhem Land Escarpment covers the eastern half of the Top End of the NT and is the landscape most familiar in Kakadu National Park. The easternmost edge of the Arnhem Land plateau has tropical savanna bordering the cliff edges. The top of the escarpment is carpeted with clumps of spinifex grasses growing out of cracks in this sandstone conglomerate massif. The habitat on top is not uniform, however. There, swales break up the cover of spinifex, where a stunted microhabitat of eucalypts grows, some of which take on a mallee form. This spinifex and eucalypt assemblage is home to some of Australia's most restricted-range bird species, such as Chestnut-quilled Rock-Pigeon, White-lined Honeyeater, and especially the highly sought after, and extremely elusive, White-throated Grasswren. Another specialized bird is the well-named Sandstone Shrike-Thrush, which eats, sleeps, nests, and sings from the red sandstone rocks and is intimately tied to the these northern escarpments. This is also the realm of the Black Wallaroo, a scarce and localized species confined to this habitat, which is a plain, dark, Euro-like wallaby. The bases of some of the outcrops within the Arnhem Land Escarpment are bordered with humid monsoon forest, such as at Nourlangie Rock in Kakadu National Park, which can hold Black-banded Fruit-Dove, Green Oriole, and Orange-footed Scrubfowl. The Kimberleys is a much more remote escarpment in n.WA with outliers to the western edge of the NT. Generally, the faunal assemblage is similar to that found within Arnhem Land, with either similar species or distinct races of the same species. Black Grasswren replaces the White-throated Grasswren in the Kimberleys, and the White-quilled Rock-Pigeon found in the Kimberleys is a sister species of the Chestnut-quilled Rock-Pigeon found in Arnhem Land. Similarly, the Kimberley Honeyeater was formerly considered a distinct race of White-lined Honeyeater but is now regarded as distinctive enough from the closely related Arnhem species to be given full species status of its own, and is therefore now seen as a species endemic to the Kimberleys. Sandstone Shrike-Thrush is also present. Other animals are also represented by endemic races or species, and found only there, including the Short-eared Rock-Wallaby and the fearsome Northern Death Adder.

MAMMALS

A. Red Kangaroo *Macropus rufus* 2–2.5 m/6.5–8 ft

Red Kangaroo is the largest land mammal in Australia, and the world's largest marsupial. **Marsupials** are an order of mammals that are at their greatest diversity in the Australasian region—some 70 percent of the species are found there, and most Australian mammals are within this order. Red Kangaroo stands around 1.5 m/5 ft tall, and males are larger than females. Although often reddish brown, it can also be gray, and so the pelage color is not always useful for identification. It is best identified from other large kangaroos by its boldly marked muzzle, characterized by striking black-and-white horizontal markings along its side—which from the front can appear rather like a mustache—and its pointed ears. Furthermore, Red Kangaroo hops with a horizontal gait, while the other large species tend to hop with an upright posture. It has a wide range over much of the interior of mainland Australia. It is absent from wetter coastal areas and is confined to the semiarid and arid interior. It is nomadic and usually found in small parties, although huge groups can congregate if resources allow. Like many other kangaroos and wallabies it is nocturnal, and so its abundance is often not fully realized until after dark.

B. Eastern Gray Kangaroo *Macropus giganteus* 1.8–2.4 m/5–7.8 ft

A huge kangaroo, standing around 1.8 m/5 ft tall, is outsized only by the enormous Red Kangaroo. Eastern Gray is generally lead gray in color, lacking the reddish tones of many Red Kangaroos, although some Reds can also display gray pelages, lacking red tones, making this an unreliable indication of species. Eastern Gray has a long muzzle and pointed ears, much like the Red Kangaroo, although it lacks Red's bold stripes along the sides of the muzzle. Eastern Grays also usually inhabit wetter, coastal areas, although they can overlap with Red in w. NSW and sw. QLD. This species also hops in an upright position, unlike the more horizontal carriage of Red. It is a common and conspicuous species in eastern Australia from around Cooktown (n. QLD) south to VIC, where it can be found in farmlands, open woodland, and even golf courses, where large mobs can gather and are most evident when active at night. Eastern Gray is the fastest known kangaroo, having been recorded moving at speeds of around 60 km/h (35 mph), and is also very agile when hopping, being able to leap distances of up to 9 m/30 ft in a single bound!

C. Euro *Macropus robustus* 1.5–2 m/4.9–6.5 ft

Also known as Common or Eastern Wallaroo. Although this is another large, heavyset kangaroo, it is significantly smaller than the preceding two giants and differs most notably in the shape of the ears: while the two previous kangaroos display long, pointed ears, the Euro is characterized by wide, rounded ears that are an excellent ID. It can be differentiated from another heavyset wallaby, the Red-necked, with which it often occurs, by its plain face, lacking the bold facial stripes of Red-necked. Euro also often has a shaggy and unkempt appearance relative to other wallabies. It is common and widespread over much of the mainland, being absent only from the south coast and the extreme north, (e.g. Cape York Peninsula of QLD).

A. Agile Wallaby *Macropus agilis* **L: 10.5–11.7 m/4.9–5.5 ft.**

The species on this page are medium-sized wallabies, significantly smaller than kangaroos, and notably larger than pademelons. To ID them, attention should be given to facial pattern, ear markings, and general coloration. Agile is the common wallaby of the tropical north. As its alternative name suggests (Sandy Wallaby), it is light sandy colored above, with a uniform sandy brown tail, and a whitish underside. It shows a striking facial pattern: on the side of the muzzle is a broad white line bordered above by a thick black stripe that runs to the eye. It also displays bold black tips to the ears, and a white stripe on the thigh, (lacking in many wallabies). The generally pallid coloration, striking facial pattern, and markings on the ears are all useful ID tools, best used in combination. Agile Wallaby is a common species within flat areas of tropical savanna and other grassy habitats in northern Australia, (from extreme n. WA eastward to the c. QLD coast). It is largely nocturnal, and gregarious, and is therefore most often observed foraging within groups in the late afternoon.

B. Whiptail Wallaby *Macropus parryi* **L: 1.6–1.9 m/5–6 ft.**

Arguably the most gorgeous wallaby, as suggested by its other name: Pretty-faced Wallaby. It displays a broad white stripe along its muzzle, bordered above by an equally broad black line running from the nose to the eye. The back of the ears are strikingly patterned: all black with a thick white line across their center, a pattern not found in any other wallaby species. Overall, Whiptail Wallaby is grayish brown (much darker than the pallid Agile Wallaby, for example), with whitish underparts, and paler, whitish limbs and tail, which are distinctly tipped black. It is locally common within hilly country in grassy open woodland from around Cairns (QLD) to just south of Brisbane (QLD). Unlike many other wallabies, Whiptail is active by day and night, and is most likely to be observed feeding in groups on hillsides within open wooded areas.

C. Red-necked Wallaby *Macropus rufogriseus* **L: 1.5–1.7 m/5–5.5 ft.**

A medium-sized eastern wallaby, best identified by its facial pattern and coloration of the shoulders: it has an indistinct white line along the side of the face, and a distinct reddish shawl across the shoulders. Although other medium-sized wallabies also show a white facial line, they do not also possess the ruddy coloration on the shoulders. Red-necked Wallaby is heavier set than Whiptail Wallaby, with a relatively thick tail that is uniformly colored and lacks the dark tail tip displayed by some other medium-sized wallabies. It is common in eastern Australia, from s. QLD south through the coastal zone of NSW, and VIC, with an isolated population in far western VIC and se. SA. It also occurs on TAS, where the distinctive subspecies is often referred to as "Bennett's Wallaby", which is smaller and longer furred than on the mainland. Red-necked Wallaby can be found in wet eucalypt forest and scrub, where it is generally active at night or around dawn or dusk, when it is most likely to be found foraging alone, as it is not a social species.

B

A. Black-flanked Rock Wallaby *Petrogale lateralis* **80–112 cm/31.5–44 in.**
Also known as Black-footed Rock Wallaby. Rock Wallabies are a diverse group
(sixteen species) of small wallabies—larger than pademelons but much smaller
than medium-sized species such as Agile Wallaby—that inhabit rocky areas. They
possess modified pads on their feet that are large, spongy, and granulated, which
gives them a good grip on treacherous rocky surfaces. Many are highly local and
can be identified by range alone. Black-flanked is a variably dark animal, largely
dull gray in color, although sometimes washed brown on the rump and upper tail,
and with a pale wash across the shoulders. There is also a diagnostic pale whitish
line running from the shoulder down the sides of the animal that is unique to the
species. The head is mainly grayish, although brown on top with a pale line along
the side of the muzzle. It is the most widespread of the rock wallabies, although still
highly local and patchy in its range. The core of the range is in the rocky ranges in
central Australia, where it is most likely to be seen within the MacDonnell Ranges.
It also occurs patchily in the ranges of WA and SA, where it is more rarely seen.
Black-flanked is a gregarious and nocturnal species, most likely to be seen foraging
in large groups once the heat of the day has dissipated.

B. Mareeba Rock Wallaby *Petrogale mareeba* **90–125 cm/35.5–49 in.**
Mareeba Rock Wallaby is the most readily seen species in a complex of seven very
similar, highly localized wallabies found on the coast of e. QLD. All seven species
(**Cape York, Godman's, Sharman's, Allied, Unadorned, Herbert's, and Mareeba
Rock Wallabies**) look alike and are considered impossible to differentiate in the
field, although they are genetically distinct, and identified on their tiny geographic
ranges. They appear largely dull brown or gray in color above, with a lighter pale
gray underside, a pale line on their flanks, and a long, dark-tipped tail. The head is
brownish with a thin black line running from the crown to the nape, and a clear
pale line running along the side of the muzzle. They are social wallabies, most
likely to be observed in groups, although they are largely nocturnal and emerge
from cool crevices once the shadows have cooled the rocks. Mareeba Rock Wallaby
is found within the ranges of the western Atherton Tablelands (QLD), where they
are easily found at Granite Gorge Nature Park just outside Mareeba.

C. Lumholtz's Tree-Kangaroo *Dendrolagus lumholtzi* **110–130 cm/43.5–51 in.**
Tree Kangaroos are odd tree-dwelling species with long tails (used for counterbal-
ance), and long, powerful forelimbs that aid climbing. Although awkward when
moving, quadrupedally, on the ground, they are efficient climbers. Lumholtz's Tree
Kangaroo is a highly localized species, confined to montane rainforest on the
Atherton Tablelands of ne. QLD, where it occurs from Kirrama to Mossman. Overall, Lumholtz's is a brownish animal with a distinctly paler, buff-colored underside,
which contrasts with the solid black face. It is nocturnal, so not easily found except
on designated night walks or by chance day roosting around tourist hot spots such
as Lake Eacham, Malanda Falls, or Curtain Fig.

A. Red-necked Pademelon *Thylogale thetis* **58–113 cm/23–44.5 in.**

Pademelons are a distinct group of small wallabies, considerably smaller than both the giant kangaroos and the other, larger wallabies. When foraging slowly, pademelons usually move on all fours. On the top side Red-necked Pademelon is largely dull brown, grizzled with gray, which contrasts with a lighter, off-white coat below. It has a characteristic warm reddish brown shawl across the nape and shoulders, which aids differentiation from Red-legged Pademelon, with which it overlaps in many areas. Red-necked and Red-legged Pademelons are both common east Australian wallaby species, although Red-necked is the most readily seen, as it tends to forage in open areas more often than the rainforest-dwelling Red-legged, which generally prefers to remain in deep cover. Red-necked is a largely nocturnal wallaby, found within rainforest edges and wet eucalypt forest in coastal eastern Australia from s. QLD south down the northern and central coast of NSW, where it is most often observed foraging at forest edges at dawn or dusk.

B. Red-legged Pademelon *Thylogale stigmatica* **70–105 cm/27.5–41 in.**

Red-legged Pademelon is a rainforest wallaby confined to eastern Australia, largely similar to Red-necked Pademelon, with which it overlaps in many areas. Red-legged however, is a ruddier-colored animal, with most of the body being reddish brown, except for grayish brown on the upper back and shoulders. This aids ID, as Red-necked is a largely grayish animal but is rufous washed across the nape and shoulders. Furthermore, Red-legged has a rust-colored face, whereas Red-necked has a grayish cast to the face. Red-legged also displays a pale buff-colored stripe along the hip, lacking in Red-necked. Red-legged is a fairly common wallaby in the eastern rainforests of the coastal zone, from the tip of Cape York (QLD) south down the coast to far northeast NSW. However, it is generally shy, preferring to keep within the rainforest, making it far less easily observed than its cousin the Red-necked.

C. Rufous-bellied Pademelon *Thylogale billardierii* **88–104 cm/34.5–41 in.**

Also known as Tasmanian Pademelon, this species is confined to TAS, where the other two pademelon species do not occur. It is a small reddish brown wallaby, with buffish underparts and distinctly washed rufous across the belly. Although now confined to TAS, it formerly occurred in s. VIC and se. SA but is now extinct on the mainland. Rufous-bellied Pademelon is common and widespread throughout TAS in areas of thick vegetation, usually alongside clearings. This nocturnal marsupial occurs in rainforests, heaths, and eucalypt forest and scrublands, where it is most often observed feeding along forest edges around dawn and dusk, or in car headlights at night. This is one of the most commonly found roadkill species in Tasmania.

C

A. Musky Rat-Kangaroo *Hypsiprymnodon moschatus* **28–43 cm/11–17 in.**

Musky Rat-Kangaroo is a tiny, quirky marsupial that looks like a strange cross between a kangaroo and a rat. Its marked oddity has led taxonomists recently to place it within its own unique, single-species family. The combination of quadrupedal movement (using all four limbs when moving around), a sharply pointed snout, and a scaled, naked-looking tail lend it this distinctly ratlike appearance. It is a tiny animal, being the smallest of all the macropods (a group of marsupials that includes kangaroos and wallabies), largely ruddy brown in color, that can readily be identified by its tiny size and ratlike features. It has a restricted range, confined to rainforests centered on Cairns in ne. QLD. Musky Rat-Kangaroo can be locally abundant (e.g., Lake Barrine) within its tiny range, where it roams in both montane and lowland forests. It is a solitary and diurnal marsupial, unlike many other species that largely forage at night. It is also odd in regularly giving birth to twins, whereas most other macropods raise just a single joey. Musky Rat-Kangaroo is most readily observed during early mornings, when it is at its most active. It is most often found foraging for fallen fruits and seeds among the dark, damp rainforest leaf litter.

B. Quokka *Setonix brachyurus* **65–110 cm/25.5–43.5 in.**

Quokka is a tiny, odd marsupial that looks rather like a giant rodent and has a highly restricted range: it occurs only in far southwestern mainland Australia and on several islands off the southwest coast (Rottnest and Bald Islands). It is short and plump, with a relatively short tail for a wallaby; it has a broad face with characteristic, wide, puffed-out cheeks; a short pointed muzzle; and rounded ears. The Quokka is grayish brown above, and paler buff colored below, and is washed rufous across the face, nape, and shoulders. It also displays a black line across the top of the head. In its extremely limited range it is unlikely to be confused with any other wallaby by virtue of its small size and characteristic shape. Quokka is largely nocturnal, and can be gregarious, occurring in groups where good food sources allow. Quokkas are notoriously tolerant of humans, often appearing fearless, and can be remarkably approachable on the island of Rottnest (just off the mainland city of Perth), which is their stronghold and where they are most likely to be encountered. On Rottnest they can easily be seen loafing around the main street or hanging around the cafes to clean up after the tourists! So common and conspicuous were Quokkas on Rottnest that some of the first Dutch explorers in the seventeenth century named the island after them. They named it "Rottenest," for rat's nest, as they had mistakenly thought the Quokkas were giant rats!

A. Common Ringtail Possum *Pseudocheirus peregrinus* **60–70 cm/23.5–27.5 in.**
Possums are plump, squirrel-like marsupials that are generally arboreal in nature.
Possums can best be identified by examining their structure. Most have variable fur
color, making this of little use in ID. Ringtail possums are distinctive, as they possess oddly shaped tails that taper to a fine point at the tip, which is contrastingly
white across the final third. The tip of the tail is prehensile, used to grasp when
climbing. Contrastingly, brushtail possums have uniformly colored, bushy tails.
Common Ringtail is variably colored, from gray to rufous above, and always shows
contrastingly paler underparts (ranging from buff to whitish). It has notably
rufous-washed limbs, which are a major ID feature. Common Ringtail is common
and widespread in eastern Australia, from the tip of Cape York (QLD), south to
VIC and TAS, and westward into far southeast SA. It favors forested environments,
usually with an extensive shrubby understory, and also occurs in gardens and
scrubby areas, where it is a nocturnal and social species.

B. Mountain Brushtail Possum *Trichosurus cunninghami* **75–92 cm/29.5–36 in.**
Brushtail possums differ from the ringtails in possessing uniformly colored, bushy
tails that lack the pale, prehensile tip of ringtails. Mountain and Common Brushtail
Possums are very similar species that are best told apart from each other by structure, as pelage color varies widely within both species. Mountain is a massive possum, the largest in Australia, with a particularly broad bushy tail, relatively short
ears, and a relatively short, stubby snout compared with Common. Mountain
Brushtail is a common but local and specialized species: it inhabits rainforest in
southeast Australia (from around Newcastle in NSW to w. VIC), where it replaces
Common Brushtail. It is nocturnal and unlike most other possums, more readily
comes down from the trees to forage on the ground. Often seen in Lamington
National Park, where feeding stations allow them to be readily observed at night.

C. Common Brushtail Possum *Trichosurus vulpecula* **60–90 cm/23.5–35.5 in.**
A plump, bushy-tailed possum, similar in appearance to the local Mountain Brushtail. Common Brushtail is one of the most familiar marsupials in Australia, being
widespread and common, and occurring in a wide variety of habitats. It possesses a
broad, bushy tail that lacks the finely tapered tip of ringtail possums. Common is
smaller overall than Mountain Brushtail, with a less bushy tail, distinctly longer
ears, and a relatively longer snout. It is widespread over much of the coastal areas
on the mainland and TAS, although it is absent from drier inland areas. The two
brushtails also differ in their calls: Common has a distinctive series of rattling
coughs and hisses, while Mountain gives a much shorter series of calls lacking this
rattling quality. Common Brushtail occurs in almost all areas that have trees,
although within the range of Mountain Brushtail Possum it is replaced by that species within rainforest. It is commonly observed in gardens and parks within most
city suburbs.

C

A. Striped Possum *Dactylopsila trivirgata* **56–61 cm/22–24 in.**

A striking animal, rather like a large black-and-white squirrel, it is a tree-dwelling marsupial with a long, bushy tail (the tail is more than 30 cm/11.5 in. long, longer than the total body length). Although a scare and local animal, restricted to rainforests and eucalypt forests in ne. QLD, it is familiar to many Australians by virtue of its distinctive coloration. Striped Possum is a white animal with broad and bold blackish stripes running down the face, upperparts, and limbs. The black-and-white patterning on the face makes a striking white Y- shape. The long, bushy tail is blackish on the upper side and white on the ventral side, and has a contrasting, extensive white tip. Striped Possum also gives off a strong, pungent odor. It is an uncommon species with two small, isolated populations: one on the Atherton Tablelands and lowlands around Cairns, and another centered on Iron Range in the Cape York Peninsula. It is most likely to be found while one is searching for other mammals on a designated night walk spotlighting animals on the Atherton Tablelands (e.g., around Curtain Fig, Crater Lakes NP, and Malanda Falls).

B. Sugar Glider *Petaurus breviceps* **31–40 cm/12–15.5 in.**

Gliders are arboreal, possumlike marsupials with big black eyes, large rounded ears, and bushy tails. They are characterized by a membrane of loose skin between the fingers and toes that allows them to glide considerable distances between trees. Subtle movements of the membrane and the tail enable it to steer. Sugar Gliders have been known to glide up to 100 m/330 ft in a single flight. It is a silvery gray animal above with paler, creamy underparts, and a distinctive black line running from the nose down to the middle of the back. The tail is mostly concolorous with the upperparts, fading into black and then white at the very tip. Sugar Glider overlaps with the similar **Squirrel Glider** *Petaurus morfolcensis* in the eastern and southeastern sections of the mainland. The latter is a larger glider with cleaner white underparts and a longer snout, and it lacks the white tail tip that Sugar Glider exhibits. Sugar Glider generally inhabits eucalypt forest and woodland, although it also occurs within rainforest in QLD. It is found in coastal northern Australia from n. WA eastward through the north of the NT to the tip of the Cape York Peninsula (QLD). In coastal eastern Australia it occurs from the tip of Cape York south to s. VIC, and west to se. SA, and is the only glider that is found on TAS. It is a common and widespread animal—with a stronghold around Boondall Wetlands in Brisbane—though nocturnal, so it is best found by joining designated mammal spotlighting tours.

A. Northern Brown Bandicoot *Isoodon macrourus* **45–60 cm/17.5–23.5 in.**
Bandicoots are ratlike marsupials that move on all fours; have a long, pointed snout; prominent fleshy ears; and naked-looking tails. They typically scurry around on the floor in the manner of a rat, too, lacking the awkward bounding gait of Musky Rat-Kangaroo. They are however, much larger than rats, with shorter tails and a more attenuated snout. Northern Brown is the largest bandicoot, brownish above, usually grizzled gray, and sometimes with a rufous cast to some of the upper coat. Below, it is much paler, and creamy in color. Size alone should aid ID of this ratlike creature. It is a common northern species found from n. WA around the coast to c. NSW. This bandicoot occurs in wet areas of eucalypt forest, rainforests, woodlands, and grasslands, where it is nocturnal and generally solitary.

B. Tasmanian Devil *Sarcophilus harrisi* **80–90 cm/31.5–35.5 in.**
An iconic Australian mammal, with a large head, prominent pink ears, and stunted limbs that give it an awkward, piglike gait, Tasmanian Devil is the world's largest carnivorous marsupial, equipped with strong jaws and sharp teeth, and the most powerful bite of any animal. It is a blackish animal with a variable amount of white on the chest and at the base of the tail, (some individuals lack white). Although largely solitary, devils will gather at a carcass, where they become notoriously feisty and cantankerous, often bickering and baring their substantial teeth, and snarling and growling at one another in a comical manner. As well as taking live prey, devils also scavenge and so have become frequent roadkill when foraging on highways. Upgrading of dirt roads to paved highways has often increased mortalities, owing to increased traffic speeds and greater difficulty in detecting oncoming vehicles. Confined to TAS, it was once widespread, although it has declined dramatically since the 1990s, when a facial cancer ravaged the population. The stronghold is in far northwest TAS, although devils still occur throughout TAS in a wide range of habitats, including eucalypt forest, scrubland, and even urban areas. Tasmanian Devils are strictly nocturnal and are best looked for at specific feeding areas or patrolling remote highways at night for roadkill.

C. Northern Quoll *Dasyurus hallucatus* **45–66 cm/17.5–26 in.**
Quolls are odd, boldly spotted feline carnivorous marsupials. There are four species in Australia, all of which display strong spots on their coats, unlike any other marsupial. They can largely be identified on range, as there is little overlap. The largest species, the Spot-tailed Quoll, is the only species that has a spotted tail. **Northern Quoll** is the smallest, found patchily in northern Australia from WA eastward to s. QLD. It is found mainly coastally in eucalypt forest, where it is more numerous in rocky areas. **Western Quoll** is confined to sw. WA, where no other quolls occur; **Eastern Quoll** is now confined to TAS, where it overlaps with Spot-tailed; and **Spot-tailed** occurs in eastern and southeastern Australia and TAS, where it overlaps with the smaller Eastern (on TAS) and, marginally, with Northern (around Cairns). All species are strictly nocturnal and generally scarce, most often seen by chance, crossing highways at night.

A. Koala *Phascolarctos cinereus* 70–85 cm/27.5–33.5 in.

One of the most instantly recognizable, iconic Australian marsupials. A rotund, densely furred, grayish, and tailless animal, with a lighter, whitish underside, characterized by its large furry ears and prominent leathery black round nose. There is some variation in the population: southern Koalas are generally browner and larger with thicker fur to cope with the colder southern climate. Its bearlike appearance led early European explorers to wrongly name it Koala Bear or Native Bear, although it is not a bear at all. Koalas are notoriously fussy animals, feeding on the leaves of just a handful of eucalypt species, which has led to their becoming endangered as their habitat becomes increasingly fragmented. It is a notoriously sluggish animal that requires long periods of time to digest the gum leaves on which it feeds, and so it sleeps high in the trees for 18–20 hours a day on average. Generally arboreal, Koalas will descend to the ground when needed, at which time they are extremely vulnerable, especially in urban areas (e.g., around Brisbane), where they become frequent road casualties. Koalas occur throughout eastern and southern Australia, from the Atherton Tablelands (QLD) south to s. VIC. There are also small, isolated populations in se. SA. Although widespread, Koala is very patchy within this range, owing to extensive fragmentation of its habitat: eucalypt forest and woodland. Koalas are remarkably hard to find in the wild when sleeping, often motionless, high in the trees by day. Once located though, Koalas may often be viewed for hours, as they move little, and can often remain in the same area for days on end.

B. Common Wombat *Vombatus ursinus* 80–120 cm/31.5–47 in.

Although occupying a separate family, the wombats are the most closely related animals to the Koala. Unlike Koalas, though, wombats are ground-dwelling animals. They are pudgy, tailless animals with a large pit bull–like head: broad, with small, triangular ears that protrude from the top of the head. Wombats have short, stunted legs, and a portly body covered with coarse fur. They walk on all fours, making them appear rather like a stocky dog. Common Wombat is a heavyset (weighing up to 40 kg/88 lb) grayish brown herbivorous grazing animal. It is crepuscular or nocturnal and sleeps in deep burrows in the ground by day. Although found in the southeast on the mainland, where it occurs in coastal NSW and e. VIC—with a tiny population in se. SA as well—it is scarce and shy there, and is far more readily seen on TAS, where it is widespread and common, and more frequently forages during the day. Common Wombat inhabits forest, heaths, and scrubby country, where it is most often encountered grazing during the late afternoon at places like Narawntapu National Park (TAS), where it is remarkably abundant, and famously fearless.

A. Short-beaked Echidna *Tachyglossus aculeatus* **31.5–44.5 cm/12.5–17.5 in.**
Another very strange Australian animal. Like the extremely different looking Platypus it is also one of only five monotreme (egg-laying mammals) species on Earth. The echidna generally lays one egg in a burrow in the ground. An odd, porcupine-like mammal, unlikely to be confused with any other: a plump, grayish brown animal covered with thick straw-colored spines with an obvious cylindrical snout at the front end that is uses for foraging. Also known as "Spiny Anteaters," echidnas feed on a variety of soil-based insects, including ants, termites, and beetle larvae. They are found throughout the continent, including TAS— where they are markedly more abundant than on the mainland—in a wide variety of habitats. The echidna is most likely to be encountered crossing roads, where its slow movement allows it to be easily approached. Its behavior on approach is quite remarkable: the animal tucks in its snout, curls up into a spiky ball, and shuffles itself into the ground, making it almost impenetrable, and freezes until the threat moves away.

B. and C. Platypus *Ornithorhynchus anatinus* **41–55 cm/16–21 in.**
A very unusual aquatic mammal that inhabits clean, clear freshwater streams, lakes, and dams. One of only five species of egg-laying mammals (known as *monotremes*) on Earth, and only two species of which occur in Australia. Unique, furry like a rat, with large webbed feet, but quite unlike any other mammal, as it possesses a prominent beak. The latter feature is the origin of its other name: Duck-billed Platypus. It also has a broad flattened tail that resembles that of a beaver. They are found on the east coast from n. QLD to TAS, although they are usually difficult to observe, being mainly nocturnal and often shy. In some areas there are a few diurnal populations, usually involving females, where they can be more readily observed. When they surface, just the top of the "beak" and the upperpart of the body and tail can be seen, and they rarely surface for long periods. Their location in an area can sometimes be tracked by following the bubbles between periods when they surface and listening for the soft splashing noises each time they surface. They feed mainly on aquatic invertebrates caught underwater, which are then stored in the cheeks and brought to the surface, where they chew on them. Interestingly, males possess a poisonous spur on their hind feet that they use to subdue females to copulate with them. Popular tourist spots with platforms and viewing areas where platypuses are frequently seen include Yungaburra and Tarzali Lakes in QLD, and Latrobe and Burnie in TAS.

A. Black Flying Fox *Pteropus alecto* 24–28 cm/9.5–11 in.

Flying foxes are massive bats, and the Australian species are among the largest ones on earth. They are in the suborder "megabats," which forage at night by sight (and not echolocation) for nectar, pollen, and fruit, often covering great distances (sometimes over 50 km/30 mi), and are therefore very important seed dispersers. Flying foxes have large wingspans (some over 1 m/3 ft across), thick fur on their bodies, and doglike faces, with prominent ears and pronounced snouts housing a powerful nose used to detect pollen and fruit. Flying foxes regularly roost together in massive groups known as *camps,* where they are rarely still, regularly squabbling with one another and fidgeting, making them popular tourist attractions in some areas. Black Flying Fox is largely blackish brown in color over much of the body except for the nape, which shows a paler reddish brown color. Some individuals also show indistinct pale spectacles around the eyes. It is a coastal species occurring across the whole of the north coast as well as the upper half of the WA coast. On the east coast it is found from the tip of Cape York (QLD) south to c. NSW. It inhabits rainforests, eucalypt forests, and woodlands, and is best looked for at traditional camp sites. Black Flying Foxes are regarded as pests by mango farmers.

B. Gray-headed Flying Fox *Pteropus poliocephalus* 23–29 cm/9–11.5 in.

A strikingly large bat, with grizzled gray body color, which is generally paler gray on the head, and with a distinctive ginger collar, which is the best feature for ID. It is unique among Australian flying foxes in possessing extensive fur all the way down its legs to its toes. Like other flying foxes, it forages mainly on eucalypt pollen and nectar, and native fruits, and also forms conspicuous camps of thousands of individuals during the day outside the breeding season. It is one of the most commonly encountered flying foxes by tourists, as there is a large summer camp of more than twenty thousand animals within the Royal Botanic Gardens in Sydney, and other large camps also exist within Brisbane. It occurs coastally in eastern and southeastern Australia, from just north of Rockhampton (QLD) south to se. VIC, where it inhabits a variety of habitats, including rainforests, woodlands, and wetlands. This species is often regarded as a pest by commercial fruit farmers.

C. Spectacled Flying Fox *Pteropus conspicillatus* 23–24 cm/9–9.5 in.

A massive bat, with a wingspan of up to 1.2 m/4 ft, that is confined to ne. QLD. It is dark bodied, with blackish brown fur, and is therefore similar in general coloration to the sympatric Black Flying Fox. However, Spectacled usually shows striking straw-colored spectacles, and a broad straw-colored collar, which differentiates it from that species. It is restricted to the coast of ne. QLD, from Tully northward to Cape York, where it, like other flying foxes, is best located at traditional camps, where it roosts during the day. Several large camps are well known and readily accessible in the region, including one within the city of Cairns, and another along the Daintree River.

A. Water Buffalo *Bubalus bubalis* 2.5–3.5 m/8–11.5 ft

A Southeast Asian species introduced into the n. NT that was once a serious pest owing to wetland destruction, although it is now highly restricted to aboriginal land there, after recent culling programs. A big, all-dark cow, usually associated with wetlands, that possesses characteristic long, backswept, triangular horns.

B. Dingo *Canis lupus dingo* 1.1–1.5 m/3.5–5 ft

A wild dog that was introduced to Australia thousands of years ago, considered responsible for the extinction of many large marsupials on the mainland, most notably the Thylacine (Tasmanian Tiger). Dingoes are powerfully built dogs with a short bushy tail and triangular pointed ears that are naturally held erect. Dingoes vary widely in pelage color from ginger to sandy to almost black, and are usually characterized by a pale underside, white feet, and a white tail tip. It is very difficult to determine Dingoes from some of the similar domestic dog breeds and hybrids between them. It occurs throughout the continent, being most abundant in drier areas, and absent only from TAS, although it is being threatened by extensive inter-breeding with domestic dogs.

C. Red Fox *Vulpes vulpes* 90–120 cm/35.5–47 in.

Introduced by English settlers to Victoria in the 1860s and now widespread across the southern half of the mainland. A distinctive animal with large pointed ears held erect above the head, thick red fur, and a broad bushy tail. Coloration is largely reddish and often grizzled with grayish hairs, whitish underneath, with the tail darkening to black near the tip, and usually white at the very tip. It appears "booted," as the limbs are black on the bottom half. Red Fox occurs in a wide variety of habitats and has been responsible for the decimation of some native mammal populations, such as Quokka.

D. European Rabbit *Oryctolagus cuniculus* 35–50 cm/13.5–20 in.

A distinctive mammal with characteristic long ears that was introduced into Victoria in the nineteenth century and now occurs in grasslands and agricultural areas across most of the southern half of the continent. Rabbits have decimated populations of other native mammals, most notably the Bilby, causing rabbit-proof fences to be built to control them. These measures proved futile though, as rabbits simply burrowed under or jumped over them. It is unlikely to be confused with any native mammal, although it could be mistaken for another introduced species, **European Hare** *Lepus europeaus*, which is considerably larger, with longer ears distinctively tipped white, and black on the tip of the inner ear.

E. Feral Pig *Sus scrofa* 1.1–2 m/3.5–6.5 ft

Also known as Wild Boar. A Eurasian species introduced in the nineteenth century and now a serious pest numbering in the millions, though conversely, rarely seen. Generally dark grayish to black in color with the characteristic stunted legs and large head that give it a front-heavy appearance, pronounced snout, and short tail. Older animals may also possess tusks. Found in northern Australia (patchily in WA, n. NT) and eastern Australia (almost all of the east except s. VIC), and always close to water, where it inhabits agricultural lands and eucalypt woodlands, and around floodplains.

A. Australian Fur Seal *Arctocephalus pusillus* 1.3 (F)–2.2 m (M)/4.3–7.2 ft

Seals are divided into two distinct groups: *true seals* and *eared seals*. Fur seals and sea lions fall within the family *Otariinae*, which are known as eared seals. The group is characterized by prominent, visible ears and maneuverable foreflippers that allow them to walk and run on land, which true seals cannot. Fur seals display extraordinary sexual dimorphism: males are significantly bigger than females— some are *five* times the size of females (up to 360 kg/800 lb in male Australian Fur Seal). Seals are typically aggressive, with males defending a harem of females. Fur seals are so named because they possess a double layer of fur, which historically (in the 1800s) led to their being hunted for their valuable pelts. Male fur seals in breeding condition display a thick mane of coarse hair around the neck. The two regularly occurring fur seals, Australian and New Zealand, need to be distinguished from each other as well as from Australian Sea Lion, with which they can overlap. Both fur seals are smaller than sea lions, with distinctly more pointed faces, longer ears, relatively longer whiskers, and display more uniform coloration. Differentiating New Zealand Fur Seal from Australian is problematic where their ranges overlap (i.e., in s. VIC and TAS). Compared with New Zealand Fur Seal, Australian is larger, with relatively shorter whiskers; a broader muzzle that is less sharply pointed and is usually slightly upturned; a larger, more prominent nose; and more rounded foreflippers. The males also often show a two-tone effect on the foreneck and chest. Australian Fur Seal occurs primarily at sea and along the rocky coastlines of s. VIC and TAS, although wandering individuals may be found further afield. These fur seals are best found by joining an organized boat trip to well-established rookeries.

B. New Zealand Fur Seal *Arctocephalus forsteri* 1 (F)–2 m (M)/3.3–7 ft

Readily distinguished from **Australian Sea Lion** *Neophoca cinerea*, with which it may overlap through most of its range, as the latter species is larger (up to 2.5 m/8.2 ft in males) and is also distinctly two-tone in both males, which often exhibit a pale buff crown, and females, which are darker on the upper side than on the ventral surface. The sea lion also possesses a more doglike face with a shorter, blunt muzzle. Australian Sea Lion also has smaller ears and relatively smaller flippers relative to both fur seals. New Zealand Fur Seal is the smallest of the three species, with the most pointed muzzle, longest whiskers, triangular-shaped foreflippers, longer hindflippers , and dark uniform coloration, compared with the extremely similar Australian Fur Seal, with which it overlaps in the southeast corner of Australia and TAS. New Zealand Fur Seal has a wider range in Australia than Australian Fur Seal, occurring along the coastlines from southern QLD around to the southwest corner of Australia, and TAS. Within this range, the strongholds are in three main areas (where they breed): off the coast of SA, s. TAS, and s. WA.

A. Southern Right Whale *Eubalaena australis* 14–17.5 m/46–57.5 ft

A massive black whale that is readily identified, as it is the only large Australian whale lacking a dorsal fin. It has a long, arched mouth (often exposed at the surface of the water) and has extensive white, barnacle-like callosities on the head, which are made up of lice-infested roughened skin, a feature unique to right whales. It produces a broad V-shaped blow when surfacing, and when diving, it often exposes the tail fluke just before disappearing below the surface. It possesses short, broad-based, triangular flippers. Southern Right Whale occurs in May to October along the south coast between Perth and Sydney, where it is often visible from shore.

B. Humpback Whale *Megaptera novaengliae* 14–18 m/46–50 ft

The most familiar whale on earth owing to its acrobatic nature and frequent surface activities. Its characteristic is extremely long flippers, which are white on the underside and regularly exposed at the surface. It is two-tone, dark gray on the upper surface and pale on the ventral side. The Humpback breaches more often than other whales, frequently exposes its tail fluke, and regularly reveals its distinctive flippers. The upper jaw or rostrum is knobbed on the surface, with a double blowhole behind it, which is often exposed when the whale is surfacing. It has a small triangular dorsal fin, which is not exposed until well after the head breaks the surface. When diving, it frequently ends by raising its massive tail fluke spectacularly. The tail fluke is broad, deeply forked, and has distinctive backswept terminal points at either side. The blow of this species is broad and bushy. Humpback is a winter visitor to Australia that can be encountered anywhere along the western or eastern coasts or in TAS.

C. Common Bottlenose Dolphin *Tursiops truncates* 2–4 m/6.5–13 ft

Bottlenose are large gray dolphins, with tall, arched dorsal fins, and long beaks. Two similar species occur in Australia: Common, which can be found on all coastlines, and **Indo-Pacific Bottlenose** *T. aduncus*, which occurs along the north, west, and upper east coasts. Overall structure is similar, although Common is generally bigger; has a shorter, broader beak, separated from the melon (forehead bump) by a dark crease; has proportionally smaller flippers; a shorter, more narrow-based dorsal fin; and lacks spotting on the underside. Common Bottlenoses are notoriously friendly and acrobatic, performing frequent activities on and above the surface, while Indo-Pacific are generally much shyer and less active. Not all Indo-Pacifics possess spotting, and so it is important to examine multiple individuals in a pod.

D. Striped Dolphin *Stenella coeruleoalba* 2.5–2.7 m/8–9 ft

A medium-sized dolphin with a striking body pattern: dark blackish gray above, separated from the pink to white underside by a broad pale blue-gray blaze along the flank. Just above the pale underside there is also a clearly demarcated black line running from eye to anus. Striped Dolphin further differs from bottlenose species in being shorter beaked. It is gregarious, usually encountered in single-species pods that may also be acrobatic but rarely mixes with other dolphin species. Occurs around all but the southern coasts and TAS.

BIRDS

A. Emu *Dromaius novaehollandiae* 150–190 cm/59–75 in.

Emu is the national bird of Australia. Australia's answer to the Ostrich, it is also a massive flightless bird in shape rather like that African species. It is a fast bird, running at speeds of up to 50 km/h (31 mph). It is one of only two large flightless land birds in the country, along with the rainforest-dwelling cassowary. Emu is the second largest living bird on Earth, outsized only by the Ostrich. It stands over 2 m/6.5 ft tall, with a stride of over 2.7 m/9 ft, and weighs up to 45 kg/99 lb. Emu is widespread in woodland and open country throughout inland Australia, rarely in the coastal zone, and unlike the cassowary, *never* in rainforest. Emu is from the distinctly odd Ratite family that is unusual among birds in that the males incubate the eggs and take care of the young after hatching. The female takes no part in this process at all. Emu is a generalist and will feed on fruit and plant matter, as well as insects. It is typically seen in the Australian outback crossing red dirt roads or feeding in small groups (two to six birds) within open country and seemingly quite unafraid when approached slowly with a vehicle. However, one step out of the car and its true speed and grace can be appreciated when the Emus are found to have moved away some distance in no time at all!

B. Southern Cassowary *Casuarius casuarius* 170–175 cm/67–69 in.

Shorter in height than the Emu (cassowary is 1.5–2 m/5–6 ft tall), although the cassowary is a heavier bird, weighing up to 90 kg/190 lb, and outweighed only by the Ostrich of North Africa. Cassowaries are heavyset birds, with coarsely feathered black bodies and striking bright blue- and red-colored naked necks and heads, and a distinctive large triangular knob or helmet on top of the head. They have powerful legs with three-toed feet that possess a lethal 5-inch-long claw on their inner toes that they can use with devastating effect to defend themselves. It is a fearsome rainforest creature that has been known to attack dogs and even humans when alarmed, so it should always be kept at a distance. Despite its large size, it can be surprisingly hard to find. Cassowary occurs only at low densities, localized within the rainforest belt of the Wet Tropics of n. QLD, and is also generally reclusive. Like the Emu and other members of the Ratite family, the males alone incubate the eggs and take care of the young. When the stripy brown cassowary chicks are very young, the male can be aggressively defensive of its offspring. The striking cassowary feeds mainly on fallen fruits in the tropical rainforests, and in a few famous areas has been known to visit gardens where food is laid out for them. At these few special places they can abandon their usual shy habits and be remarkably trusting.

A. Malleefowl *Leipoa ocellata* **55–60 cm/21.5–23.5 in.**
The three markedly different birds on this page are all from an Australasian family, the **megapodes**, which build massive earth mounds to incubate their eggs. Malleefowl mounds reach 4–5 m/13–16 ft across and are 60 cm/24 in. high. It is a rotund, long-necked terrestrial bird with powerful legs and feet used for mound excavation. It is intricately and distinctively patterned, which if seen well, is easy to identify: cryptically marked above with intricate chestnut, white, and black markings across the upperparts. Underneath it is much plainer and pale, with a distinctive black stripe running down from the throat to the breast. This shy and wary species blends in very well with its surroundings: undisturbed areas of mallee woodland and scrub in southern Australia. There are three discrete populations, one in sw. WA, another spotty population in SA (mainly in the south), and another in nw. VIC and s. NSW. In all areas it is a rarely seen species, by virtue of its scarcity, furtive behavior, and camouflage. It is a weak flier, preferring to rely on its cryptic coloration to avoid detection. It creeps away slowly when disturbed rather than flying, and quickly melts into its surroundings.

B. Australian Brush-Turkey *Alectura lathami* **60–70 cm/23.5–27.5 in.**
A distinctive, large, turkeylike megapode with a large black body, bright red bare skin on the head and neck, and a vivid lemon yellow collar. It builds a large earth mound (up to 4 m/13 ft across and 2 m/6.5 ft high) to incubate its eggs. They can be nuisance, as they often take advantage of well-manicured gardens in which to build these huge "incubators." Brush-Turkeys are poor fliers, spending most of their time on the ground, and preferring to run from danger or flap clumsily away. They are commonly found in the rainforests and woodlands of eastern Australia, from extreme northern QLD down into ne. NSW. They have powerful legs and feet that they use to construct their large mounds and scratch the forest floor for food like invertebrates, fruits, and seeds. Unlike many other rainforest creatures it is not shy, and can be bullish and even a pest around picnic grounds.

C. Orange-footed Scrubfowl *Megapodius reinwardt* **42–47 cm/16.5–18.5 in.**
A small and common megapode (or mound builder) found in tropical areas of northern Australia. It is a plain, grayish brown bird with a distinct crest and prominent orange feet, which are its most conspicuous feature. It uses its powerful, brightly colored feet to build truly massive mounds in which to incubate its eggs. The mounds are larger than those of all the other Australian mound builders, measuring some 12 m/39 ft across and up to 5 m/16.5 ft high! The mounds are often the first clue to the scrubfowl's presence in an area. Scrubfowl are commonly found within botanical gardens, town parks, forests, and tropical woodlands in humid parts of northern Australia.

A. Australian Bustard *Ardeotis australis* **80–120 cm/31.5–47 in.**

Bustards are tall, thick-set birds found throughout the Old World and are the heaviest of all flying birds. This species, Australia's only bustard, stands 3 ft tall. Bustards have long necks and legs, and heavy rotund bodies, and spend most of their time wandering slowly on the ground in open habitats. Australian Bustard is found throughout the inland in grasslands, tropical savannas, pasturelands, and open woodlands. It seems especially fond of rural airfields and gravel roads. It has a bizarre display, in which the male inflates a large gular sac that droops down spectacularly from the neck and touches the ground, fans out its breast feathers, and raises its tail over its back, while strutting around slowly and making a number of strange grunts, croaks, booms, and even lionlike roars! Although they can be tricky to find as they stand motionless in tall grassy areas during their normal foraging behavior (when they are best approached in a vehicle), at such display times they emerge into the open and can readily be seen as they try to attract the females in this most impressive fashion.

B. Bush Thick-Knee *Burhinus grallarius* **54–59 cm/21–23 in.**

Thick-knees (or stone-curlews) are large, cryptically plumaged, gangly, long-legged shorebirds, or waders, that blend in well to their surroundings. Of the two Australian species this one prefers a variety of *dry* habitats, whereas the bulkier Beach Thick-Knee is associated with coastlines. Bush Thick-Knee is not choosy, as it is found in a range of dry areas including rainforest, woodlands, pastures, parks, and gardens throughout most of Australia except for the extreme south and desert areas. Their cryptic plumage makes them easy to overlook, and they are also most active at night, so they can appear rarer than they are at times as they rest in shaded areas of the leaf litter during the day. They are not especially shy, though, and are perhaps best seen at well-known locations where they rest in the daytime. They can be quite approachable, as they rely heavily on their camouflage to avoid detection (e.g., in cemeteries and parks in Cairns).

C. Beach Thick-Knee *Esacus magnirostris* **54–56 cm/21–22 in.**

Another long-legged wader or shorebird, found very locally in coastal areas of north Australia (from n. WA round to n. NSW). It is considered threatened in Australia owing to human disturbance of its coastal habitats (beaches, flats, and mangroves). A heavyset Thick-Knee (or stone-curlew) with a massive bill (compared with the Bush Thick-Knee, which inhabits drier habitats) that it uses to feed primarily on crabs along the shoreline, which it stalks slowly and deliberately, in heronlike fashion. Despite its huge size (it is one of the largest shorebirds on Earth) and its striking plumage—it has a piercing yellow eye, and bold black-and-white patterning on the wing—it can be hard to find, as it is a shy bird that often roosts by day in dense mangroves, and pairs can occupy territories that cover long stretches of coastline.

B

C

A. Australian Shelduck *Tadorna tadornoides* 56 (F)–72 (M) cm/22–28 in.

Shelducks belong in the same family as ducks, geese, and swans. They are somewhere between a goose and duck in size and are boldly patterned, colorful ducks that are equally at home on the land as in the water. Australian Shelduck is strikingly patterned and shows marked sexual dimorphism, that is, the male and female differ in their appearance. This plump duck is blackish bodied. The male has a bright buff area on the lower neck, and the female is bright, rich chestnut on the lower neck and chest. Both sexes have a dark blackish hood; however, the male has a completely dark head, with a subtle green sheen, *and no pale markings around the eye,* whereas the female has a variable amount of white around the eye. When they take flight they are no less striking, with big white flashes at the front of the wing. The Australian Shelduck feeds primarily by grazing on pasture out of the water but will also sometimes feed on aquatic vegetation in shallow areas by upending. It occurs around swamps, dams, and streams, where it is most often encountered in groups. Australian Shelduck is found over much of the south, although it is much scarcer within the inland parts of its range. Good places to find it include the shorelines of TAS and sw. WA, and the highlands of s. NSW. Like many wetland birds on the desertlike continent of Australia, it responds to changes in local water levels by moving and migrating over large areas to seek out suitable wetlands. At such times groups of shelducks fly between sites in a distinctive V-formation.

B. Radjah Shelduck *Tadorna radjah* 49–61 cm/19–24 in.

A small white shelduck closer to most ducks in size. In common with other shelducks it is also boldly marked, and patterned quite unlike any other duck in Australia. Radjah Shelduck is white headed with clean white underparts except for a conspicuous chestnut breast band, and has dark chestnut upperparts. At a distance it essentially looks black and white. Like many other shelducks, the sexes differ in appearance and can be told apart in the field: the male has a broader dark chestnut breast band than the female, although otherwise they look very similar. They are found only in northern Australia, where they are common in parts of the NT but quite local and scarce in e. QLD. They feed around the margins of wetlands, including pools, lagoons, tidal areas, and swamps, and are often seen perched up on banks and dikes around the fringes of these areas. A good site includes Fogg Dam in the NT, and anyone partaking in the Yellow Waters river cruise in Kakadu National Park (NT) will almost certainly get great looks at this striking duck. They are much less reliable and nomadic in QLD.

A. Magpie Goose *Anseranas semipalmata* **70 (F) –99 (M) cm/27.5–39 in.**
One of only two geese in Australia but regarded by many as being its own family. A massive white goose with a contrasting black head, neck, and wings. A large waterbird with a wingspan of over 1.5 m/5 ft; an odd, helmetlike knob on the crown; and a strange hooked bill, quite unlike that of any other goose. Thus for many years this unique waterbird was given its own family, although more recently it has been aligned into the family with other geese, ducks, and swans. One of the most conspicuous waterbirds of tropical northern Australia (where it is fairly common) owing to its striking coloration and its congregation in truly massive numbers, sometimes flocking in groups of thousands. It was once extremely widespread throughout NSW and VIC, but through hunting has become endangered in southern Australia. Although now still most abundant in the tropical north (n. WA, n. NT, and n. QLD), through significant protection measures the Magpie Goose is slowly spreading south once more and can be found in lower numbers in s. QLD and n. NSW. Magpie Goose feeds principally on aquatic vegetation that it finds by wading into the water or swimming and picking vegetation from the surface or upending for deeper food items. They are seen just as readily grazing on flats on land as they are in the water, and they often also perch in trees, something other geese do not normally do.

B. Cape Barren Goose *Cereopsis novaehollandiae* **75–90 cm/29.5–35.5 in.**
One of only two geese in Australia, this large pale goose is unique to Australia, where it is found only locally in the extreme south of the mainland and on TAS, where it is perhaps most readily seen. It is named after the tiny Tasmanian island of Cape Barren, where it was first discovered by early European explorers. Cape Barren Goose is a distinctive bird, generally all pale gray in color, with a scattering of dark markings on the upper side of the wings, and a dark bill with a prominent lime green upper section to the beak (known as the "cere"). Unlike some other geese the Cape Barren rarely swims and usually forages and grazes on land for its food. However, if they have young and are alarmed, the birds may take to water and can therefore swim when they need to escape a threat. Owing to their adaptability to feed on agricultural lands, they have recovered after recent declines and now appear to have a stable, if local, population in southern Australia. They usually nest on islands off the mainland and in TAS. Although large grazing flocks occur on the mainland during the nonbreeding season, they split off into flocks and breed on offshore islands.

A. Green Pygmy-Goose *Nettapus pulchellus* **32–38 cm/12.5–15 in.**
The smallest duck in Australia, and one of the smallest duck species in the world. Green Pygmy-Goose has a tiny, pink-tipped bill; dark, green-glossed upperparts; and conspicuous white cheek patches. It is sexually dimorphic: males have a dark neck and a reduced white area on the face, while females have a paler neck and a larger white face patch. It is locally common on large wetlands with abundant floating vegetation such as water lilies, in the tropical north of Australia from Broome in n. WA eastward to around Rockhampton in QLD. They are usually observed swimming among mats of floating vegetation and are rarely seen on land. They prefer to perch on submerged logs and branches well away from the edges of wetlands.

B. Maned Duck *Chenonetta jubata* **45–50 cm/17.5–19.5 in.**
Also known as Australian Wood Duck. A small-billed, gray-bodied duck, with bold black stripes on its back, and a distinctive rust-colored maned head in males (pale brown in females). Bold scaling on the lower neck and upper breast extends down onto the belly in females. A familiar species commonly found over much of Australia, except for humid northern areas and interior desert areas. Easily found around a variety of habitats, most notably around small farm dams, and wooded areas near water. It is the most land-based duck, often seen grazing out of water.

C. Blue-billed Duck *Oxyura australis* **36–44 cm/14–17.5 in.**
Male Blue-billed is a distinctive diving duck, similar in appearance to its American cousin, the Ruddy Duck: deep red wine colored with a black head and conspicuous powder blue bill. Females are less distinct: all dull brown with indistinct pale barring. They sit low in the water and usually hold their tail submerged. However, these stiff-tailed ducks sometimes hold it cocked, particularly in display, when it may also be fanned. This uncommon species inhabits large, well-vegetated wetlands in southern Australia (s. WA, locally in SA, and VIC and s. NSW, and TAS), where it is typically secretive, usually sticking close to the vegetated edges, where it can be hard to track, as it dives frequently. It can occur on more open waters when not breeding.

D. Pink-eared Duck *Malacorhynchus membranaceus* **37–45 cm/14.5–17.5 in.**
A peculiar Australian duck with bold plumage pattern and distinctive shape, by virtue of its large shovel-shaped, spatulate bill, which it uses for filter feeding. The body is boldly barred—the source of its old name, the "Zebra Duck"—and the head is pale with a large dark eye patch, and indistinct pink ear patch, visible only at very close range. Unlike many other duck species, males and females are alike. It is a widespread, though highly nomadic species, generally confined to inland Australia (except the driest desert areas) but wanders coastward during exceptionally dry periods inland. They occur on a variety of wetland habitats from large permanent lakes to temporary floodwaters and sewage ponds, where they are most often encountered in large flocks, usually dabbling on the water's surface or perched on emergent logs and branches. The **Australian Shoveler** *Anas rhynchotis* has a similar shape, but the female is dappled brown, and the male is brown with a gray head and a white vertical stripe at the base of the bill.

A. Plumed Whistling-Duck *Dendrocygna eytoni* 40–60 cm/16–23.5 in.

One of two whistling-duck species in Australia. **Whistling-ducks** are also sometimes called *tree-ducks* and are a subfamily within a larger family that also contains other ducks, geese, and swans. They are called whistling-ducks because they have strange, nasal whistling calls quite unlike those of most other duck species. All are tall with long, gooselike necks, and they spend more time in trees than other, more "traditional," duck species. Plumed Whistling-Ducks tend to forage on aquatic vegetation by grazing around the edges of wetlands (while the similar Wandering generally spends more time in the water). Plumed can also be distinguished from the similar Wandering (which frequently shares the same wetland areas) by its flashy, long, upswept plumes that protrude prominently from its flanks, and by the all-pale neck that lacks the dark upper border that Wandering Whistling-Ducks possess. It is a widespread species found in a variety of wetland areas and swamps throughout the tropical north of Australia and down the east side of the continent. It is often encountered in huge single-species flocks numbering hundreds of birds.

B. Wandering Whistling-Duck *Dendrocygna arcuata* 55–60 cm/22–23.5 in.

Like all whistling-ducks the Wandering has a strange, un-duck-like, high-pitched, whistling call. It is also tall, with long legs for a duck, and has the elongated neck characteristic of all whistling-ducks. This species has a home range similar to that of Plumed, with which it often occurs. It is most common in wetland areas of tropical northern Australia but is also found farther south along the eastern side of the continent. Like Plumed it also feeds predominantly at night, although unlike its congener, it prefers to feed in open water, where it dabbles and dives for aquatic vegetation. It is a darker bird than Plumed, with a dark rufous body, and possesses only short plumes along the flanks. Its pale foreneck contrasts strongly with a dark border down the back of the neck, quite unlike Plumed.

C. Black Swan *Cygnus atratus* 110–140 cm/43.5–55 in.

Many birds in Australia seem odd and very different from our perceptions of similar ones elsewhere in the world, and the Black Swan is the exemplar. It is the only swan species in the world that is predominantly black; all other eight species are completely white or nearly so. It is otherwise swanlike in appearance, with a long, graceful neck and rotund body like all the others. Largely black in color, with a bold reddish bill, and broad white fringes to the wings, which are normally noticeable only when the bird takes flight. A truly massive waterbird, with a wingspan of up to 2 m/6.5 ft. Common and conspicuous on larger wetland areas throughout most of Australia including TAS, except for the interior of the west. In northern Australia it tends to favor freshwater environments, although in the south it can also occur in saltwater habitats. Black Swan is most numerous in the south of its range. It is rarely alone and usually congregates in large groups.

A. Pacific Black Duck *Anas superciliosa* **47–60 cm/18.5–23.5 in.**
Australia's most common dabbling duck, similar to the familiar female mallard of North America and Europe. Dabbling ducks forage for food at the surface by swimming and upending, and do not dive. A brown duck, with a striking face pattern, it possesses a black cap and two horizontal black lines across the side of a buff face. Many ducks have an iridescent wing patch known as a *speculum*, best seen in flight, although it is sometimes revealed as a small, square patch toward the rear of the body sides when swimming. Pacific Black Duck has a deep glossy purplish green speculum. Males and females are alike. It is one of Australia's most familiar waterbirds and is found around a variety of wetlands across the entire continent.

B. Gray Teal *Anas gracilis* **42–44 cm/16.5–17.5 in.**
Teal are a group of small, round-headed dabbling-ducks. This is the "plain Jane" of ducks, with a uniform grayish brown body and a two-toned face: dark on the cap, with a whitish throat and neck, and a blood red eye. The contrasting throat can be used to differentiate this species from female Chestnut Teal. Males and females are identical. A common species that can be found on any type of wetland throughout Australia and TAS, where it is most often seen in flocks. Gray Teal is usually shyer than other teal species.

C. Chestnut Teal *Anas castanea* **35–50 cm/14–19.5 in.**
A strikingly dimorphic duck: males are distinctive with a deep green head and chestnut underparts, and a striking white flank patch. Females are wholly grayish brown like many other female ducks, particularly Gray Teal, although Chestnut is warmer toned with a uniformly colored head and neck. Chestnut Teal is a southern species, found in the southwest and southeast mainland, and TAS, and is most abundant in saline and coastal areas.

D. Australasian Grebe *Tachybaptus novaehollandiae* **23–25 cm/9–10 in.**
Grebes are slim diving waterbirds that prefer to flee danger underwater rather than in flight. Australasian is the smallest Australian species, which is distinctive in breeding plumage, with a piercing yellow eye in a dark head, and a bold chestnut stripe running down the sides of the neck, although dull and indistinct in winter, when it can readily be mistaken for another small grebe, the **Hoary-headed Grebe** *Poliocephalus poliocephalus*. However, Australasian displays a yellow eye in all plumages. The dark-eyed Hoary-headed further differs when breeding by showing a dark head covered with thin, frosty white striping. Both are found across the continent, although they are more abundant in the south.

E. Great Crested Grebe *Podiceps cristatus* **48–61 cm/19–24 in.**
A large, striking grebe with chestnut neck frills, and a bold dark crest when breeding. When not breeding, it is dull and best identified from the smaller grebes by its larger size and longer, daggerlike bill. The dramatic, synchronized courtship dance involves flaring of the crest and neck frills while the pair face each other, bobbing their heads regularly and touching bills at times, and climaxes when the pair rise high up in the water with vegetation in their bills and treading water. It is patchily distributed in eastern Australia (most abundant in the southeast) on large freshwater wetlands and occasionally also occurs in tidal bays.

C

E

A. Purple Swamphen *Porphyrio porphyrio* **35–39 cm/14–15.5 in.**

The birds on this page are **gallinules**: long-legged, long-toed, plump waterbirds, often with brightly colored bills that extend onto the forehead in the form of a hard shield. They are best identified by the color of the body, bill, and undertail coverts. Gallinules are often aggressive in defense of their territories. Although some dive for food, many are perfectly comfortable grazing on land, walking with tails cocked, exposing their undertail. They feed mainly on aquatic vegetation and invertebrates. Many species flick their tails nervously while swimming or grazing. The Swamphen is the largest mainland gallinule, purplish in color with a vivid scarlet bill, frontal shield, and legs, and white undertail coverts. A common bird unlikely to be confused with any other owing to its large size and purple color that is found all over eastern Australia and TAS but is absent from large areas of the west; it occurs only in n. and sw. WA. It is usually encountered in parties grazing around the edges of swamps, boggy pastures, and even urban lakes and ponds.

B. Dusky Moorhen *Gallinula tenebrosa* **35–40 cm/14–15.5 in.**

A small gallinule, all blackish gray in color with bright white undertail coverts, and bright red shield and bill that has a bold yellow tip. It can be found both grazing on land and also feeding regularly by upending for food. While it is swimming and on land the bright white undertail coverts are always highly visible, as the tail is often held cocked. A common and abundant gallinule over eastern Australia (all of QLD and NSW, and much of TAS) that is absent from large sectors of the west, being found only in sw. WA. It is found around a variety of freshwater wetlands including urban ponds and lakes, where it is most likely to be encountered.

C. Tasmanian Native-Hen *Tribonyx mortierii* **43–51 cm/17–20 in.**

A huge flightless gallinule found only on TAS. As it is unable to fly, the Native-Hen runs, dives, or swims to escape danger. This conspicuous gallinule is dark bodied with a bold white flank stripe that is its most prominent ID feature. It also has black undertail coverts, exposed always, as they permanently cock their tails when grazing. Moorhens and swamphens both show white undertail coverts. The bill is dull greenish, and the legs are gray colored. It is locally common on TAS over much of the island, although absent from the southwest (which is dominated by rainforest, which it avoids). Native-Hens feed mostly by grazing around the edges of marshes, marshy paddocks, grassy margins of farms and woodlands (usually near water), where small parties are normally conspicuous and easily found.

D. Eurasian Coot *Fulica atra* **35–39 cm/14–15.5 in.**

A slaty gray gallinule with a conspicuous white bill and shield that often dives for its food. Coots have an odd foot structure: the huge, clumsy-looking toes have flattened lobes that are adapted for powerful swimming and diving. Found commonly throughout mainland Australia (including TAS) and absent only from the interior of WA and w. SA. A generalist occurring on many wetland areas with abundant aquatic vegetation, such as freshwater lakes, reservoirs, town parks, and sewage ponds, as well as brackish lagoons and saline offshore waters. Most commonly encountered in rafts on large lakes.

B

D

A. Wandering Albatross *Diomedea exulans* 110–135 cm/43.5–53 in.

Albatrosses are massive, graceful, seafaring birds, some of which are among the largest flying birds on Earth. They are the great ocean wanderers, sometimes spending years at sea, and covering vast distances over the ocean in search of food that is very patchily distributed, so they can occur over wide geographic areas when not confined to their remote nesting areas. No albatrosses breed on mainland Australia; most occur as offshore migrants during the austral winter, when Australia offers great opportunities to encounter these enigmatic species. Albatrosses are a distinct family of birds within a larger group or order of birds called **Tubenoses**. Tubenoses are all seabirds that have a well-developed nasal passage that gives them a strong sense of smell, which is unusual among birds, which generally have little or no sense of smell at all. This allows the albatrosses to detect prey items such as squid, fish, and krill at sea that are very spottily distributed over the oceans. Adult birds are best identified by their huge size and greater extent of white on the upper wing, but great care is needed to distinguish them from other races such as *gibsoni* and *antipodensis*, which are regarded by many as a separate species, and from the two regularly occurring forms of Royal Albatross in our region. One of the trickier birds to ID, as multiple features are required to make a firm ID. It is most likely seen on pelagic trips into deeper waters in the southern half of the continent. Wandering Albatross is most often seen cruising low over the surface of the sea, where it rarely needs to flap its massive wings as it takes advantage of the ocean winds to glide effortlessly for long periods.

B. Black-browed Albatross *Thalassarche melanophris* 80–95 cm/31.5–37.5 in.

Black-browed Albatross is part of a group of smaller albatrosses known as "mollymawks." It is one of the more distinctive of the small albatrosses, as it always has a thick black area or "brow" around the eye, and its underwings have a very broad dark border around them (adults) or are almost wholly dark (juveniles), whereas the other small albatrosses have a largely white underside to the wings with a narrow dark border to them. The upperwings are solidly dark, like those of the other mollymawks. Adult Black-browed has an all-white head and bright orange-yellow bill, which is grayish and indistinct bill in juveniles. Like some of the other small albatrosses, they can often be observed from land where they come to regularly forage for cephalopods (including squid), fish, and krill. Like all albatrosses, they are most often seen gliding gracefully and effortlessly (rarely flapping their wings) low over the sea, although if they have found food, or when resting, they may be seen sitting on the surface of the ocean. Australia's most commonly seen albatross from land, around the southern coastlines.

A. Yellow-nosed Albatross *Thalassarche chlororhynchos* 75 cm/29.5 in.

Both the small albatrosses on this plate are also mollymawks. Substantially smaller than Wandering Albatrosses but also equally confusing and difficult to ID without experience. No albatrosses breed in continental Australia or TAS; they visit Australian waters only as migrants during the austral winter, usually between April and November. Yellow-nosed is the smallest Australian species, with a wingspan of up to 2 m/6.5 ft. Adult Yellow-nosed have all-dark upperwings and a wholly dark tail, an all-white head, and a distinctively colored large bill: all dark with a yellow outline on the upper edge, the "yellow nose." Like all albatrosses, it is most likely to be seen from a boat trip into deeper southern Australian waters, although it may be seen from land when blown inshore during periods of strong onshore winds. Albatrosses are well known to fishermen, as they often follow boats, and this one is no exception. In common with all the other Australian albatrosses, Yellow-nosed feeds on fish and a variety of cephalopods, including squid. Albatrosses glide low over the surface of the water in search of these food items, which they often locate with their strong sense of smell. Once they locate food, they drop down onto the sea and pick the items from the surface of the ocean while sitting on the water.

B. White-capped Albatross *Thalassarche cauta* 95 cm/37.5 in.

Sometimes called Shy Albatross. Another small albatross, or mollymawk, although larger than Yellow-nosed that may be seen in the same waters on occasion and shares a similar appearance: both have all-dark upperwings, dark-bordered largely white underwings, and a dark tail. Where they differ is at the front end. The head of White-capped is usually shaded with gray (all white in adult and juvenile Yellow-nosed), and the bill is predominantly pale yellowish (adult) or pale gray (young birds) in White-capped with a dark marking near the tip. One of the more frequently seen albatrosses from mainland areas (along with Black-browed and Yellow-nosed) in appropriate conditions (strong onshore winds), although much more frequently seen from cruises into deeper offshore waters around the southern half of Australia. White-capped Albatross feeds on squid, fish, and also barnacles and crustaceans, which are taken while sitting on the surface of the water by surface-feeding (picking from the surface), or by surface-plunging (making shallow dives just below the surface). Albatross taxonomy is very complex, and not yet fully understood, with many different races centered on isolated breeding populations. The Shy Albatross complex contains multiple races and phases, many of which are represented in Australian waters.

A. Australasian Gannet *Morus serrator* 84–91 cm/33–36 in.

Gannets and boobies are large seabirds that share the same family. They have long, sharply pointed wings and heavy bills, and have the striking habit of diving dramatically from great heights above the ocean to plunge into the water to pursue their prey. The three species of gannets around the world are all large (larger than their booby cousins), heavy-billed, long-tailed seabirds, mostly white in color with bold black markings, and a distinct yellow hue to the head. The Australasian Gannet is the only regularly occurring gannet species in Australia. It, too, is almost all white, except for a broad black border to the hind wing, and a largely black pointed tail, both of which are best viewed in flight. It also has a black outline to the front of the face, and a yellow head. They are superficially similar to some of the graceful albatrosses when seen at distance, most notably the Wandering Albatross. They are best distinguished by shape: albatrosses have longer, narrower wings that are more uniform in width along most of their length, squarish tails, and thick, uniform-width bills that are blunt ended. Gannets by comparison have shorter, broader wings that gradually come to a pointed tip, long pointed tails, and sharp, triangular-shaped bills. These characteristic combines to give albatrosses and gannets different profiles in flight, which is how they are most often seen at sea. On close inspection the gannet also has a yellow head that albatrosses do not possess. Many of the albatrosses also have dark backs (e.g., Black-browed, White-capped, Yellow-nosed), unlike the white-backed gannet. Furthermore, although gannets do glide for short periods, they tend to flap regularly in flight, while the albatrosses can glide great distances without flapping. The Australasian Gannet is a coastal southern species that occurs from the central coast of WA south and east around to the s. QLD coastline. These pelagic birds are most likely to be seen in flight either blown in close to shore after windy conditions, or from a boat trip into deeper waters, where they are more regular than along the coastlines. They are only exceptionally seen away from coasts.

B. Brown Booby *Sula leucogaster* 65–75 cm/25.5–29.5 in.

Boobies are seabirds in the same family as the gannets. Although similarly shaped, boobies are smaller and stockier. Their feeding style is similar to that of the gannets, although boobies usually dive for fish from less dramatic heights. Brown Booby is a brown seabird with a dark brown hood, chest, and upperparts, and contrasting white underparts and wing linings that make for quite a striking bird even at some distance. It has a prominent horn-colored bill that is blue at the base in male birds, and has a piercing yellow eye. Brown Booby occurs coastally all across the tropical seas of northern Australia, (from the central coast of WA eastward around to the north coast of NSW). They breed on remote offshore islands and roost on sandy cays and small islands, and so are most likely to be seen on cruises to offshore reefs (e.g., Michaelmas Cay). Brown Booby is the most likely member of this family to be found roosting in harbors along the northern Australian coastline.

A. Hutton's Shearwater *Puffinus huttoni* 36–38 cm/14–15 in.

Shearwaters are long-winged seabirds from a group known as *tubenoses*, which possess a very strong sense of smell that enables them to locate food. They are gregarious, so they are most often found in flocks. Small shearwaters have a fluttering flight action, broken up by short glides. Hutton's is bicolored: solid blackish brown on the upper side and largely white below. One of two similar species, along with **Fluttering Shearwater** *P. gavial*, which need to be distinguished from each other with great care (wingspans of around 75 cm/29 in.): Hutton's has a longer body and neck, and more slender wings. Generally, Fluttering has brighter white wing linings with less dark smudging within this white area. Thus, Fluttering usually shows extensive white on the underwing, while this area is more limited in Hutton's. Fluttering therefore is a species showing more color contrast, displayed also on the head, which is sharply demarcated between the white throat and dark head and neck. In Hutton's this area is more diffuse; the dark color often bleeds onto the throat, and even sometimes gives Hutton's a hooded appearance. Experience is often required to ID these birds to species, and both can be found in the same flock. Hutton's occurs around all the coasts of Australia, although it is most abundant in the southeast, where it overlaps with Fluttering.

B. Short-tailed Shearwater *Puffinus tenuirostris* 42–45 cm/16.5–17.5 in.

The following two species are larger (wingspans 1 m/over 3 ft), dark shearwaters that are characterized by a more languid flight interspersed with longer glides than the smaller shearwaters. Short-tailed is a large, almost wholly dark brown bird with a subdued paler panel on the underwing. Good views, great care, and experience are required to differentiate Short-tailed from Sooty Shearwaters. Both are dark with a similar shape and body pattern. However, the underwings of Sooty usually show a large and conspicuous pale area, although extra care should be taken when judging this on bright days, because reflections can make the dark underwings of Short-tailed appear paler than they actually are. Furthermore, if seen very close, the bill structure can aid ID: Short-tailed has a short, relatively thick bill compared with that of Sooty. It is abundant in coastal waters from s. QLD to sw. WA, where they are most likely to be seen in large flocks, during offshore boat trips, where several shearwater species may be present.

C. Sooty Shearwater *Puffinus griseus* 43–46 cm/17–18 in.

A large, dark chocolate brown shearwater, with the slower flight typical of larger shearwaters, lacking the fluttering quality of the small black-and-white species. Sooty Shearwater is characterized by bold white panels visible on the underwing, which starkly contrast with the dark overall body color. The underwing pattern aids differentiation from the very similar Short-tailed. Further, subtle differences from Short-tailed are the slimmer, longer bill, larger size, and longer, more slender and pointed wings. Overlaps in range with Short-tailed along the southern half of the east coast, TAS, and the entire south coast, where it is also most likely to be found from a headland or on pelagic trips into deep waters. Care should also be taken to distinguish it from the **Wedge-tailed Shearwater** *Puffinus pacificus*, a common shearwater off the east coast, best identified by its longer, diamond-shaped tail.

C

A. Australian Pelican *Pelecanus conspicillatus* **160–180 cm/63–71 in.**

The only pelican in Australia, where it is the largest waterbird. It is also the largest of all the eight pelican species in the world. It weighs up to a massive 15 kg/33 lb, boasts a huge wingspan of nearly 2.5 m/8 ft, and has a lengthy bill of nearly 48 cm/19in.! A typical pelican: mostly white in color, with contrasting black markings on the wings (most visible in flight), with the distinctive, instantly recognizable, large pink bill with a huge throat pouch for catching fish. Pelicans usually fish in formation: a group of birds "herd" fish into an area so they can catch them. Once the group has channeled the fish into an appropriate position, the pelican plunges its bill into the water, capturing both large amounts of water and the fish in its large bill pouch. It siphons the water out from the pouch by pressing it against its chest. Once only the fish remains, the pelican then repositions it within the pouch and swallows it lengthwise. The remarkable throat pouch of the Australian pelican is capable of taking in over 13.5 L/3 gal of water. Like many Australian birds that live on this desertlike continent, which undergoes massive shifts in the availability of water annually and seasonally, the pelican can be highly nomadic, traveling vast distances in search of water. It is found permanently throughout most coastal areas and moves inland during flood years to breed within vast colonies.

B. Great Frigatebird *Fregata minor* **86–100 cm/34–39.5 in.**

One of two very similar species of frigatebird in Australia. **Frigatebirds** are oceanic birds, found mostly out to sea, and less often close inshore, that are famed for several distinctive family features: the males of all frigatebirds possess bright scarlet gular sacs on their throat that they inflate with air to dramatic effect to attract females. Second, they are famous for their "robbery," scientifically termed *klepto-parasitism*, whereby they harass other seabirds and cause them to drop their prey (usually squid or fish) in the process, and then the frigatebird swoops down quickly and steals the food from the hapless seabird. They are distinctively shaped birds with a long hooked bill, narrow sharply pointed wings, and a deeply forked tail, giving them an unmistakable silhouette. In all plumages the significantly smaller **Lesser Frigatebird** (70–80 cm/27.5–31.5 in.) can be distinguished from the Greater in that they have a thin white line extending from the flanks onto the inner wing that is completely absent in Greater. The females are most easily distinguished, as the female Lesser has a dark throat, and the Greater has a white throat concolorous with its white chest patch. Both frigatebirds are found at sea off northern Australia, and are most likely seen either on boat trips into deeper Australian waters (e.g., Great Barrier Reef cruises) or coming into roost around coastal ports such as Darwin (NT) and Weipa (QLD).

A. Australasian Darter *Anhinga novaehollandiae* **86–94 cm/34–37 in.**
Darters, or "snakebirds," are a distinct family of cormorant-like birds, being large, long-necked, black fish-eating birds, although darters are much slimmer bodied, with long, thin snakelike necks, and finer, pointed bills compared with the cormorants. Darters also sit low in the water when swimming, with just their necks usually visible. Like cormorants they often perch at the edge of wetlands and stretch their wings out for long periods to dry them. Darter also has a bold white line that runs from the bill onto the upper neck. Young birds are strikingly buff, although both adults and young birds are best identified by their distinctive sinuous necks and slender build.

B. Little Black Cormorant *Phalacrocorax sulcirostris* **55–65 cm/21–25.5 in.**
Cormorants are black or pied fish-eating birds with long necks and tails, hooked bills, and short legs with webbed feet, that have the conspicuous habit of perching with their wings outstretched to dry them. Little Black is the smallest Australian species, easily identified by its small size, and all-black color, lacking pale facial markings. A common and gregarious species, continent-wide, in both freshwater and saltwater environments, where they are most likely to be encountered in groups.

C. Great Cormorant *Phalacrocorax carbo* **80–85 cm/31.5–33.5 in.**
The largest cormorant, best identified by its size, and generally all-blackish coloration except for a prominent pale facial patch and pale band above the thighs (in adults). Young birds are all brownish and lack the bold markings, and so are best identified by size alone. Great Cormorants are found widely in freshwater and coastal environments, throughout the continent except for western desert areas, where they are often seen resting on piers or jetties, or in dead trees.

D. Black-faced Cormorant *Phalacrocorax fuscescens* **60–69 cm/23.5–27 in.**
A large pied cormorant species that is confined to the south coasts and TAS. Superficially similar in appearance to another large species, **Pied Cormorant** *P. varius*, which occurs throughout all the wetter parts of the mainland although is absent from TAS, and therefore overlaps with Black-faced along the south coast. Black-faced Cormorant can be differentiated, though, by a black, not peach-colored, face and also has a blackish-colored (not horn-colored) bill. Black-faced Cormorant is a marine and coastal ground-nesting species.

E. Little Pied Cormorant *Phalacrocorax melanoleucos* **55–65 cm/21.5–25.5 in.**
A small black-and-white cormorant that is the most abundant cormorant in Australia. Most readily identified by its small size, which can be striking when in direct comparison with the much larger Pied/Black-faced. Further differences from the other two black-and-white cormorants are that Little Pied has a yellow bill and more white on the face that extends above the eye. It is found throughout the mainland and TAS on small and large bodies of water both in coastal, saline habitats and freshwater environments. It is a colonial, tree-nesting cormorant species.

A. Pacific Heron *Ardea pacifica* 75–105 cm/29.5–41.5 in.

Also known as White-necked Heron. **Herons** are large, long-necked, long-legged fish-eating birds. They fly with necks tucked in, not stretched out like cranes or storks. Pacific Heron has a dark blackish blue body and a long all-white neck and head. The gray legs and huge size help to distinguish this heron from considerably smaller young pied herons (which also possess an all-white head and neck). In flight the dark wings have a small but conspicuous white window on the leading edge of the wing, which shows as a distinct shoulder patch when perched. It is a common and widespread heron throughout the continent except for the eastern interior of WA and extreme w. SA, where it is found on flooded fields, small farm dams, and many other small pools and flooded areas. It is rarely found in tidal areas, and usually favors small wetlands or marshy areas.

B. Great-billed Heron *Ardea sumatrana* 100–110 cm/39.5–43.5 in.

The largest heron in Australia, standing over a meter (3.5 ft) tall. A large, dark heron with a dusky gray head, neck, and body with dull grayish legs and bill, and a dull whitish breast. The sheer size and overall dull coloration (lacking white on the head or neck) distinguish this massive waterbird from any other heron. Young birds are all brown and therefore could be confused with the similarly colored juvenile Black-necked Stork. However, storks have much thicker bills with a markedly different shape, and fly with their necks extended. Great-billed Heron is an uncommon bird of the coastal tropical north of Australia (n. WA, n. NT, and n. QLD), found in forest-lined creeks, mangroves, and tidal areas, usually where there is plenty of surrounding cover. When encountered, this large, shy heron is usually found quietly feeding alone along the banks of creeks or large rivers.

C. White-faced Heron *Egretta novaehollandiae* 66–68 cm/26–26.5 in.

A common and familiar light ashy gray heron with a bold white face, piercing pale eye, and yellow legs. The overall pale coloration is quite unlike that of any other species. Young birds lack the white face, although are all pale gray like adults, so equally distinctive. It is a common and widespread heron in a variety of wetland habitats throughout Australia (including TAS). It occurs in both freshwater and saline environments, and can be found in many habitats, including tidal flats, small farm dams, saltmarshes, flooded pastures, harbors, and beaches. Less wary and more approachable than many other herons.

D. Pied Heron *Egretta picata* 43–55 cm/17–21.5 in.

A handsome and striking little black-and-white heron. Pied Heron has a dusky gray body, white neck, and a dusky gray cap. It also has bright yellow legs and bill, and a piercing yellow eye. Although superficially similar to the much larger Pacific Heron, the gray cap of adult Pied Heron separates it from that species. Juveniles are more similar to Pacific Herons, lacking the gray cap of adult Pied Herons, although they have yellow legs and lack the bold white shoulder of Pacific Heron. It is a northern species confined to the tropics of NT and n. QLD, where it occurs in the coastal zone. Pied Herons occur on both tidal saline environments and freshwater wetlands, where they are usually encountered in flocks. It is a distinctly gregarious species relative to other herons, and rarely found alone.

B

D

A. Great Egret *Ardea alba* 83–103 cm/32.5–40.5 in.

Egrets are white herons, which display delicate plumes in the breeding season, best distinguished from one another by relative size and examination of the bill and legs. Great Egret is the largest egret species. In breeding plumage the dark legs are flushed reddish on the upper section from the knees up. The bill in breeding plumage is blackish, and the lores are pale green, while the bill and facial skin are yellow when not breeding. Crucially, in the Great Egret the bare facial skin patch extends beyond the eye. The fine breeding plumes grow out from the back and extend down beyond the tail. They never possess breast plumes. A common and widespread species over almost all of Australia, found on both saltwater and freshwater wetlands (often found well inland), where they are most often found wading in the shallows.

B. Intermediate Egret *Mesophoyx intermedia* 55–70 cm/21.5–27.5 in.

Intermediate in size between smaller Little, and larger Great Egrets. In breeding plumage it has an orange bill, green lores, and dark legs washed reddish from the knees upward. It also grows fine breeding plumes both from the breast (unlike Great) and the back. Nonbreeding Intermediate has blackish legs and yellow bill and facial skin. Importantly, the facial skin patch does not extend beyond the back of the eye (unlike on Great). Both Great and Intermediate have a similar structure, and often hold their kinked necks in the shape of a question mark. A common egret over n. WA, much of the NT, and all of eastern Australia and TAS, where it often outnumbers both Great and Little Egrets, and largely absent from southern Australia. Likely to be found wading in the shallows, where they fish much like Great Egrets: freezing for long periods then suddenly reaching out lightning quick to grab a fish.

C. Little Egret *Egretta garzetta* 55–65 cm/21.5–25.5 in.

A small heron with black legs and bill, and yellow facial skin. In breeding plumage the facial skin flushes red or orange-red at the height of the season. Furthermore, when breeding, Little Egret grows fine breeding plumes that extend from both the breast and back, and also grows a few plumes that grow out from the nape. When fishing, this egret can be quite acrobatic: quickly and suddenly dashing after fish while raising its wings in the process, a distinctive behavioral feature that is quite different from the slow deliberate feeding style of both Intermediate and Great Egrets.

D. Cattle Egret *Bubulcus ibis* 70 cm/27.5 in.

A small egret with colorful breeding plumage that is rich rufous on the head, neck, breast, and back. At this time it also has reddish legs, and the bill flushes red, too. The bird also grows short spiky plumes on the back of the head and breast that are not long and fine like the breeding plumes of other egrets. When not breeding, the Cattle Egret has an entirely white body, dark legs, and yellow bill and facial skin. A common and spreading species, found around the coastal zone of almost all of mainland Australia, and absent from much of the interior and the coasts of SA and western WA. It is a very social egret, often seen in large flocks in farm fields foraging on the ground around livestock. It is one of the most widespread birds on Earth, and has adapted well to expanding farmlands.

A. Royal Spoonbill *Platalea regia* 75–80 cm/29.5–31.5 in.

Spoonbills are large, white, long-legged, heronlike waterbirds, similar in appearance to egrets, but are in fact in a separate family altogether (Spoonbills and Ibises) and have a distinctively shaped bill that makes them strikingly different. All spoonbill beaks are quite literally shaped like a spoon and are used to forage in a distinctive feeding action. The birds sweep their slightly opened bill widely from side to side, then snap it shut whenever the inside of it comes into contact with prey items like crustaceans, fish, or insects. There are two different species of spoonbill in Australia, which differ in the color of their oddly shaped bills. Royal Spoonbill has a black face, legs, and bill, and **Yellow-billed Spoonbill** (*P. flavipes*) has a yellow bill and legs, making the two easily told apart. Both grow delicate breeding plumes in the breeding season, when Royal has long white plumes that hang down from its nape, while Yellow-billed has buff-colored plumes that grow down from the chest. Royal Spoonbill is found on a variety of wetlands and in coastal areas in eastern and northern Australia, and only the northern section of WA, and is generally absent from TAS. Yellow-billed Spoonbill is rarely coastal, being more common inland, and is often found on smaller wetlands and dams than those where Royal occurs. Unlike Royal, it is also present in s. WA and n. TAS. Royal Spoonbill is generally more regularly encountered than Yellow-billed.

B. Striated Heron *Butorides striata* 43 cm/17 in.

Also known as Mangrove Heron. A tiny grayish heron with a black cap that is found throughout large sections of Asia and South America as well as Australia. It is confined to coastal areas of northern and eastern Australia, where it can be difficult to detect as it sits quietly and motionless on the edges of mangroves and tidal areas, on the hunt for crabs, mollusks, and small fish. Unlike some larger herons and egrets, it often sits in a hunched posture with the neck tucked in tight and the body crouched low while hunting, so its long neck is rarely seen until it suddenly lurches out to snatch its prey. Most likely to be seen at the edge of stands of mangroves, or along the edge of a tidal channel, at low tide.

C. Rufous Night-Heron *Nycticorax caledonicus* 55–65 cm/21.5–25.5 in.

Also known as Nankeen Night-Heron. As the name suggests, this heron is mainly nocturnal, feeding at night, and sleeping well hidden in dense tree cover by day. This handsome heron is found in a variety of wetlands (tidal and freshwater) over all of eastern and northern Australia, even occurring in Australia's biggest cities, and also patchily in w. WA, although it is largely absent from desert areas. It is a strikingly marked waterbird with richly colored rufous upperparts, bright white underside, and a neat black cap. In breeding plumage, in common with many other herons and egrets, it grows delicate white breeding plumes that protrude from the nape. Although difficult to find by day as they sleep motionless in thick vegetation, they are perhaps best found at traditional roost locations, or emerging to feed along rivers at dusk.

A. Black-necked Stork *Ephippiorhynchus asiaticus* **110–135 cm/43.5–53 in.**

This eye-catching bird, also sometimes called "Jabiru" by Australian birders, is the only stork in Australia. A huge, long-legged, boldly patterned black-and-white bird, with striking bright red legs, the Black-necked Stork is nearly 1.3 m/4 ft tall and has a monstrous 2 m/7 ft wingspan. It is therefore unlikely to be confused with any other Australian bird. Only the cranes are of similar shape and so tall, but not black and white. Unlike cranes, storks do not occur in large flocks but are usually found alone or in pairs. They are most often found around an assortment of freshwater wetlands, from wet pastures to large lakes and reservoirs, and more rarely also on tidal flats along the coastlines. They are found mainly in tropical northern Australia and down the east side of the mainland, being much more abundant in the north of their range. Black-necked Storks are especially abundant in the NT, and are usually seen on boat cruises in Kakadua National Park.

B. Sarus Crane *Grus antigone* **112–115 cm/44–45.5 in.**

One of two crane species in Australia, the Sarus is also found across much of Asia. Although widespread globally, this is the less common of the two cranes, first recorded in Australia in the late 1960s. The core of its range is in ne. QLD. The Sarus, in common with other cranes, is a massive bird, standing nearly 1.5 m/5 ft tall, and has a huge wingspan of almost 2.5 m/8 ft. Both crane species are remarkably similar in appearance: large pale gray birds with striking red heads. At large roost sites in QLD both species can occur side by side, where they flock in the hundreds. They are best told apart by leg color and examination of the head and neck. The legs of Sarus are a dull reddish pink, and the red on the head crucially extends down onto the upper neck. Furthermore, Sarus lacks the distinctive flap or dewlap on the chin that Brolga shows. As these are truly massive birds these features can often be seen even at long range. Both Sarus Cranes and Brolgas are best looked for at communal roost sites, where they gather in large numbers and draw attention to their presence with their frequent trumpeting calls. They are also frequently found feeding in red-stained agricultural fields, and are often easy to find courtesy of their large size and open habitat.

C. Brolga *Grus rubicunda* **77–134 cm/30.5–53 in.**

The Brolga is endemic to Australia (found only there). More widespread than the Sarus, the Brolga is found extensively in northern tropical Australia and down the eastern side of mainland Australia, although neither species is present on TAS. It is best differentiated from the Sarus by its dull grayish legs, red that is limited to only the head (*not* extending down onto the neck), and by its distinctive head shape with a prominent dewlap on the underside of its chin (which is lacking in Sarus). In parts of northern QLD they can be seen flocking in the hundreds with Sarus Cranes, which makes for a spectacular sight, as both species often bugle to each other loudly and dance with one another as part of their elaborate and striking displays, creating a truly amazing wildlife scene.

C

A. Glossy Ibis *Plegadis falcinellus* **65–75 cm/25.5–29.5 in.**

Ibises are fairly long-legged wading waterbirds with long, down-curved bills somewhat like that of a curlew in shape (a kind of shorebird). Ibises are counterintuitively grouped in the same family (*Threskiornithidae*) as the heronlike spoonbills, in spite of their markedly different bill shapes. All three Australian species of ibis are found around the edges of wetland areas, but are also at home feeding in pastures. The Glossy Ibis is distinct from the other Australian species in being wholly dark in coloration, with almost no white at all. The Glossy Ibis generally appears all black, although it is actually deep reddish brown and glossed with purple-green on the back and wings, which can usually be discerned only in strong sunlight. They are most often found in single-species flocks probing in shallow wetlands for frogs and fish, or foraging in pastures for insects. They are found throughout most of Australia, except for the interior of the west, and parts of the extreme south of the mainland, and are absent from TAS, although are generally uncommon. Unlike the other two ibis species, Glossy is never around human habitations, whereas the other species can regularly be found around towns and farmlands. Glossy is also the shyest of the species. When moving between feeding sites Glossy Ibis may fly in single-species flocks in V-formation.

B. Australian Ibis *Threskiornis molucca* **65–75 cm/25.5–29.5 in.**

Also known as Australian White Ibis. A common and familiar white ibis, found in a range of wetlands and also regularly in town parks of the east, where they are often highly visible, tame, and approachable. An adaptable ibis, it has a more varied diet than other species, feeding on a variety of fish, crayfish, mollusks, and frogs, in addition to insects and even garbage in urban areas. Easily recognizable by virtue of its almost wholly white body with a contrasting black neck and head, and striking black wing tips in flight. They are most often seen like most ibis in flocks, sometimes mixing with Straw-necked Ibis, and are easy to find, as they feed in open habitats, including parks and gardens. Found throughout northern and eastern Australia, where they are most abundant, although only patchily in coastal and northern WA. They are absent from the most arid parts of the continent.

C. Straw-necked Ibis *Threskiornis spinicollis* **60–70 cm/23.5–27.5 in.**

Another familiar, common, ibis species that like the Australian also turns up regularly in town parks and gardens. Unlike the Australian Ibis, with which they sometimes flock, Straw-necked is largely dark in coloration, with white mainly on the underside and sides of the neck. At close range are seen the strange straw yellow plumes on the neck that gives it its name. Found in a wide variety of freshwater wetlands and fields over much of Australia, except for the dry interior of the west, where no ibis occur. It is usually found in flocks foraging for fish, mollusks, and insects that can include grasshoppers, crickets, and locusts. Like Australian Ibis, and unlike Glossy, Straw-necked are also quite approachable and often tame round towns.

A. Osprey *Pandion haliaetus* 50–65 cm/19.5–25.5 in.

A distinctive, fish-eating hawk that occurs along most Australian coastlines, although rarer in the southeast and TAS. It is rarely seen away from water. Generally coastal, although it can be found along large rivers and substantial inland wetlands. When fishing, it soars high initially to locate schools of fish, then swoops down and glides low over the water before plunging spectacularly into the water to grab its prey, causing considerable splashing in the process. Osprey is able to plunge deeper than 1 m/3 ft and has phenomenal grip in its sharp and powerful talons, so that is can firmly grasp its slippery prey. When it emerges from the water, it does so with the fish clasped firmly in its talons, facing forward, and flies directly to a nearby prominent perch. From underneath, Osprey appears largely white with a dark line through the eye, and faint, scattered dark markings on the underside of its white wings. They often perch prominently and construct huge, highly visible nests of sticks in open places, such as atop power poles, electrical pylons, and other conspicuous structures. Although once considered threatened, the Osprey is becoming an increasingly familiar site in coastal eastern Australia.

B. White-bellied Sea-Eagle *Haliaeetus leucogaster* 75–85 cm/29.5–33.5 in.

Another raptor of coasts and wetlands that preys on fish in addition to snakes, turtles, and small mammals. It is a large bird of prey that flies with a distinctive flight action, soaring on upward-held wings that make a deep V shape when seen head-on (osprey flies with flatter, M-shaped wings in comparison). Sea-Eagle is massive with very broad wings and a relatively short, wedge-shaped, tail. It is uniform pale gray on the upper side of the wings, while the head, neck, and underside of the body are bright white. The underwings are also white, with a broad black border on the back edge. They are most often seen gliding high over the sea or along coastlines singly or in pairs, or sitting on a high prominent perch around wetlands and in coastal areas. They are found on all the coastlines of Australia, including TAS, and occur some distance inland from the coast in the east, where they can be found around larger wetlands and dams. A more wary bird than Osprey, with which is shares many habitats, and is less often seen around human habitations than that species.

C. Wedge-tailed Eagle *Aquila audax* 85–105 cm/33.5–41.3 in.

The largest raptor in Australia. All dark in color, with a distinctive, long, diamond-shaped tail. Can be identified by a combination of the massive size, the tail shape, and all-dark appearance. Occurs widely across Australia and TAS in a range of habitats, although is perhaps most abundant inland within open country. "Wedgies" are known to feed on a variety of prey including lizards, small mammals, and rabbits, and also carrion. Indeed, one of the most common ways in which to see them is feeding on roadkill along an outback road, where one or two birds may be attending the carcass much in the manner of a vulture. Alternatively, one or two birds may be seen flying high in the sky, where their distinctive tail shape and deep dihedral silhouette help ID them.

A. Black Kite *Milvus migrans* 45–55 cm/17.5–21.5 in.

The first three species are similar **kites**: long-winged, soaring raptors with fingered wing tips, the first two of which are frequent scavengers, especially around roadkill. Black is often confused with Whistling Kite but is darker overall, having an all-dark body and underwings except for a small window on the outer wing. However, Black's main feature is the tail, which is deeply forked. When perched it is a darker bird than Whistling, with an obvious dark smudge around the eye, lacking in that species. Black Kite is widespread over mainland Australia, being absent only from se. WA, se. NSW, e. VIC, and TAS. It is found in open grasslands, farmlands, timbered watercourses, and other open habitats. The consummate scavenger, flocks of them regularly gather around slaughterhouses and rubbish dumps. It also regularly attends bush fires, where, interestingly, some kites have been observed taking embers from the flames and dropping them into unburned areas.

B. Whistling Kite *Haliastur sphenurus* 50–60 cm/19.5–23.5 in.

Similar to Black Kite, although with a paler body and pale wing linings on the underwing in flight. Whistling also shows a prominent pale vertical wedge on the underside of the secondaries in flight, which in combination create a distinct pale M shape on the underwing. Importantly, it has an unmarked rounded tail, quite unlike Black. It is very widespread over the mainland, being absent only from the most arid areas of WA, although Whistling does occur on TAS, where Black Kite is absent. It frequents open woodlands, plains, open forests, timbered watercourses, and even tidal flats, and is usually encountered singly or in pairs, flocking less often than Black Kite. Whistling has a closer affinity with watercourses than does Black Kite.

C. Brahminy Kite *Haliastur Indus* 45–50 cm/17.5–19.5 in.

A striking kite, with a rufous body and clean white head. In flight the rufous upperwings contrast noticeably with black wing tips. Brahminy Kite is strictly coastal and found from c. WA eastward around the top of Australia to n. NSW. Its strong affinity for coastal areas is reflected in its former name: "Red-backed Sea-Eagle." Brahminy Kites occur around tidal flats, mangroves, beaches, estuaries, harbors, and coastal forests, where they are most likely to be seen soaring alone or in pairs high above the coastline.

D. Australian Kite *Elanus axillaris* 35 cm/13.5 in.

Also known as Black-shouldered Kite. A distinctive small, slender-winged, black-and-white kite that hunts by hovering for prey (such as rodents and grasshoppers). A mainly white bird with pale ashy gray upperparts, and a bold black shoulder patch, visible as a distinct bar in flight. A widespread and common bird found throughout the mainland in open woodlands, farmlands, and grasslands with scattered trees, where it is most likely to be noticed hovering for prey, or perched on an exposed branch or wire.

A. Australian Kestrel *Falco cenchroides* **30–35 cm/12–14 in.**

The only Australian kestrel species, also called Nankeen Kestrel. **Falcons** are small, swift raptors that have narrow, pointed wings and long tails. **Kestrels** are a subgroup of falcons that have a characteristic hovering hunting style, which helps ID them. Males and females are quite different: both are rufous birds, but the male has a contrasting dove gray head and tail that stand out in flight especially. Both sexes have a strong dark subterminal tail band and contrasting black tips to the upperwings, which are striking features in flight. The rufous coloration and hovering behavior make this falcon easily recognized. It is common and widespread throughout the mainland and TAS in open country.

B. Australian Hobby *Falco longipennis* **30–36 cm/12–14 in.**

Hobbies are agile, narrow-winged, long-tailed falcons that hunt at high speed, scything through the air to swoop on prey. Its typical falcon shape (narrow, sharply pointed wings), upperpart coloration (dark gray), and hunting style make it readily confused with Peregrine, which has broader wings and a shorter tail, and lacks the rufous underparts of Hobby. The rufous underside of hobby distinguished it from all other falcons. Hobby is widespread over open wooded habitats and scrubby areas and even wanders into urban environments over most of mainland Australia and TAS. It is usually observed in flight, either alone or in pairs, when hunting on the wing over open areas.

C. Peregrine Falcon *Falco peregrinus* **35–50 cm/12–19.5 in.**

The fastest bird on earth, reaching up to 320 km/h (200 mph) in stooping flight. Hobbies and peregrines do not hover like kestrels. A large, dark-backed falcon, much like a hobby on the upperparts although with heavily barred or streaked underparts that are dull buff, not rich rufous. It is also is more heavily built than hobby, with broader, shorter wings. It is found sparsely throughout Australia and TAS, occupying many habitats, although it is most common where rocky outcrops provide vital nesting sites. In some towns and cities in Australia they hunt pigeons (where buildings provide nest sites), and haunt large flocks of shorebirds in tidal areas, putting the fear of death into them when they appear, causing the shorebirds to flea en masse, creating a spectacular scene.

D. Brown Falcon *Falco berigora* **40–50 cm/15.5–19.5 in.**

A thick-set brown falcon that is broader winged than all the other falcons pictured here. It is variable: some birds are almost entirely dark brown, others are rufous above (i.e., similar to a kestrel), or dark brown with a pale buff head. In most plumages it can be distinguished from the other falcons by its dark brown upperparts. In the rufous morph it lacks the obvious dark subterminal band on the upper tail that kestrel possesses, and has dark "trousers," not white like the Kestrel. Although they can hunt by hovering, like kestrels, they do this for only short periods, and are always more powerfully built than the slender kestrel. They also regularly soar, which can then give them a hawklike appearance, too, and then take prey generally by gliding down and capturing their quarry on the ground. It is widespread throughout the mainland and TAS in a range of habitats that includes open woodlands, farmlands, and grasslands.

A. Masked Lapwing *Vanellus miles* **30–37 cm/12–14.5 in.**

Shorebirds are long-legged ground-dwelling birds that find their food by probing into the ground or snatching prey from the surface. Some frequent tidal flats, and others feed on drier ground. Most shorebirds can feed during the day or night. There are two large groupings of shorebirds: sandpipers and plovers. **Lapwings** are a subgroup of shorebirds in a family called **Plovers and Lapwings**. The lovers and sandpipers can be distinguished from each other morphologically by their bill shapes, and also by their feeding style. Plovers have short stubby bills, and feed by searching for their prey while standing motionless, then suddenly running after a prey item once spotted. The sandpipers usually have finer, longer bills, and find their prey by feel when probing in the mud. Sandpipers therefore have a more continually active feeding style, unlike the "stop-start" style of plovers and lapwings. Many lapwings exhibit strange facial wattles of brightly colored skin, and many feed in dry areas and not tidal flats. The Masked Lapwing is found widely in the eastern half of the continent, where it is most commonly found in pairs on lawns in gardens, towns, and airports, making them a familiar sight to Australians. It is distinctively patterned: a large plover with a black cap, gray-brown back, gleaming white underparts, long reddish legs, and a yellow bill. However, its most noticeable feature is the bright canary yellow facial wattle that hangs down from the sides of the head. In flight this lapwing has plain wings lacking any bold markings on the upperwing. A pleasantly common, easily recognized shorebird that is often tame and approachable where it occurs in urban areas. When breeding, lapwings can be vigorously defensive of their nest, which comprises nothing more than a shallow scrape in the ground. They can react impressively, becoming loud and obnoxious and even dive-bombing some intruders while calling continually and harshly the whole time.

B. Banded Lapwing *Vanellus tricolor* **25–29 cm/10–11.5 in.**

A scarce, localized lapwing of inland grasslands and agricultural lands. Similar to Masked: both have grayish backs and largely white underparts. However, the smaller Banded has more black in its plumage, with an almost wholly black face except for a white flash behind the eye, and a broad black band across the chest that lends the birds its name. In flight they can also be differentiated, as Banded displays a bold white band across the upperwing, whereas Masked has plain wings. The Banded also has a yellow bill and lacks any extravagant facial wattles. Most commonly found in the south of mainland Australia, where it is highly nomadic in response to water levels and therefore changing vegetation, and so is quite unpredictable in its appearances. It is a scarce species that is not encountered frequently. Like the Masked Lapwing it is most likely to be seen in pairs, foraging on the ground. The inconspicuous Banded Lapwing is most likely to be found during the breeding season, when it harsh alarm calls draws attention to its presence in an area.

A. Red-kneed Dotterel *Erythrogonys cinctus* **17–19.5 cm/6.5–7.5 in.**

Dotterels are small shorebirds—alternatively called plovers—that are characterized by short, stubby bills and the typical stop-start feeding style that all plovers exhibit. A tiny, boldly marked plover most often seen around inland wetlands. Like the larger Banded Lapwing this dotterel has a grayish back and a black head, though this species lacks the white blaze behind the eye, which also differentiates it from Black-fronted. The contrasting white throat is its most striking feature, bordered by a black chest below that extends down the flank in a bold stripe that gradually fades into dark chestnut at the rear. It also has a blood red bill with a black tip, in common with the Hooded Plover and Black-fronted Dotterel. However, Hooded Plover has a complete black hood with a dark throat that differentiates it from that species. In flight the dotterel also has a bold, broad white hindwing. This handsome little wader is most likely to be found in small numbers around the edges of dams, swamps, billabongs, and sewage ponds well inland from the coast, although like many of Australia's waterbirds it is nomadic and wanders widely in response to water conditions.

B. Black-fronted Dotterel *Elseyornis melanops* **16–18 cm/6.5–7 in.**

A small plover found across much of Australia, around small dams, large freshwater wetlands, and occasionally also in tidal areas. This tiny boldly marked shorebird has a brown cap, bold white line over the eye, black line through the eye, bold white throat bordered by a black Y-shaped chest band underneath, and all white underparts. The upperparts are gray brown with a distinct chestnut area on the shoulders. It also has a reddish bill with an obvious dark tip, in common with the other birds on this page. Best distinguished from the other plovers here by its brown (not black) cap , bold white supercilium (lacking in the all-black-headed Hooded Plover), broad chest band with no markings along the flank (unlike Red-kneed Dotterel), and bold rufous patches on the shoulders. In flight it shows a white band across the center of the wing. Most often encountered in small groups around the edges of freshwater wetlands. In common with many dotterels, when the nest is approached, the Black-fronted Dotterel feigns a broken wing, and leads the intruder away from the area.

C. Hooded Plover *Thinornis cucullatus* **19–23 cm/7.5–9 in.**

One of Australia's most wanted shorebirds, endemic to the country, and scarce and localized. This handsome grayish shorebird has a contrasting all-black hood bordered by a clean white collar on the nape, and is bright white below. Hooded Plover has a reddish bill with a black tip. It is easily identified by virtue of its all-black head and throat. The other plovers or dotterels with large amounts of black on the head also have large sections of white on the throat and therefore do not have a hooded appearance like this species. It is a very particular shorebird, found only locally in coastal areas of the extreme south of the mainland (where it is mainly found in the east), and on TAS. It is the most wary of the plovers and therefore generally only occurs in relatively undisturbed coastal areas. Pairs are usually found along sandy beaches.

A. Red-capped Plover *Charadrius ruficapillus* **14–16 cm/5.5–6.5 in.**
Plovers are a shorebird family characterized by plump bodies, short stubby bills, and a distinctive feeding action: they search for prey while frozen still for periods, suddenly running after prey when sighted, creating a distinct "stop-start" style. Red-capped is a small, slim-billed plover with a rich chestnut cap and nape, bright white forehead, pale sandy upperparts, white underparts, and blackish bare parts. When not breeding they lack the rich color on the cap and are completely sandy colored on the upperparts. They are most likely to be confused with sandplovers, although both sandplover species are much larger, longer legged and longer billed, with striking breeding plumages quite unlike that of Red-capped. Red-capped is also more hyperactive, with a faster-paced feeding style than the sandplovers. It is a resident species found throughout the continent, on freshwater and saline lakes, and tidal areas. It is generally more common in the coastal zone on sand or mudflats.

B. Greater Sand-Plover *Charadrius leschenaultia* **22–25 cm/8.5–10 in.**
Sand-plovers are large pale plovers that have striking breeding plumages but are plain and indistinctive when not breeding. The sand-plovers are very difficult to separate from one another although they often occur together, when their different structures can be compared directly. At all ages Greater is larger headed, longer billed (longer than the distance between the bill and the eye), and marginally larger bodied (photo B, *left*). The structure is always the best distinguishing feature, although it is best used when both species are present and possible to compare directly. Both sand-plovers are larger and heavier billed than Red-capped Plover. In breeding plumage the face has a black mask that encloses a small white forehead patch. Some breeding Lesser races lack the white forehead patch. Greater has a narrow chestnut breast band that is always broader in Lesser, and does not have a black upper border, unlike some Lessers do. Greater is generally more washed out in breeding plumage relative to Lesser. Both sand-plovers are common nonbreeding migrants from Eurasia to Australian and TAS coastlines, where they are usually encountered in tidal areas and often observed together.

B. Lesser Sand-Plover *Charadrius mongolus* **18–21 cm/7–8.5 in.**
The smaller of the sand-plovers, best distinguished from the similar Greater by structure (photo B, *right*): at all ages Lesser is shorter legged, shorter billed (equal in length to the distance between the bill and the eye), and smaller headed, with a slighter frame. When in bold breeding dress, Lesser has several distinct races, one of which lacks a white forehead patch that Greater always possesses at this time. Furthermore, Lesser sometimes displays a thin black upper border to the broad chestnut breast band, lacking in Greater, which shows a narrower chestnut band. In breeding plumage Lesser is always brighter and bolder than similarly plumaged Greaters. In nonbreeding plumage structure is the best ID feature. It is a fairly common nonbreeding migrant to Australia between August and May, when they are often encountered in mixed groups with other sand-plovers, and are most often seen on mudflats.

A. Pied Oystercatcher *Haematopus longirostris* 42–50 cm/16.5–19.5 in.
Oystercatchers are a family of very distinctive, strikingly patterned shorebirds characterized by pied or black plumage and carrot-colored bills. Oysters and a variety of bivalve mollusks form a major component of their diet. In Australia there are two regularly occurring species, Pied and Sooty, which are easy to separate, as Pied is black and white, while Sooty is an all-black oystercatcher. They are both found along all the coastlines of Australia, including TAS. The two separate by their preferred habitat: Pied occurs on sandy shorelines and muddy coastlines and estuaries, while Sooty prefers rocky shorelines. Pied Oystercatchers are usually encountered in pairs or small groups, and like many other oystercatchers, are very vocal. Their piercing, piping calls are heard most often when they are disturbed from their well-hidden nesting sites, which are nothing more than a shallow scrape on the ground. Pied is generally more approachable than Sooty Oystercatcher.

B. Sooty Oystercatcher *Haematopus fuliginosus* 40–52 cm/15.5–20.5 in.
Sooty Oystercatcher is an entirely black shorebird with a bright orange beak and legs that generally prefers rocky shorelines, which the only other oystercatcher, Pied, generally avoids. However, in some areas they can be seen foraging together on the same beaches. Sooty never shows any white in its plumage, unlike Pied. It feeds mainly on mollusks although it will also capture crabs and feed on starfish, small fish, and even sea urchins. Sooty is generally more wary than Pied Oystercatcher, less often allowing close approach.

C. Pied Stilt *Himantopus leucocephalus* 33–37 cm/13–14.5 in.
The following two species, although very different in appearance, belong to the same family: **Stilts and Avocets**. They are tall, elegant, long-legged pied shorebirds, although they have strikingly different bill shapes. Pied Stilt, previously called Black-winged, has a fine, *straight*, black bill. Otherwise, the stilt has a long white neck with a bold black patch on the nape, all blackish back, and incredibly long, stiltlike, bright bubble-gum pink legs that are the defining feature of stilts. It is found in a range of wetland habitats throughout the continent, and is absent only from the driest part of the interior, where it is most often encountered in flocks. They are readily recognized by virtue of their long legs, which give them both a characteristic silhouette on the ground and in flight, when these trail noticeably beyond their tails.

D. Red-necked Avocet *Recurvirostra novaehollandiae* 40–48 cm/15.5–19 in.
Avocets are a discrete group of elegant shorebirds with very long necks and legs, and a distinctive upturned bill, which lend them a unique outline. Just one avocet occurs in Australia. Red-necked Avocet is an immaculate bird with a neat pied body and crisp chestnut head and neck. They occur in an array of wetland environments, both in freshwater and saline areas, from inland swamps and large lakes to small dams and coastal salt pans. They feed with a distinctive feeding action, wading into deeper waters and sweeping their oddly upturned bill from side to side to forage on aquatic insects and crustaceans. They can also forage while swimming, almost in the manner of a duck, by floating on the surface, with their long legs hidden below the water and picking up aquatic prey from the water's surface.

B

D

A. Terek Sandpiper *Xenus cinereus* 22–25 cm/8.5–10 in.

This page covers four **sandpipers**, a subgroup of shorebirds characterized by relatively long, slim bills and an active feeding style, in which they continually probe into the mud. These characteristics separate them from another shorebird subgroup, plovers, which are plumper birds with thicker, shorter bills, and a slower, stop-start feeding action. Terek is a medium-sized gray sandpiper, with a distinctive upswept orange-based bill. It often also displays a dark shoulder patch, and has relatively short orange legs (for a sandpiper). They are usually found in small groups feeding actively on tidal flats, where the bill shape is often the best form of ID. It is an uncommon nonbreeding migrant to Australia during August to April, possible along the entire mainland coastline, but is most abundant on the north and east coasts.

B. Gray-tailed Tattler *Tringa brevipes* 24–26 cm/9.5–10 in.

A medium-sized gray sandpiper, with a straight bill and yellowish or dull orange legs. In breeding plumage it displays distinctive fine barring on the underparts, which, along with bill structure, aids ID. Outside of breeding plumage however, it can best be differentiated from the similar Terek Sandpiper by its straight, not upturned, bill. This common coastal bird occurs along the entire Australian coast as a summer migrant (September to April) from Siberia, and frequents tidal flats, rocky shores, mangroves, and estuaries.

C. Common Greenshank *Tringa nebularia* 30–34 cm/11.5–13.5 in.

This large, long-legged pallid gray sandpiper is one of Australia's most common shorebirds, occurring along the entire coastline, and also often found on inland wetlands across much of the continent (absent only from desert areas). It is recognized by its overall pale coloration, long, lanky, greenish legs, and long, thickish, slightly upturned bill. Terek Sandpiper is also pale with a markedly more upturned bill, although it differs in the color of the bare parts and is also much smaller, and shorter legged. This common shorebird is a nonbreeding visitor (from its Siberian and European breeding grounds), occurring around a variety of freshwater wetlands and coastal areas. It is often encountered alone or in small parties that when disturbed fly up with a distinctive loud "tew-tew-tew" call, exposing a contrasting white rump triangle in flight.

D. Common Sandpiper *Actitis hypoleucos* 19–22 cm/7.5–8.5 in.

A small brown and white sandpiper that constantly bobs its tail. This behavior is often the easiest way to ID the bird. It is brown above and clean white below with a characteristic white spur at the bend of the wing. It has a straight, medium-length bill and yellow-green legs. It also has a distinctive jerky flight, with shallow wingbeats regularly interspersed with short glides, revealing a white wing bar. They are less gregarious than many other shorebirds, usually encountered either alone or in pairs. It is found through much of the continent (including TAS), absent only from desert areas. This uncommon bird is particularly fond of muddy edges of freshwater streams and creeks, and is often seen perched on a low exposed limb at the water's edge bobbing its tail conspicuously. However, they also can occur on large tidal flats.

A. Ruddy Turnstone *Arenaria interpres* 22–24 cm/8.5–9.5 in.

Turnstones are distinctive plump-bodied, short legged, sandpipers when in bold breeding plumage, at which time the upperparts are black and ruddy, the head is black and white, and the rest of the underparts are bright white except for a thick black chest band. It has orange legs and a black bill that is unusually shaped: it is short and wedge shaped with a broad base and a fine tip, and is slightly upturned. In nonbreeding plumage it lacks the bright upperpart colors and is largely grayish brown with a paler breast, when the orange legs and bill structure stand out as the most prominent features. At all ages the plump frame, distinctive bill shape, and feeding style aid ID: it turns over stones on rocky shorelines with its well-adapted bill, a unique feeding action. Turnstone is a high Arctic breeder that is a nonbreeding visitor to Australia between August and April, where it is fairly common along the entire coastline of both mainland Australia and TAS.

B. Great Knot *Calidris tenuirostris* 26–28 cm/10–11 in.

Knots are sandpipers with conspicuous breeding plumages, although are dull colored and difficult to ID in nonbreeding colors, when structure is the best indication of species. Knots are medium-sized, plump sandpipers with short, straightish bills that are relatively blunt tipped compared with those of other sandpipers. In breeding plumage Great Knot has thick black, bold markings from the throat down, and dark upperparts with a distinctive contrasting chestnut patch on the shoulder. Nonbreeding, they are indistinct gray birds with bold arrow markings down the flanks (that are bolder and more extensive than those of the similar Red Knot). Its bill shape is similar to that of the closely related Red Knot, but Great has a longer bill that is often slightly decurved, and has a larger body size, which are all useful ID features. In flight it has a bright white rump, unlike the duller barred rump of Red Knot. It is a nonbreeding migrant to Australia between September and March, where it is commonly found along the coasts and TAS. Large flocks of knots tend to favor tidal flats and estuaries, and are most likely to be encountered within big mixed-species flocks of shorebirds.

C. Red Knot *Calidris canutus* 23–25 cm/9–10 in.

Red Knot possesses a very distinctive breeding plumage with rich chestnut underparts unlike that of any other similarly shaped shorebird, *except* for the breeding plumage of Curlew Sandpiper, which differs in having a distinctly longer, obviously down-curved bill, and a clean white rump in flight. Red is similar in shape to Great Knot but markedly smaller with a relatively shorter bill that is *not* noticeably down curved. In nonbreeding plumage the two knots are very similar, being dull grayish, when the size and bill structure are the best indicators of species. The Red Knot also usually has weaker markings on the flanks, and in flight sports a pale barred rump, not pure white like that of Great Knot. It is a nonbreeding migrant to the coastlines of Australia and TAS from August to April, when it is a common shorebird frequently found in large flocks in the tidal zone, and often associates with other shorebird species.

A. Far Eastern Curlew *Numenius madagascariensis* 60–66 cm/23.5–26 in.
Australia's largest shorebird, an enormous brown sandpiper with a very long, down-curved bill. A combination of huge body size and incredibly long, down-swept bill make it very different from all other shorebirds except Whimbrel. However, the curlew is noticeably larger in body size and has a different bill shape: it gradually curves down starting from the base rather than kinking down near the tip. Curlew is also plain faced, lacking the Whimbrel's bold crown stripes. In flight they are readily told apart, as the Far Eastern Curlew is plain brownish all over and lacks the contrasting white wedge on the rump that a Whimbrel shows. This large wader breeds in Asia and is a common nonbreeding migrant to Australian coastlines between August and May, where it is most likely to be seen in tidal areas. Generally found in small parties, although on the north coast they often form large flocks.

B. Whimbrel *Numenius phaeopus* 40–45 cm/15.5–17.5 in.
A large sandpiper with a long, down-turned bill, similar in shape to Far Eastern Curlew. However, the much smaller Whimbrel is grayer overall, with bold black head stripes, and displays a clean white rump in flight that contrasts with the otherwise plain grayish coloration of the rest of the body. The Whimbrel breeds in Siberia and is a fairly common nonbreeding, migrant to Australia's coastlines during the austral winter (August–April). Like the curlew, most commonly found on tidal mudflats, where they can sometimes be seen in large flocks. Quite a vocal wader that rarely fails to call when it takes to flight.

C. Bar-tailed Godwit *Limosa lapponica* 39–45 cm/15.5–17.5 in.
Godwits are tall, large-bodied sandpipers, characterized by long, slightly upturned bicolored bills (pinkish at the base with a black tip). Their long legs and bills allow them to feed in deeper waters than those in which many other shorebirds feed. Bar-tailed Godwit is the greatest migrant on earth, having the longest recorded nonstop flight of any bird: over 7,000 miles (almost 9 days) without pausing to feed! The godwits are similar in coloration: chestnut in breeding plumage (unlike most other shorebirds) and nondescript grayish in nonbreeding dress. Bar-tailed has solid chestnut underparts in breeding plumage (with no white belly patch), and in nonbreeding has mottled upperparts (not plain like a Black-tailed). In all plumages the Bar-tailed has plain wings and a subtle, finely barred tail in flight, with a white wedge-shaped rump visible above that. It is a common summer migrant (September–April) mainly to coastal Australia, although it also occurs inland in smaller numbers. Both godwits are gregarious shorebirds most likely to be seen in small flocks on coastal tidal flats.

D. Black-tailed Godwit *Limosa limosa* 36–43 cm/14–17 in.
Similar in appearance to Bar-tailed Godwit: large bodied, long legged, with a long upswept two-tone bill. However, this species has a white belly contrasting with the chestnut underparts in breeding plumage, and in all plumages has bold white wing bars and a black tail, making it most distinctive from Bar-tailed when in flight. Another common Asian and Siberian breeder that migrates to coastal Australia in September to May.

A. Red-necked Stint *Calidris ruficollis* 13–16 cm/5–6.5 in.

This page covers three sandpipers that like most within this group are all very active birds, often feeding continually by probing in the mud with their long, slim, fine-tipped bills. Red-necked Stint is a tiny bird, the smallest sandpiper in Australia, best identified by size and structure. It is very short billed and short legged relative to many other sandpipers. It is all grayish with no distinct markings when in nonbreeding plumage, but turns rusty in breeding colors, with a warm rufous throat. It is a common nonbreeding visitor between August and April, occurring along the coastlines of both mainland Australia and TAS, and also often turns up on freshwater wetlands across much of the continent (though not in desert areas).

B. Sharp-tailed Sandpiper *Calidris acuminate* 18–22 cm/7–8.5 in.

A medium-sized sandpiper that is warm colored, with a bright rufous cap and bold eyebrow, and is generally brown with rusty tones, unlike many other nondescript gray shorebirds. Unlike many sandpipers that have dark legs, Sharp-tailed displays yellowish or greenish legs, although care should always be taken with mud-colored limbs that may appear dark. It has a relatively short bill, which looks straight, or can be mildly decurved, and is notably pale at the base, which can be hard to discern except at close range. Most other similarly sized sandpipers have uniformly dark bills. In breeding plumage it is very distinctive, with bold dark arrow markings scattered down the breast but are especially striking along the flanks. In nonbreeding it is less distinct, lacking bold arrow marks and having just fine streaking on the sides of the neck, and in young birds can be washed rich rufous across the chest. When observed in freshwater areas, care should be taken to distinguish this from the uncommon but closely related **Pectoral Sandpiper** (*C. melanotos*), which differs at all ages in having a solid breast band of dark streaks across the throat, neck, and breast, contrasting strongly with a clean white underside below. Sharp-tailed never shows a solid band like this, being largely unmarked below, except in breeding dress, when the striking boomerang patterning below makes it very different. Sharp-tailed is a common migrant both to coasts and inland, throughout almost the entire continent, except for the most arid areas.

C. Curlew Sandpiper *Calidris ferruginea* 18–22 cm/7–8.5 in.

A distinct sandpiper in breeding dress, when it is brick red below, similar to breeding Red Knot. However, it differs from this knot in structure, being long legged, and with a longer, finer-tipped, down-curved bill. It is also has a more slender frame than the plump knot. In nonbreeding attire it is a nondescript gray bird best distinguished from other similar shorebirds by size. It is considerably larger than a stint but smaller than a knot and structurally longer legged with a long, fine-tipped, down-curving bill, and has a bold and striking pale supercilium, something that is mostly lacking in many other gray sandpipers. It is a migrant to Australia between August and April, and is possible along all coastlines. It is most abundant in coastal areas, although does also regularly wander inland.

C

A. Australian Pratincole *Stiltia isabella* **19–24 cm/7.5–9.5 in.**
Pratincoles are ternlike shorebirds that feed by hawking insects on the wing, in addition to pursuing prey on land. They have narrow pointed wings and a light, fluttering flight, remarkably different from that of other shorebirds. Australian Pratincole is a plain-headed, sandy brown bird with a deep chestnut band across the belly, and long wings that extend far beyond its tail when sitting. In flight the square tail is white with a broad black band across its center. The only other pratincole, **Oriental** *(Glareola maldivarum)* has a black-bordered yellow throat, rich chestnut wing linings on the underwing, and a deeply forked tail. Oriental is a wet-season (November–January) nonbreeding visitor from Asia to northern Australia, where it can occur in huge flocks. Australian Pratincole is a widespread nomad most abundant in open arid regions on mainland Australia, where it is usually seen in flocks.

B. Little Penguin *Eudyptula minor* **40–45 cm/ 15.5–17.5 in.**
The only regular penguin in Australia. The smallest penguin species in the world, sometimes called Blue or Fairy Penguin. This flightless bird has a two-tone appearance: soft deep blue above and clean white below. It is highly pelagic, coming to land only to breed. They are at their most graceful at sea, when their nimble movements through the water display them in their true natural environment: at sea pursuing fish and crustaceans. Like all penguins they stand upright and have modified, flipperlike wings marvelously adapted for swimming and life at sea, but appearing clumsy and awkward on land. Even when breeding they spend long hours at sea, usually coming onto dry land only for the night, when these flightless birds are safer from predators. The Little Penguin nests in colonies on the coast of the southern mainland and TAS, where they are most easily seen on organized penguin tours to well-known nesting sites, (e.g., Bruny Island and Phillip Island). They are remarkably tame and can often be seen to within inches on such walks making for a truly fantastic wildlife experience.

C. Comb-crested Jacana *Irediparra gallinacean* **20–27 cm/8–10.5 in.**
Jacanas are a tropical family of long-legged waterbirds that are characterized by their remarkable, oversized feet and incredibly long toes that allow them to walk on floating vegetation, leading to their nickname: "Lily trotters." Australia has just one species that is unlikely to be confused with any other bird owing to its distinctive toes and bold coloration. Adults are black backed with a whitish underside, black band across the chest, and a striking vermilion red shield or comb on the forehead that glows in strong sunlight and is its most striking feature, besides its ridiculous toes. They are found in tropical northern Australia and down the eastern side of the coast into n. NSW. They are locally common on large lagoons and natural freshwater wetlands, where groups of them are usually found conspicuously walking on floating mats of vegetation, often well away from the margins of the wetland. They are especially striking in flight, when their long legs and toes trail well beyond the tail giving them a unique appearance. Especially common around wetlands in Kakadu National Park (NT).

A. Silver Gull *Chroicocephalus novaehollandiae* 43–44 cm/17–17.5 in.

The smallest and most abundant of the three regular seagulls in Australia. Silver Gull is not confined to coasts, and occurs in a variety of habitats, including tidal flats, city dumps, and lakes throughout mainland Australia and TAS. It is the only gull found in inland Australia. Distinguished from the other gulls by its much smaller size and paler, silvery gray upperparts (all others display blackish gray upperparts when adults), and a slim, bright red bill. The other two larger gulls exhibit heavy, largely yellow bills, with red only near the tip. Silver Gull is a familiar bird to Australians. Like many other gulls, it is highly gregarious and most often seen in flocks. They are regular scavengers in urban areas, frequently squabbling noisily for food scraps.

B. Pacific Gull *Larus pacificus* 50–67 cm/19.5–26.5 in.

The largest of the Australian gulls. Both the larger gull species are coastal, and very rarely found inland like the Silver Gull. Pacific is confined to coasts on the southern mainland and TAS. Both adult Kelp and Pacific Gulls are large, dark-backed gulls. Pacific is a real brute, large bodied with a thick-set, heavy bill that is often identified by its bill shape and large body size alone. Pacific has a truly massive bill with a very pronounced bump (known as the gonys) on the underside, compared with Kelp Gull. Furthermore, Pacific in breeding plumage has a deep orange-yellow bill with a large amount of red at the tip on both the upper and lower mandibles (upper and lower sections of the beak). It also always exhibits a dark tail band at all ages, unlike adult Kelp, which has a pure white tail. When in immature plumages, both large gulls (Kelp and Pacific) are confusingly patterned with variable amounts of brown, when the structure of the bill and overall body size are the best clues to ID. Most likely to be seen in small flocks along the coast, either perched on rocks along the shore, or on the tidal flats, or even resting on boats around docks.

C. Kelp Gull *Larus dominicanus* 49–62 cm/19.5–24.5 in.

Another large, dark-backed gull, similar to Pacific Gull. Kelp is less of a brute, being smaller in body size, with a much slimmer bill that has a less pronounced bump on the underside. In adults the bill is a paler yellow than Pacific's, with distinctly less red, which is confined to the lower mandible (on both sections in Pacific). The adult bird also lacks the obvious dark tail band of Pacific, making them readily identifiable in flight at this age. Immatures are an ID challenge, as both species are essentially variably patterned, brown birds, when they are best told apart by the overall size and the structure of the bill, as outlined above. Kelp Gull is also coastal, rarely straying far from there, on the southern mainland and TAS. Kelp often occupies the same harbors and coasts as Pacific, when they can be compared side by side, at which time they can appear structurally very different. Most often encountered in small groups along southern shorelines.

A. Brown Noddy *Anous stolidus* **40–45 cm/15.5–17.5 in.**

Noddies are **terns,** which are closely related to gulls, although noddies are generally more aerodynamic in shape, with narrow, pointed wings; slender, pointed bills; and forked tails. Many terns are similar to gulls in coloration: largely white with gray backs. However, these three species are all dark-backed pelagic terns that breed on sandy islands, and are only rarely seen from the mainland. Brown Noddy is one of the more distinctive terns, being all dark brown (including the underparts) except for a bold white cap. The main species in range with which it can be confused is the smaller (35 cm/14 in.), darker **Black Noddy** *A. minutus.* They are best told apart by size when sitting together, when this difference is very noticeable. Both noddies are found in the tropical seas of northern Australia. Black is restricted to the northeast, while Brown occurs around into s. WA. They both breed on islands in QLD, and Brown also has breeding colonies in WA, but may be seen anywhere between, as they are widely wandering oceanic birds. Noddies are most likely to be seen on a boat trip to the sandy cays of the Great Barrier Reef, where large numbers of Brown outnumber Black Noddies on these bird-packed breeding islands.

B. Bridled Tern *Onychoprion anaethetus* **30–32 cm/12–12.5 in.**

The following two terns are very similar, dark-backed, white-breasted pelagic terns. Bridled is gray above, not jet black (like Sooty), although this can be hard to judge except at very close quarters. The best difference is the face pattern: Bridled has a white line running from the base of the bill, over the eye, and beyond the eye. In Sooty this eye line is reduced and does not extend behind the eye. Both are pelagic species only rarely seen from the mainland (where Bridled is more likely to be seen from shore), found in the tropical seas of northern Australia (both possible from w. WA eastward around the coast to n. NSW). They both breed on offshore islands in northern Australia.

C. Sooty Tern *Onychoprion fuscatus* **33–36 cm/13–14 in.**

A striking tern similar to Bridled Tern: both have dark backs, white underparts, and narrow, pointed wings with deeply forked tails. However, Sooty Tern is jet black above (not blackish gray), and has a shorter white line on the face running from the bill over the eye, though not extending past the eye, as it does in Bridled. In island colonies juvenile Sooty Terns and Brown Noddies can be confused, as young Sooties are all dark brown but show bold speckling all over the upperparts, while juvenile noddies are all uniformly brown. Large colonies of these terns nest on offshore cays and islands in n. QLD and n. WA, where they are most easily seen by taking a pelagic boat trip (e.g., cruises out to Michaelmas Cay in the Great Barrier Reef). When visiting their densely packed nesting colonies, one can hear their distinctive yapping, doglike calls, which led to their alternative name: "Wideawake."

A. Little Tern *Sternula albifrons* 20–25 cm/8–10 in.

Terns are related to gulls, and though often similar in coloration, terns are more elegantly shaped, with more slender, pointed bills and narrow, more aerodynamic wings, that lend them a more graceful flight. All birds on this page are small terns; the first two are coastal, while Whiskered can often be found well inland. Most terns are best identified by size, head pattern, and bare-part color. Little is tiny; the smallest tern in the world. Aside from size, in breeding birds the best ID features are the black-tipped yellow bill, black cap with a large white forehead, and a bold black line connecting the bill to the eye. In Australia this tiny tern is most likely to be mistaken for the similarly patterned **Fairy Tern** *S. nereis* in breeding plumage, when Fairy lacks the black bill tip and never has a complete dark bar linking the bill and the eye (nonbreeding Fairy retains a yellow bill and again lacks this complete bar, when Little looks very different). Outside the breeding season the bill of Little is black, and it shows an all-white crown and black mask from the bill and around the nape, when it can appear quite like Black-naped Tern. However, that species is significantly larger and has a long, deeply forked tail (Little has a short, shallow-forked tail). Little Tern is fairly common along northern and eastern coastlines but absent from the coasts of s. and w. WA, w. SA, and w. TAS.

B. Black-naped Tern *Sterna sumatrana* 30–32 cm/12–12.5 in.

Black-naped is a small and dainty, crisply marked, striking tern of the north and northeast. Its most conspicuous feature is the dazzlingly white overall appearance and its striking head pattern: all white on the crown, with a bold black mask running behind the eyes and around the nape. Otherwise, it is silvery on the upperparts, and gleaming white on the underside. It is has a long and deeply forked tail, unlike that of Little Tern, which is significantly smaller. This coastal tern is patchily distributed from n. NT eastward to n. QLD and south down the coast to s. QLD. As it is generally not close inshore, it is best found on boat trips out to sandy cays on the Great Barrier Reef.

C. Whiskered Tern *Chlidonias hybrida* 25–26 cm/9.5–10 in.

A small dark tern of marshes that is most common at inland freshwater wetlands. In breeding plumage it is distinctive by virtue of its dark blackish breast and underbelly and bold white cheeks. At this time it has a dull deep red bill, solid black cap, and silvery gray upperparts. It has a short tail with a very shallow fork (it often appears unforked when spread). Outside the breeding season the bill is dark, and the cap is incomplete with a white forehead, and the underparts are white, making it less obvious. However, this is the only tern that is likely to be found in large groups hawking insects over marshes, as most others terns are fish-eaters. Whiskered Terns have a distinctive buoyant flight. Thus the behavior and habitat help differentiate it from other tern species. It is found widely across the continent, absent only from the sandy deserts of central Australia, in various freshwater wetlands, sewage ponds, well-irrigated fields, and also sometimes coastal estuaries and brackish lagoons, where they often pick insects off the surface of the water.

A. Caspian Tern *Hydroprogne caspia* **47–54 cm/18.5–21 in.**

This page illustrates three large **terns** (gull-like birds with narrower wings than gulls and a more elegant, buoyant flight). The three large terns are similar in general coloration and so are best identified using a combination of relative size, and the color and shape of the bill. All three species are found along coasts (although Caspian can also be found well inland, unlike the crested terns), where they feed primarily on fish by plunge-diving. Caspian is the largest tern on Earth, and sports a massive carrot-colored bill with a dark smudge at the tip. The body and bill size are much larger than those of any other tern. Its bill is notably heavy and thick based, quite unlike the longer, more slender bill structure of the crested terns. Caspian Terns have a square-shaped head with just a short stunted crest evident at the nape. They lack the shaggy crest displayed by crested terns. In flight the underside of the outer wing (primaries) is washed with black, which is quite contrasting and conspicuous relative to other species as well. Caspian is common and widespread on the coasts all over mainland Australia and TAS, and although it is mainly coastal, it does turn up inland, mainly in the eastern half of the continent, where it can frequent freshwater lakes.

B. Great Crested Tern *Thalasseus bergii* **40–50 cm/15.5–19.5 in.**

Australia's second largest tern, which has a slender and long, uniform yellow (not orange) bill that aids ID. Crested also never shows a dark smudge near the tip, as Caspian does. Both crested terns have a shaggy black crest that extends from the nape, making for quite a different head shape in contrast with the block-headed Caspian. The crested terns have a solid black cap in breeding plumage and an incomplete black cap in nonbreeding with a prominent white forehead. The extent of the white on the forehead in nonbreeding birds is usually smaller in Great—relative to Lesser—which possesses more black on the head in this plumage. Crested terns are best separated by relative size (Great is larger) and bill color (yellow in Great and orange in Lesser). Great Crested is a common, strictly coastal bird throughout the coasts and pelagic areas of Australia, often encountered fishing just offshore.

C. Lesser Crested Tern *Thalasseus bengalensis* **38–43 cm/15–17 in.**

The smallest of the large terns pictured here, which has a long, slim orange bill with no dark markings. It is notably smaller than the huge Caspian and also smaller than Great Crested. In all plumages the bill color and relative body size are the best ID features. In nonbreeding plumage Lesser sports a more extensive white forehead, with less black on the head at this time relative to Great Crested. Like Great Crested, this species also has a conspicuous shaggy black crest that gives it a very different head shape in comparison with Caspian. In northern Australia Lesser Crested Tern can frequently be seen close inshore, while on the eastern coasts it tends to be more pelagic; it is not often seen unless one takes a boat trip out into deeper waters. It occurs in the tropical seas of northern Australia, around to s. QLD.

A. Rock Pigeon *Columba livia* **31–36 cm/12–14 in.**

Also known as Feral Pigeon. The common town pigeon throughout the world, introduced into Australia by early European settlers, and a feral descendant of the Rock Dove of Eurasia. A familiar bird to most people, as it inhabits many cities and towns across the globe. In Australia it occupies the south and east only (from c. WA to s. WA and eastward to VIC and NSW. It also occurs in s. QLD and TAS, and is largely absent from the NT and n. WA. The classic urban bird that has adapted extremely well to living alongside humans wherever it occurs in the world. Many color varieties, the most common being dull gray with a paler gray back, solid black bars in the wings, and subtle metallic green and purple on the neck. In flight it shows a bright white rump. Less common bright rufous variants occur, although all color variations are very different from those of any other pigeons.

B. Emerald Dove *Chalcophaps indica* **23–28 cm/9–11 in.**

An attractive forest pigeon with glistening green upperparts and a distinctive double white band on its black rump visible in flight as it flashes low through the understory. Otherwise, rich salmon colored below. Emerald Doves are found in the tropical north: n. WA, n. NT, and n. QLD, and south down the coastal zone to s. NSW. It is mainly a bird of forest edges, including both tropical rainforest and wet eucalypt forest, but does turn up in tropical gardens and also occurs in scrub, coastal heaths, and mangroves. This beautiful dove is highly terrestrial, foraging mostly on the ground, often in the shade of the forest. It is most often encountered when single birds are flushed suddenly out of the leaf litter at close range, which often startles the observer. They are best found feeding around the verges of rainforest-lined parking lots or feeding along forested country roads at dawn.

C. Wonga Pigeon *Leucosarcia melanoleuca* **38–44 cm/15–17.5 in.**

A large, boldly patterned, plump pigeon of the eastern forests. All powdery blue above with a bright white underside scaled with dark markings that form a pattern quite unlike that of any other bird. The patterning of the white, when viewed front-on, appears as if the bird is being cradled in a human hand, with two white fingers positioned on either side of the neck. Wonga Pigeons occur in eastern Australia from the southeastern corner of QLD south to e. VIC, where they favor wet eucalypt forests and temperate rainforests. It is another terrestrial species, most often observed foraging along forest edges at dawn. At O'Reilly's in Lamington National Park (QLD) a number of birds have become remarkably habituated and can often be seen wandering around public feeding areas, walking within just a few feet of gathered tourists. During the day these vocal pigeons often give an incessant "wooping" call that provides a regular backdrop to the chorus in the eastern forests, and is the source of their name. Away from certain habituated areas they are shy and more often heard than seen. Interestingly, the Latin name *leucosarcia* means "white flesh." Famed naturalist John Gould explains: "Its flesh being white, and extremely delicate, it is one of the best birds for the table inhabiting Australia." Thus, this stout bird was often eaten by early explorers.

A. Common Bronzewing *Phaps chalcoptera* 31–36 cm/12–14 in.

A largish pigeon that at distance appears like an unattractive, largely grayish brown bird. However, up close there is a subtle beauty to it, with bold white facial markings: a prominent white forehead, white stripe below the eye, and delicate scaling on the upperparts. There is also intricate patterning on the wings, and parts of the wing have a bronze and metallic sheen. Although widespread in open forests and woodlands over the entire continent except the most arid desert areas, it is inconspicuous, as it forages on the ground. It is most often first seen when disturbed as it bursts into the air with a clatter of wing noise, and exposes rich cinnamon underwings as it flies off at high speed. If it is seen to alight in a tree following such disturbance, it often sits on a branch nervously bobbing its head. Also often seen feeding along the edges of dirt roads or around farm dams during late afternoons.

B. Crested Pigeon *Ocyphaps lophotes* 31–36 cm/12–14 in.

The following pair of species are striking ground-dwelling pigeons characterized by a long pointed crest that sticks up prominently from the top of their head, and strikingly barred plumage. Crested is a largely gray pigeon, with pink hues on the underparts, red skin around the eye, and a thin black topknot, quite unlike the rich ochre-colored Spinifex Pigeon. Crested Pigeon is a widespread, common, and conspicuous species found over much of the continent, except for the Cape York Peninsula (QLD), TAS, and the tip of the NT. It occurs in a range of open habitats from farmlands to gardens and golf courses, avoiding few habitats except closed forest. Crested Pigeon generally forages on the ground, usually in groups, bobbing their head as they walk along. When disturbed, Crested Pigeons fly with a rapid low flight characterized by long glides, and tilting regularly. Once they alight again, they raise their long tails in a conspicuous fashion that characterizes this species. Crested Pigeons frequently perch on roadside wires, and as they occur around many urban areas, are a familiar sight.

C. Spinifex Pigeon *Geophaps plumifera* 20–23 cm/7.5–9 in.

A handsome reddish inland pigeon that is even more striking than the more widespread Crested Pigeon. Mostly ruddy colored with a pointed rufous topknot and a striking face pattern: bare red skin surrounds a pale eye, and the face is striped black and white, with some subtle blue markings. Bold black bars are spread across the wings and sides of the mantle, and some races also show a bold white bar across the chest. Its reddish coloration mirrors the red dirt and rocky outcrops in its habitat: rocky and hilly areas, and spinifex grasslands within the north of the outback. It is inconspicuous when it forages on the ground and is well camouflaged within the arid landscapes that it inhabits. It occurs patchily within the NT, c. and n. WA, extreme western QLD, and far northern SA. Spinifex Pigeon is never far from water in its arid environment and is therefore best located around shrinking water sources late in the dry season, when these nomadic birds become more concentrated.

B

A. Peaceful Dove *Geopelia placida* 19–23 cm/7.5–9 in.

The first three species are all small, relatively long tailed doves. Peaceful Dove is a heavily barred dove, with blackish bars on the nape and down the back. These bars extend around onto the throat, unlike in the main species with which it can be confused, Bar-shouldered Dove. It also has a ring of pale blue skin around the eye. Peaceful Dove is a common species over much of northern and eastern Australia, found over a wide variety of habitats, including open woodlands, tropical savanna, eucalypt forests, edges of rainforest, agricultural lands, and parks and gardens. This tame dove is very terrestrial, often observed feeding on the ground. Once disturbed, it flies up with a whir of rapid wingbeats, showing a long black tail with white sides as it flies away at high speed. The distinctive, oft-repeated, "doodley-doo" call of Peaceful Dove is the common and iconic sound of the Australian countryside.

B. Bar-shouldered Dove *Geopelia humeralis* 26–30 cm/10–11.5 in.

A significantly larger dove than both Diamond and Peaceful Doves, with heavily barred brown upperparts, a contrastingly pale blue-gray head, and a distinct chestnut nape, which lacks any barring on the throat. The size, chestnut nape patch, and plain unbarred throat help differentiate this species from its smaller cousin, the Peaceful Dove. This widespread bird is found throughout much of northern and eastern Australia in eucalypt forest, tropical savanna, scrubland, mangroves, and parks and gardens. It is most likely to be found feeding on the ground in small groups.

C. Diamond Dove *Geopelia cuneata* 19–23 cm/7.5–9 in.

A small gray inland dove, subtly dotted with white on its dull gray wings, which forms a distinctive pattern. Diamond Dove also shows a distinct red ring around the eye, and a contrasting white belly. When disturbed, it flies up with rapid wingbeats, creating a noticeable whirring sound, and displays a large chestnut flash in the outer wing and long, white-sided tail. It is found in drier areas throughout much of the Australian mainland, is normally not found along the wetter coastal regions, and is absent from extreme southwest Australia. It is a common and widespread dove, though notably shyer than the preceding species, that occurs in open woodlands, mulga, scrubland, and timbered watercourses. It is irruptive, that is, numbers fluctuate dramatically in response to local weather conditions.

D. Spotted Dove *Streptopelia chinensis* 29–33 cm/11.5–13 in.

A large brownish introduced Asian dove, with a distinct black patch that is boldly spotted with white on the sides of the neck, and pale gray underparts washed with soft pink. The neck patch differentiates this dove from all other pigeon species. When it takes flight it shows a long blackish tail with a striking broad white band at the tip. It is a common species in the coastal region of eastern Australia, from ne. QLD south to VIC, and westward into se. SA. There is also another isolated population in extreme sw. WA. Spotted Doves are found largely in urban environments, and are most commonly encountered around towns such as Brisbane, Sydney, and Perth.

D

A. Chestnut-quilled Rock-Pigeon *Petrophassa rufipennis* 28–31 cm/11–12in

This long-tailed pigeon is very dark brown over the whole of its body, with indistinct white flecking over some of the head and upper body. The only bold marking is a conspicuous chestnut marking on the outer wing, usually visible only in flight. This local species is restricted to rocky areas around sandstone escarpments in the tropical north of the NT. This pigeon is mostly likely to be found by walking across rocky areas, where singles or pairs may be seen scurrying across the rocks or bursting into flight with a loud whirr of wings when disturbed. It has a distinctive low flight interspersed with long glides, during which it displays its most prominent feature: the chestnut primary patch. It is very local and uncommon, and best looked for at Gunlom Falls in Kakadu National Park.

B. Brown Cuckoo-Dove *Macropygia phasianella* 38–45 cm/15–17.5 in.

A long-tailed, all–rust brown dove found in coastal eastern Australia. In its range there are no other all-brown pigeon species. The long tail gives rise to its name as a cuckoo-dove, which is a group of brown, long-tailed doves that occur in Australasia and Asia. This is the only cuckoo-dove in Australia. This common dove is confined to the eastern coastal forest belt (from n. QLD south to e. VIC), where it occurs around the margins of temperate and tropical rainforests, and eucalypt forests. Brown Cuckoo-Dove forages both terrestrially and in the canopies of trees.

C. Squatter Pigeon *Geophaps scripta* 26–31 cm/10–12 in.

Squatter is a ground-feeding boldly marked brown-and-white pigeon that forms a sister species with the similar **Partridge Pigeon** (*G. smithii*). These two species do not overlap in range and can therefore be identified by locality. Squatter Pigeon is an uncommon brown pigeon with a white breast and contrastingly marked black-and-white face that forms an uncommon pattern: a large white cheek patch dissected by a black vertical line through its center. There are two races that differ in the color of the eye ring: birds in n. QLD have a red eye ring, while southern birds possess a pale bluish gray eye ring. They are most often encountered in small parties feeding on the ground, where they can allow close approach, often freezing motionless, then bursting up suddenly with a whirr of wingbeats if approached too close. It occurs in eastern Australia from n. QLD south into the far north of NSW, where it is usually found near water sources, in open woodlands, on tropical savanna, around rural homes, and in open grassy areas. A good method of finding them is to drive along dirt roads in the late afternoon, where small groups of Squatters can often be found quietly feeding along the verges, or checking around small dams, where they may gather to drink late in the day. Both species also regularly feed within recently burnt areas. In the west, Squatter Pigeon is replaced by Partridge Pigeon, which occurs in the tropical north of the NT and WA. They are very similar in appearance, and behavior: Partridge Pigeon possesses a large patch of bare skin around the eye, which is red in most of its range, or yellow in the Kimberleys. Partridge Pigeons should be looked for around burns and road verges within Kakadu National Park (NT).

A. Wompoo Fruit-Dove *Ptilinopus magnificus* 35–50 cm/14–19.5 in.

This page covers four strikingly marked pigeons. The first three are fruit-doves, characterized by colorful plumage, which feed mainly on fruits within the canopy. Wompoo is a strange oversized fruit-dove (it is the largest pigeon in Australia), often simply called Wompoo *Pigeon*. It is named after its distinctive guttural call: "wolompoo," often heard when clusters of them gather in fruiting trees. This massive pigeon has green upperparts; a pale powder gray head; a deep maroon throat, chest, and belly; and contrasting bright lemon yellow vent. A scattering of yellow markings form an incomplete bar on the wing. It is an eastern species, found in closed forests from northern n. QLD south down the coast to n. NSW. It is fairly common, and most often encountered in groups in the canopies of large fruiting trees, when their distinctive calls and regular loud fluttering of wings often draw attention to them.

B. Rose-crowned Fruit-Dove *Ptilinopus regina* 21–25 cm/8.5–10 in.

A small, beautiful dove that is mainly green, with a blue-gray head, rose pink crown, and a bright orange-yellow belly. It is a tropical species found within monsoon forests in n. WA and the NT, and within rainforests on the eastern seaboard. Like other fruit-doves it is most likely to be found in the canopy of fruiting trees, where they draw attention to themselves with their soft cooing calls, but can be frustratingly difficult to locate, as they are small and blend in well with the large leaves around them.

C. Black-banded Fruit-Dove *Ptilinopus alligator* 33–42 cm/13–16.5 in.

Also known as Banded Fruit-Dove. Like all fruit-doves it is typically striking, being largely black in color with a white head and neck. Both perched and in flight it essentially appears like a black bird with a white hood. It is uncommon and highly localized, confined to monsoon rainforest and eucalypt woodlands around the western edge of the Arnhem Land Escarpment (within Kakadu NP), at sites like Nourlangie Rock. They are most likely to be found by following their hooting calls, or listening for the flapping of their wings that may betray their presence around fruiting trees. A shy bird that is often hard to locate except when moving between fruiting trees, such as figs.

D. Torresian Imperial-Pigeon *Ducula spilorrhoa* 38–44 cm/15–16.5 in.

Also known as Pied Imperial-Pigeon. **Imperial-Pigeons** are a group of large Australasian pigeons. Torresian is the only regular imperial-pigeon in Australia and is outsized only by the strange Wompoo Fruit-Dove. Torresian is mainly ivory white, except for contrasting black on the outerwings, tail, and undertail. It occurs in rainforests, mangroves, offshore islands, eucalypt woodlands, and parks and gardens, specifically in coastal areas in the far north of the mainland. Torresian Imperial-Pigeon is often observed in small flocks flying around coastal towns (e.g., in Cairns and Darwin), or perched on overhead cables.

A. Red-tailed Black-Cockatoo *Calyptorhynchus banksii* **55–60 cm/21.5–23.5 in.**
Black-cockatoos are massive, almost prehistoric-looking parrots that fly with labored, deep wing beats, whose raucous flight calls often lead to their detection. Many display prominent color panels in their tail, visible in flight. Black-cockatoos are gregarious and social species, often found in flocks, that regularly forage on the ground. Red-tailed is a huge, noisy cockatoo with a prominent crest. It is the iconic black-cockatoo of tropical Australia (with another tiny population in sw. WA). In its northern range it is the only black-cockatoo. Males are solid black with a scarlet tail panel, while females are browner with narrow barring on the underparts, and fine pale speckling on the head and wings, and have an orange tail panel. It occurs in open forests and woodlands and is most often found when large flocks of them gather to roost in the evenings or visit waterholes when their massive shape, striking tail patterns, and regular strident calls are hard to miss.

B. Slender-billed Black-Cockatoo *Calyptorhynchus latirostris* **54–56 cm/21–22 in.**
Also known as Carnaby's Black-Cockatoo. Slender-billed is a large black-cockatoo that displays a pale cheek patch and white panels in the tail. Its black body feathers are fringed white. It is one of two very similar black-cockatoos in WA, which differ in their bill shapes: Slender-billed has a shorter and broader bill adapted for cracking open the seeds of *Hakea*s, *Banksia*s, *Dryandra*s, and other introduced pine species; **White-tailed (or Long-billed) Black-Cockatoo** *C. baudinii* feeds on *marri* nuts, apples, pears, and wood-based grubs, and has a longer, slimmer bill. Both species are confined to sw. WA: Slender-billed in pine plantations, open woodlands, karri forests, sandplain woodlands, and mallee; White-tailed in karri forests, farmlands, and wandoo woodland. They are both fairly common and most likely to be observed in flocks foraging within banksias

C. Yellow-tailed Black-Cockatoo *Calyptorhynchus funereus* **56–65 cm/22–5.5 in.**
A huge black-cockatoo with yellow cheek patches and yellow tail panels, and a labored, almost pterodactyl-like flight. In the southern part of its range it does not overlap with any similar species, and it is the only black-cockatoo with yellow markings. It is a bird of the coastal zone from s. QLD south through e. NSW into VIC and TAS (it is the only black-cockatoo in TAS). This cockatoo occurs in pines, eucalypt forests, temperate rainforests, heathlands, scrublands, and farmlands, where they are usually picked up in groups passing over in flight when their loud squeals draw attention to them. Arguably, the shyest of the black-cockatoos, only rarely allowing close approach.

A. Galah *Eolophus roseicapilla* **35 cm/14 in.**
One of two pink Australian cockatoos. Galah is deep fuchsia pink below, soft pow-dery gray above with a solid creamy white cap. A gorgeous, familiar bird that is both delightfully common and widespread, and is almost impossible to miss on a trip to Australia. Galahs are found throughout the mainland in open country with sparse trees and often frequent town parks, where they can be found feeding in flocks on the ground, sometimes with other cockatoos like Sulfur-crested or corel-las. They are usually tame and approachable.

B. Pink Cockatoo *Lophochroa leadbeateri* **39 cm/15.5 in.**
One of only two pink cockatoos. Also known as Major Mitchell's Cockatoo. A daz-zling bird with lightly dusted salmon pink underparts (that vary greatly in their intensity depending on the light conditions), a white back, and a unique, remark-able red-and-yellow crest. A wide-ranging but scarce species of interior Australia that is more abundant in the south than the north. Pink Cockatoo is a bird of arid or semiarid country with sparse tree cover, most often encountered in groups, either roosting in trees or feeding on the ground.

C. Sulphur-crested Cockatoo *Cacatua galerita* **48–55 cm/19–21.5 in.**
The familiar large white "cocky" of eastern Australia. All white with a sulfur yellow crest and blackish bill. In flight the underwings and undertail are lightly washed with yellow. These boisterous and highly vocal birds are hard to ignore where they occur, as noisy flocks draw attention to themselves wherever they are. They are common in a coastal arc from n. WA through n. QLD and down eastern Australia to s. NSW and TAS. They are generalists, adapting to many habitats, including within many urban areas of eastern Australia. For example, large marauding flocks occur in Sydney, where they sometimes damage properties. They can also be found feeding with other cockatoos like Galahs and corellas wherever they overlap.

D. Little Corella *Cacatua sanguinea* **35–40 cm/14–15.5 in.**
Corellas are small white cockatoos with stunted crests, pale bills, an odd blue patch of bare skin around the eye, and variable amounts of pink in their plumage. Little Corella is the ubiquitous white cockatoo of the Australian grain fields. It is found patchily across much of the mainland except the southwest corner of WA. The main species with which it is commonly confused is the larger Sulfur-crested Cockatoo, which has a large yellow crest and lacks the blue eye skin that the Corella possesses. Little Corella has just a short white crest (which is often held down and therefore inconspicuous), a horn-colored bill, and also has a subtle rose pink wash between the bill and the eye. Like Sulfur-crested Cockatoo, it is also washed with yellow on the undertail and underwing, so it can look similar in flight. It favors a range of open habitats, from agricultural land to scrubby country and is often found in noisy flocks in these areas (sometimes numbering in the thou-sands), which are regularly seen foraging on the ground for grain, seeds, and bulbs.

A. Budgerigar *Melopsittacus undulates* **17–19 cm/6.5–7.5 in.**
A familiar long-tailed native parrot that is a popular cage bird. Bright green in the wild with a delicately barred yellow head and prominently scaled yellow wings and upperparts. In flight the long tail, bright green coloration, and conspicuous pale wing bars stand out. Budgerigar ranges widely in more arid parts of Australia, occurring across much of the mainland, except the wetter coastal regions. However, it is highly nomadic and irruptive, and therefore often absent from many suitable areas. It favors grasslands, farmlands, mallee, and open woodlands within inland Australia, where it regularly forages on the ground in groups, which can swell to epic numbers (reaching tens of thousands) after a flush of new feeding areas following heavy rains.

B. Cockatiel *Nymphicus hollandicus* **29–32 cm/11.5–12.5 in.**
A familiar native bird, commonly found in the cage-bird trade. Although in the cockatoo family, it appears more like a parrot, being much smaller and longer tailed than most cockatoos. Mainly gray with large conspicuous white panels in the wing (which are visible even at some distance), a conspicuous long lemon yellow crest and face, and a prominent chestnut cheek patch. Females lack yellow on the head. It is a common inland species, found over semiarid open country with scattered trees across much of the continent, but is absent from the most arid, desert areas and coastal regions. Cockatiels are usually encountered in small groups either foraging on the ground or perched in open dead trees, where their distinctive shape and striking combination of colors make them unmistakable.

C. Rainbow Lorikeet *Trichoglossus haematodus* **25–32 cm/10–12.5 in.**
Lorikeets are spectacular, highly arboreal parrots, with specially adapted tongues for feeding on nectar. A large, striking, long-tailed parrot that is adorned with a myriad of vivid colors: mainly bright green, with a deep blue hood, pale lime green collar, bright coral-red bill, orange breast, and a large dark blue belly patch. There are two distinct populations: one in the eastern coastal zone south in an arc around to extreme se. SA, and another in the tropical north of NT and WA. This latter population is markedly different, with deeper red breast and a red collar, and is sometimes considered a separate species, Red-collared Lorikeet also inhabits tropical woodland, open forest, and heaths. They are most often detected in noisy groups as they fly overhead, when they are arguably even more colorful, with vivid red underwings, long pale lime green bars on the wings, and long bright green tails. They are noisy and common birds, familiar to many, as they regularly visit blooming shrubs within town parks and gardens.

D. Musk Lorikeet *Glossopsitta concinna* **20–22 cm/8–8.5 in.**
A small lime green nectar-feeding parrot with a relatively short tail and bright red facial markings. The pattern of the scarlet face patches are the key to ID: the forehead is bright red, and there is a broad crimson cheek patch that leads from behind the eye. It is conspicuous around blossoming eucalypts when noisy gatherings occur, and can be detected from the racket produced, and where these tiny, hyperactive parrots regularly dart in and out of the trees at high speed, calling and moving often. It is confined to southeastern Australia, and TAS.

B

D

A. Hooded Parrot *Psephotus dissimilis* 26–28 cm/10–11 in.

All parrots on this page are small, long-tailed species that are primarily ground-feeding birds. Hooded Parrot is a distinctive, beautiful ultramarine parrot confined to the Top End of NT. Males are unmistakable: bright turquoise with striking gold wing patches and a black cap. Females are duller: green birds lacking the bold wing patch and solid caps of males. It occurs in paperbarks, open woodlands, and areas of eucalypts on rocky ridges, with a grassy understory and an abundance of termite mounds (in which they nest). It is an uncommon bird most often found in pairs or small groups, except when roosting communally. The stronghold of the species is centered on the town of Pine Creek, where they sometimes visit birdbaths.

B. Mulga Parrot *Psephotus varius* 27–32 cm/10.5–12.5 in.

Male Mulga Parrot is an all–bright green bird with a bright yellow bridge across the top of the bill, scarlet nape patch, yellow shoulder patch, and a red-and-yellow vent. The head markings and shoulder patch help to distinguish it from Red-rumped Parrot, with which it is most likely to be confused. Note that males of both species show red on the rump. Females are dull greenish brown and distinguished from the similar female Red-rumped by its red shoulder patch and pale pinkish red nape patch. Females of both species show green rumps. Mulga Parrot inhabits scrubland and open woodland like mallee and mulga, as well as timbered water-courses. It is fairly common, though shy and conspicuous, within dry arid country in the southern half of the mainland, where it is most likely to be found in pairs or family parties.

C. Red-rumped Parrot *Psephotus haematonotus* 24–30 cm/9.5–11.5 in.

Male and female Red-rumped Parrots are rather like dull Mulga Parrots. The male is a bright green parrot with a red rump, lemon yellow belly and vent, and a subtle royal blue wash on the shoulder and forehead. Males are distinguished from male mulgas by their lack of red on the nape and vent, and absence of a yellow shoulder patch. Females are dull brownish green with little color except for some green on the rump. The lack of any strong shoulder mark or reddish nape patch differenti-ates this species from female Mulga Parrot. Red-rumped is a common southeastern species, where it occurs in farmlands with scattered trees, grassy woodlands, and other open woodlands, and also in areas of red gums (often along watercourses). Most likely to be found in pairs or small flocks, and more readily perches in the open (compared with Mulga Parrot),. It is often conspicuous and approachable, and is more regularly found around country towns.

D. Bluebonnet *Northiella haematogaster* 26–34 cm/10–13.5 in.

Predominantly olive-brown with a prominent blue face and bright yellow belly and vent, with variable amounts of bright scarlet scattered across this vivid yellow area. The wings are deep blue, and it often shows a dark red shoulder patch. The blue face and wings and red underbelly help distinguish Bluebonnet from any other parrot. A southeastern species found in semiarid, dry country across e. SA, n. VIC, w. NSW, and sw. QLD. It is found in areas of open wooded country, mulga, farm-lands with scattered trees, and tree-lined watercourses, but is most abundant in mallee regions.

A. Australian Ringneck *Barnardius zonarius* **31–42 cm/12–16.5 in.**
A large green parrot with a long square-ended tail and a conspicuous yellow ring-neck or collar. There are many forms, sometimes regarded as distinct species, with western birds displaying darker hoods above the yellow collar (which is common to all forms). These darker-headed forms are called "Port Lincoln" Parrot and "Twenty-eight Parrot" (named after the call). In the east there are two distinct forms: the southern form, "Mallee Ringneck" (s. QLD, NSW, VIC, and w. SA) is more colorful, with blue upperparts, a soft reddish patch on the green chest, and a red bridge across the top of the bill. The northern form in the east (w. QLD) is known as "Cloncurry Ringneck" and lacks the red areas and the blue upperparts, but shows a bright yellow underside. It is a common, though inconspicuous, species, most often found along vegetated watercourses, as well as open woodland, mallee, and farmlands with scattered trees. They forage for seeds on the ground and so are best detected when inadvertently disturbed, when they fly up in groups with distinctive deep wingbeats and often emit raucous calls as they do so.

B. Red-winged Parrot *Aprosmictus erythropterus* **30–32 cm/12–12.5 in.**
A stunning green parrot with large scarlet panels in the wing, a contrasting black back (in males only), and an orange bill. This dashing parrot is striking in appearance both perched and in flight. They fly with slow, deliberate wingbeats and display a zigzag flight pattern, which allows the observer to savor their most conspicuous feature, the scarlet wings, as well as reveal their square-shaped tail. It occurs in open woodlands, tropical eucalypt forest, and tropical savanna in northern and eastern Australia. Unlike many other Australian parrots, Red-winged does not usually forage on the ground but feeds on blossoms within trees.

C. Australian King-Parrot *Alisterus scapularis* **40–44 cm/15.5–17.5 in.**
A large, striking parrot with a long, square tail. Males and females are strikingly different: males are bright scarlet birds, except for a forest green mantle, tail, and wings with a slim, lighter green shoulder stripe. Females are all dull green with a red belly and undertail. Despite their striking appearance they can be quite inconspicuous as they forage within trees in rainforest, eucalypt forest, or densely vegetated parkland, usually giving themselves away when they burst out from cover in flight or through their high-pitched piping calls. Found in wet eastern coastal regions from Cairns (QLD) to Melbourne (VIC). In some areas, most notably Lamington National Park (QLD) and Pebbly Beach (NSW), a number of wild individuals have been habituated around feeding stations and can be seen at absurdly close quarters.

A. Crimson Rosella *Platycercus elegans* 35–38 cm/14–15 in.

Australia is often known as the "Land of Parrots," and one look at this page of common Australian birds illustrates why. **Rosellas** are brightly colored parrots that have characteristic broad tails and a bouncing, deep undulating flight. Although they regularly perch in trees, Rosellas frequently forage on the ground for seeds and insects. Most Rosellas are geographically separated, and all are common where they occur. Crimson Rosella is a bird of eastern coastal Australia, from n. QLD down to s. VIC, where it inhabits rainforests, woodlands, eucalypt forests, and gardens. It is a striking bird, largely all vivid scarlet with a royal blue throat, blue tail, and blue flashes in its wings. This red parrot is scaled blackish all down its back from the nape down to the rump. It is most likely encountered feeding quietly in groups on the ground, which when disturbed, flush up with a flurry of red and a sudden outbreak of noisy calls, making them hard to miss once in flight. Orange and yellow forms (that replace the scarlet areas on the body) are found in Adelaide and inland southern NSW, respectively.

B. Eastern Rosella *Platycercus eximius* 28–33 cm/11–13 in.

Eastern Rosella is an eastern parrot found coastally from se. QLD south to VIC and TAS. Its brightest feature is the bright scarlet head, which contrasts with a clean white throat and gaudy yellowish underparts. It is yellow on the back with bold black scales down the mantle, and has a bright green rump and a blue tail. This myriad of colors makes it unlikely to be confused with any other bird. It is found in parks, open woodlands, farmlands, and gardens, and like all rosellas, is often encountered feeding quietly in small parties on the ground.

C. Northern Rosella *Platycercus venustus* 30–32 cm/12–12.5 in.

A northern parrot found in n. WA and the north of NT that does not overlap with any other rosella species. Northern Rosella has a black head and bright white throat, yellow underparts with a vivid scarlet vent, yellow upperparts scaled black on the mantle, and a blue tail and striking bright yellow rump in flight. It also has a broad blue flash in the wing visible even when perched. It is found in tropical open woodlands, scrubby areas, and grassy clearings within its small range, where it is fairly common.

D. Green Rosella *Platycercus caledonicus* 30–36 cm/12–14 in.

A Tasmanian parrot, restricted to there, where it overlaps with just one other rosella species, the markedly different Eastern Rosella, which has an all-red head. On occasion these two rosella species can be found feeding together within the same flocks. Green Rosella possesses black-scaled green upperparts, a green tail, bright yellow underparts and head with a solid blue chin and cheeks, and a small bright red forehead. In combination, these features are unlike those of any other species of parrot on TAS. It is a common rosella on TAS in a range of habitat types, from dense forests to farmlands to eucalypt woodlands and neighboring clearings. Like all the rosellas, they are most frequently observed in small groups. This Tasmanian endemic is even common in downtown Hobart.

A. Channel-billed Cuckoo *Scythrops novaehollandiae* **57–70 cm/22.5–27.5 in.**
A massive, loud, and distinctive species that is both the largest cuckoo and the largest brood-parasite on Earth. It is migratory, spending the winters on the island of New Guinea and migrating to Australia in large flocks (unlike other migratory cuckoos) to breed between August and April. A real brute that looks like a huge flying cross in flight. A gray bird with a bulbous, straw-colored bill (somewhat reminiscent of a hornbill), and red skin around the eye near the bill base. The combination of massive size and odd bill shape makes this a truly unmistakable cuckoo. It is parasitic like many other Old World Cuckoos, laying its eggs in the nests of large birds like magpies, currawongs, crows, and butcherbirds, and taking no part in rearing the young. The young of this enormous cuckoo then quickly outcompete the smaller chicks of the natural parents, which often then die from starvation. It is not uncommon therefore to see these other birds harass them when they arrive on the scene as they try to drive this parasitic bird away. They are migrants to the coastal areas of the tropical north and down the eastern side of Australia into n. NSW. It inhabits anywhere with large trees such as rainforests, eucalypt forests, open woodlands, and wooded farmlands, where congregations can sometimes be seen around fruiting trees such as figs. They are usually encountered in pairs or small marauding groups, unlike other Australian cuckoos, which are typically found singly or in pairs. Channel-billed Cuckoo usually sits high in the trees and often draw attention by its loud, raucous, and highly distinctive "awk" calls.

B. Pheasant Coucal *Centropus phasianinus* **54–68 cm/21.5–27in.**
Coucals are long-tailed, ground-foraging cuckoos characterized by black and brown coloration, and often possess deep whooping or bubbling calls. They are typically weak fliers, often running instead from danger. Unlike all of Australia's other cuckoo species, Pheasant Coucal is peculiar, as it is *not* a brood parasite, rearing its own young. Coucals are strange among cuckoos, too, in that the majority of the parental care is undertaken by the male. This species is the sole Australian representative of the coucals. In breeding plumage it is all black below with heavily streaked brown upperparts, and a heavily barred, very long tail. When not breeding, it is a brown bird heavily streaked all over and lacking the solid black of breeding dress. Pheasant Coucal is found commonly throughout the tropical north and down the eastern coastal region into n. NSW, in habitats like open woods, scrublands, heaths, swamps, and thickets. Notably, the species has benefited from sugar cane farming on the east coast of Australia, where they can regularly be found around cane fields. Generally skulking, they can be observed for long periods when at a distance, but when approached, soon drop to the ground and run away, much in the manner of the roadrunner of North America. It is most likely to be seen feeding on the ground at the edge of a road, or sunning itself on the top of low scrub in the early morning sunlight.

A. Eastern Koel *Eudynamys cyanocephalus* 41 cm/16 in.

A large, fruit-eating cuckoo that shouts its name: "koel," a loud and familiar call in its range. Males are all glossy black with a blood red eye and pale horn-colored bills. Females are brown birds with a black cap, red eye, and black moustache, and are spotted white all over. It is a long-tailed cuckoo found throughout the tropical north and down the east side to s. NSW. Koel is far more easily heard than seen in forests and other areas with tall trees, as it tends to sit well hidden when it gives its loud call incessantly from the treetops. It is a breeding migrant to Australia (from New Guinea) and is parasitic, laying its eggs in the nests of orioles, honeyeaters, Magpie-Larks, and riflebirds. It sometimes joins groups of Channel-billed Cuckoos at fruiting fig trees.

B. Shining Bronze-Cuckoo *Chrysococcyx lucidus* 17–18 cm/6.5–7 in.

Bronze-cuckoos are small cuckoos that have bronzed upperparts and typically have barred underparts. There are three similar species that overlap in eastern Australia: Shining, **Horsfield's** (*C. basalis*) and **Little Bronze-Cuckoo** (*C. minutillus*). They are all metallic green or bronzy above with extensive dark barring on a white underside. They differ markedly in the eye color: Little possesses a red iris and a noticeable red eye ring, while Shining and Horsfield's both have dull brown eyes and lack an obvious eye ring. Horsfield's further differs in having incomplete bars on the underparts, which usually do not meet in the center, and a very broad white supercilium, which create the effect of a conspicuous dark ear patch. Shining and Little are both eastern coastal species, while Little also occurs across the tropical north. Horsfield's Bronze-Cuckoo occurs across the entire continent, generally in drier habitats than the other species, and is the only bronze-cuckoo on TAS. They are all parasitic on small songbirds, such as fairywrens and gerygones, and some small honeyeaters.

C. Pallid Cuckoo *Cacomantis pallidus* 30 cm/12 in.

A largely uniform pale gray cuckoo with a dark line or mask through the eye (its boldest plumage feature), and a long boldly barred tail. Rufous morph females are rufous on the back with scattered pale mottling above. A very widespread cuckoo that favors open habitats, where it is commonly encountered perched prominently on roadside wires in both dry and wet areas of the entire continent. Parasitizes medium-sized songbirds such as orioles, cuckoo-shrikes, and flycatchers.

D. Fan-tailed Cuckoo *Cacomantis flabelliformis* 24–27 cm/9.5–10.5 in.

A gray cuckoo with a cinnamon-washed throat, neck, and breast, which are the key to distinguish it from **Brush Cuckoo** *C. variolosus*, which differs in its buff-washed underparts, and squarish tail that lacks the notched tail sides that Fan-tailed possesses. Fan-tailed occurs in the wet coastal regions of eastern and southern Australia, inhabiting rainforests, woodlands, and mangroves. Brush Cuckoo occurs in similar habitats in eastern and northern Australia, but is absent from the south. Both species are brood parasites, laying their eggs in the nests of small birds such as fairywrens, thornbills, and scrubwrens. Both species are vocal, often giving incessant, trilling calls that form a dominant backdrop to eastern forests.

A. Barn Owl *Tyto alba* 29–38 cm/11.5–15 in.

Owls are a group of ferocious birds of prey that are generally active at night, when they hunt for their prey by using their exceptionally sharp hearing, and sleep during daylight hours. Owl roosting or nesting areas may be detected by the presence of discarded pellets on the ground formed of regurgitated matter from their prey that the owls cannot digest, such as bones and fur. The Barn Owl is one of the most widespread and common Australian owls, and one of the most widespread birds on Earth, occurring on all continents except Antarctica. Ghostly white with indistinctly marked sandy upperparts and a characteristic heart-shaped face. The Barn Owl occurs in open country, such as grasslands and open woodlands throughout Australia (except for the southern deserts), where they roost and nest in hollow tree cavities and old buildings like barns, as the name suggests. They are most likely to be seen either flying around country roads at night or perched on a roadside post, when their white coloration can be dazzling in the headlights of a car. Barn Owls often begin hunting a short time before dusk, when they may also be observed quartering open areas for prey.

B. Barking Owl *Ninox connivens* 39–44 cm/15.5–17.5 in.

An owl that has the distinction of possessing a call that sounds remarkably like a series of dog barks. It also has another, disturbing, blood-curdling scream, which lent it the earlier name "Screaming woman owl"! Like a large version of the more common and widespread Southern Boobook: a small-headed brownish owl, variably spotted and streaked with pale markings, and big staring eyes. In Barking Owl the eyes are brilliant yellow, although greenish toned in the boobook. The boobook also usually displays obvious dark markings (which look rather like black-eye bruises) around the eyes, which are absent in the larger Barking Owl. It is less common than the more widespread boobook and is usually found in dry country woodlands and wooded watercourses, mainly in the north and east of the mainland, where they are significantly more abundant in the north of their range.

C. Southern Boobook *Ninox novaeseelandiae* 30–35 cm/12–14 in.

A small, relatively small headed brownish owl, with greenish yellow eyes, which are used to differentiate it from the similar, though larger, Barking Owl, which has piercing bright yellow eyes. It is the smallest of the Australian owls, closer in size to the nocturnal frogmouths than most of the other owls. The Southern Boobook also displays black markings around the eyes, reminiscent of black-eye bruises, which are usually surrounded by white markings, usually lacking in Barking. It is Australia's most common owl. It is found in a wide range of habitats throughout the mainland and TAS, including within wetter habitats such as rainforest, from which Barking Owl is usually absent. The name boobook is said to derive from an onomatopoeic rendition of its incessant call. Boobooks can usually be easily located by tracing their frequently given call.

C

A. Australian Owlet-Nightjar *Aegotheles cristatus* **21–24 cm/8.5–9.5 in.**
A strange, cryptically patterned, nocturnal bird. A tiny bird that is the smallest of all the nocturnal species (owls, frogmouths, and nightjars) in Australia. Neither a nightjar nor an owl but from an Australasian family named **Owlet-Nightjars**. In their body shape they are nightjar-like: they possess long tails and slim, protruding, nightjar-like bills but perch with an upright posture like an owl. This is the sole representative of this odd, strictly nocturnal bird family in Australia. It is fairly widespread across the continent, found throughout the mainland and TAS, wherever there are wooded areas or even small clusters of trees in open country. They are not readily found, however, and usually require dedicated searches to locate them. Unlike other nocturnal birds (i.e., frogmouths, nightjars, and owls) the eyes of Australian Owlet-Nightjars do not glow in a spotlight, making them especially tricky to find. Australian Owlet-Nightjar nests and sleeps in tree hollows, where they are perhaps most likely seen, sunning themselves at the entrance during early mornings, before sleeping during the day. Insect-eaters, they usually capture their prey at night by sallying from a perch or by dropping down onto the ground.

B. Tawny Frogmouth *Podargus strigoides* **35–50 cm/14–20 in.**
Frogmouths are large, cryptically patterned, nocturnal birds with very wide gapes, reminiscent of a frog. They use their large mouth to capture prey (such as lizards, frogs and insects) at night, by pouncing on them on the ground from an elevated perch. Frogmouths are well camouflaged, a feature they rely on when roosting during the day, as they often sleep in the open, strongly mimicking parts of the trees in which they roost (much the same as the Potoos of the Americas). Their size and coloration are highly variable, with some birds being distinctly grayer than others that are more rufous-toned, although they are always cryptically patterned, with a barklike appearance. Tawny is the only frogmouth species in Australia with big yellow eyes. It is the most widespread of the three Australian species, found throughout the mainland and also in TAS, occurring in all habitats except within dense rainforest. The other two species are confined to eastern rainforests. They are best found when roosting during the day or when nesting (frogmouth nests usually comprise just a few twigs precariously balanced on an open limb), as they often return to traditional sites to sleep and nest year after year.

C. Papuan Frogmouth *Podargus papuensis* **50–60 cm/20–23.5 in.**
A huge, highly camouflaged, nocturnal bird that is the largest Australian frogmouth. Papuan is a forest frogmouth confined to the Wet Tropics of ne. QLD. Although most often found in rainforests, they also occur in mangroves and palm forests. Like all the frogmouths it has rufous and gray forms, and also hunts by seizing prey from low branches and trunks, and by pouncing on them while on the ground, much in the manner of a butcherbird. This species has distinctive orange eyes. Papuan Frogmouth is best located in traditional nesting areas where local people can often take you to their favored haunts (e.g. on Daintree River cruises, QLD).

C

A. Laughing Kookaburra *Dacelo novaeguineae* 40–48 cm/15.5–19 in.

Kookaburras are a group of large kingfishers found in Australasia that are characterized by large bills, stout bodies, and strange, very loud calls. Laughing Kookaburra is the largest species of kingfisher in the world, and one of two kookaburras in Australia. The Laughing Kookaburra is one of Australia's most familiar and famous birds, immortalized in many Australian children's songs and stories, and it even lends its name to the national hockey team. It is an abundant and familiar endemic (i.e., found only in Australia) that is widespread in the east and TAS, and is common in every eastern town and city. Laughing Kookaburra is famed for its extraordinary call, which is, in fact, a sequence of loud calls, beginning with what has been described accurately as a "merry chuckle" and rising to a crescendo of "raucous laughter." This rollicking call is often given by a pair, which then often triggers loud reactions from other neighboring kookaburras, making for quite an explosive chorus. This remarkable song is the most familiar call of any Australian bird. Unlike many other kingfishers, the Laughing Kookaburra is not tied to water, and preys on a huge variety of animals including snakes, lizards, nestlings of birds, grasshoppers, earthworms, beetles, spiders, moths, and many other insects, as well as table scraps like cheese and raw meat! As usual with most kingfishers, spends long periods of time waiting, nearly motionless, before pouncing on its prey. Distinguished from the similar Blue-winged Kookaburra by its dark eye, dark brownish mask around the eye, and a brown, barred tail, lacking any blue on the wings or tail. Laughing Kookaburras are cavity breeders that often make hollows in the nests of tree termites.

B. Blue-winged Kookaburra *Dacelo leachii* 39 cm/15.5 in.

Another large kingfisher with very loud, raucous, obnoxious, and maniacal calls that draw substantial attention. The Blue-winged is found only in the tropical north of Australia, usually in open forest, wooded areas, and tree-lined watercourses. It is most abundant in tropical savannas. Unlike Laughing, Blue-winged is not confined to Australia, as it also occurs across the Torres Strait on the island of New Guinea, and is less associated with towns. Blue-winged is shyer and distinctly less approachable than the trusting Laughing Kookaburra. Where Laughing and Blue-winged coexist, Laughing tends to prefer wetter areas. Blue-winged occurs in dry country and often far from water, where it hunts for a huge variety of prey items, including insects, snakes, small birds, small mammals, and even bird eggs. Distinguished from the larger Laughing Kookaburra by its brighter blue wings; plain, buff-colored head (sometimes with a capped appearance) that lacks a dark "eye patch"; and a piercing white eye. The male only also has a blue tail, unlike the brown-tailed Laughing.

A. Forest Kingfisher *Todiramphus macleayii* **19–21 cm/7.5–8.5 in.**

This page covers four similar kingfishers: all blue or blue-green above with whitish underparts. Collared is the only species that is tied to water; all the others are often found far from wetlands. They are best distinguished from one another by one or more of these features: forehead markings, tone of the upperparts, rump color, underpart coloration, and wing pattern. Forest is a clean blue-and-white kingfisher, deep blue above with a darker head and a very bold white spot on the forehead. Males have a complete white collar on the nape (like Collared and Sacred), although females have no collar and have a blue nape (different from all the other species on this plate). It has a blue rump (unlike Red-backed) and has pure, gleaming white underparts (unlike the buff-tinged Sacred). Forest has a striking white patch on the upperwing in flight, while all the other species have plain, unmarked wings. Forest can be found in open forest, open woodland, and woodland edges, where it most likely to be encountered perched prominently on roadside wires. Found in coastal areas from Brisbane north around to Darwin.

B. Sacred Kingfisher *Todiramphus sanctus* **21 cm/8.5 in.**

A widespread kingfisher with buff-washed underparts and a buff collar that differentiates this species from all others. Furthermore, the pale spot before the eye is buff toned and indistinct in Sacred, although bold and white in Forest and Collared. Sacred is found in a wide variety of habitats all over Australia (including TAS) and is the most abundant, widespread kingfisher. It occurs in open woodlands, parks, eucalypt stands, and mangroves as well (which can also hold both Collared and Forest Kingfishers).

C. Collared Kingfisher *Todiramphus chloris* **23–27 cm/9–10.5 in.**

A specialist of the coastal zone, found mainly around mangroves, from which it gets its other name: Mangrove Kingfisher. The combination of aqua upperparts, small white forehead mark, and clean white collar and underparts firmly differentiates this species from all others. Collared Kingfisher is found from c. WA around the top of Australia down to s. QLD, where it is a highly vocal kingfisher that often draws attention to itself by its strident calls emanating from the mangroves.

D. Red-backed Kingfisher *Todiramphus pyrrhopygius* **23 cm/9 in.**

Red-backed Kingfisher shows a blue back, white underside, and a white collar much like several other species on the page but uniquely has a bold red rump, white supercilium, and a streaked crown. Red-backed is usually found far from water in open woodland, and occurs sparsely over much of mainland Australia, being most abundant in drier parts of the interior. It is most likely to be found sitting quietly and high on an open dead branch, from which it surveys the ground below for prey.

A. Azure Kingfisher *Ceyx azureus* 16–19 cm/6.5–7.5 in.

An abundant and handsome Australian kingfisher that is always found near water; the common riverside kingfisher. A small, dumpy kingfisher with a very short, stumpy tail and relatively massive bill. Named for its deep azure blue upperparts, this species differs from the Little Kingfisher, with which it sometimes occurs, in its bright apricot underside and prominent red feet. Fairly common along rivers, creeks, small shady pools, and mangroves in northern and eastern Australia. Usually hunts for fish from a low creek-side perch in the shade of an overhanging tree. It bobs its head regularly to pinpoint its prey, then suddenly plunges into the water before darting off at high speed to another concealed perch.

B. Little Kingfisher *Ceyx pusillus* 11–13 cm/4.5–5 in.

A tiny bird that is the smallest Australian kingfisher. This diminutive kingfisher is deep royal blue or violet-blue above; clean, shining white below; and shows a contrasting blaze of white on the sides of the neck, and a bright white spot before the eye. It is very locally distributed in the tropical north of Australia, where it is found along forest-lined creeks, at the edges of well-vegetated swamps, and in mangroves. It can be frustratingly difficult to find, as it perches low near the water, often well hidden in the shadows provided by the overhanging vegetation, causing the observer surprise when it suddenly bolts from it perch at high speed, shooting low over the water to escape, in a blur of blue and white. The prize bird of many river trips in Kakadu National Park (NT) and QLD, where they are most likely found with the help of local guides.

C. Buff-breasted Paradise-Kingfisher *Tanysiptera sylvia* 30–36 cm/12–14 in.

The jewel in the crown of Australia's kingfishers. A sensational bird decorated with a long fancy tail that characterizes all the **paradise-kingfishers**, a distinct subfamily that is largely found in New Guinea. Indeed, the Buff-breasted Paradise-Kingfisher is a migrant from New Guinea, coming to the rainforests of ne. QLD only to breed from November to March. This odd and dazzling kingfisher has the notable habit of nesting in active terrestrial termite mounds. Unlike the other kingfishers on this page, it is not tied to water and is usually found sitting inconspicuously in the forest understory, where it is often spotted when it betrays its position by its regular tail-flicking motion. A gorgeous bird, rightly prized among visiting birders, with deep blue upper side, a long ghostly white tail, burnt orange underparts, and a gaudy carrot-colored bill that simply glows in the gloomy understory.

C

A. Rainbow Bee-eater *Merops ornatus* 22–25cm/8.5–10in

Bee-eaters are an Old World family of brightly colored insectivorous birds that reach their greatest diversity in Africa. They are among the most richly colored birds on the planet, so bee-eaters are always a crowd favorite wherever they occur. The Australian "version" is no different. It is the only bee-eater in Australia. In common with all other bee-eaters it hunts from a prominent perch such as an open branch or power lines and sallies for passing insects. As the name suggests, a large portion of their diet is indeed bees, although a huge variety of other invertebrates are taken, including flies, butterflies, beetles, dragonflies, and even spiders. It is a strikingly marked bird that is delightfully common in open country over much of Australia, and is unlikely to be confused with any other bird. It is well named, for it is indeed decorated with many bright and appealing colors: the head alone boasts a prominent black mask edged in turquoise blue, a rich rufous crown merging into a subtle jade green forehead, and a bold yellow throat bordered with black and rufous. Most of the body is gemlike greenish in tone, with bright azure blue on the rump and turquoise lower belly. In addition, when the bird takes flight (as it regularly does to snatch airborne prey), it reveals a distinctive body shape, with two fine, needlelike plumes protruding from its tail, as well as vivid coral underwings that contrast with the overall greenish coloration. Thankfully it is quite common and highly visible. Small, vocal groups of these enchanting birds can often be found in town parks.

B. Dollarbird *Eurystomus orientalis* 26–29 cm/10–11.5 in.

The Dollarbird is from another colorful, largely African family, the **Rollers**. The species is named for the large silver dollar–shaped markings on its dark wings that can be seen only in flight. They are usually seen sitting bolt upright, high on an open perch, where they hawk for airborne insect prey that they catch by regularly sallying from a favored perch like a dead branch or an electrical cable. The Dollarbird preys mainly on hard insects like beetles, along with mantises, grasshoppers, shield-bugs, cicadas, ants, and many other insects. It is the only representative of the roller family in Australia and therefore is a distinctive bird quite unlike any other: a stocky, well-built bird with an all–deep blue–green glossed body, and a bright, carrot-colored bill and feet. It also has a strange rolling flight action that becomes distinctive with birding experience. It is a common breeding migrant (from New Guinea) to the tropical north of Australia, and rarer in the southeast of the country. Dollarbirds have a preference for exposed perches, and occur in all habitats through their range. In rainforests, for example, such perches are frequently high in the canopy, although these exposed perches may be lower in other habitats such as open woodland, where dollarbirds may be seen sitting. Dollarbird is a widespread global bird, occurring throughout Australasia and over much of Asia, too.

A. Noisy Pitta *Pitta versicolor* 18–26 cm/7–10 in.

Pittas are a brightly colored family of tropical birds that are often some of the most highly sought species wherever they occur. The Australian ones are no different. Both of these Australian species are spectacularly adorned birds that any visiting birder puts right near the top of his or her wish list. Pittas are plump birds with almost no tail, and long legs, and are most often seen hopping around on the forest floor, where they feed in the manner of a thrush or an American Robin: probing for insects in the leaf litter with their thick, powerful beaks. The Noisy Pitta is not uncommon in the eastern rainforests of Australia, from extreme northern Queensland into n. NSW. However, although reasonably common, and despite their brilliant coloration, they can be tough to see, as pittas are masters at hiding within the shadows of the forest floor, where they are usually found. They are perhaps most easily seen early in the morning or late in the afternoon, when they can emerge from the forest to feed on an open trail or even along the edge of a quiet road. Alternatively, when the well-named Noisy Pittas vocalize, they can perch high in trees (rarely above 6 m/20 ft) and can draw attention to themselves with their loud, far-reaching calls. At such times they may abandon their usual furtive habits and become quite visible, and can be tracked down with knowledge of these distinctive sounds ("walk to work"). This remarkable green bird of the eastern rainforests, with the vivid scarlet vent, buff yellow underside, black hood, and brilliant iridescent blue, kingfisher-like, wing flashes is unlikely to be confused with any other bird in its range.

B. Rainbow Pitta *Pitta iris* 16–18 cm/6.5–7 in.

The Rainbow Pitta is another dumpy bird with almost no tail and long legs that is spectacularly colored and therefore highly prized among visiting birders. It, too, is most at home in the leaf litter, where it probes the dirt for insects and other prey items while hopping along the floor in the fashion of a thrush or robin. Its dazzling colors make it unlikely to be confused with any other bird in its range: the humid monsoon forests, thickets, and mangroves of extreme northern sectors of WA and the NT, such as Howard Springs and Fogg Dam (NT). The most similar species, the Noisy Pitta does not occur in the same areas, and possesses a yellowish, not black-ish, breast. Like that species, Rainbow Pitta also boasts glistening blue wing patches that glow brilliantly from the understory or flash vividly in flight, and its striking crimson undertail can also create a stir as it hits the light. If you manage to see a Rainbow Pitta and hear its call, then whistled imitations can cause this alluring bird to circle you excitedly in pursuit of the unseen intruder.

A. Albert's Lyrebird *Menura alberti* 65–90 cm/25.5–35.5 in.

Lyrebirds are pheasant-like birds, the males of which sport long, lyre-shaped tails, which are intricately patterned and used during their dramatic displays at traditional calling posts in the forest. Albert's are shy forest birds, especially when displaying, when they are very hard to observe, as they raise their fine filament-like tail feathers over their head, gradually bringing them lower until their head is covered as if by a fine, delicate veil. Albert's is the smaller lyrebird, with a more northerly distribution; it is found in extreme southeastern QLD and extreme northern NSW only, where it is confined to temperate rainforest. Both lyrebirds are fabulous songsters, capable of some of the most remarkable mimicry on Earth. Although Albert's does not have quite the extensive arsenal of mimicry compared with Superb, it is known to regularly imitate Green Catbird and Satin Bowerbird among others. It mixes these imitations into a long sequence of calls with its own unique and varied vocabulary, which comprises a huge variety of high squeals, shrieks, trills, dingolike howls, and other more mellow sounds. It is a large chestnut bird with a reddish throat and long tail, found on the forest floor, where it scratches in the leaf litter with its powerful feet and claws for invertebrates and seeds. It is a poor flier, and more often runs swiftly from danger.

B. Superb Lyrebird *Menura novaehollandiae* 76–103 cm/30–40.5 in.

The largest songbird on Earth. Generally found to the south of Albert's from se. QLD down into the Dandenongs of VIC; there is an introduced population on TAS. It is the more accomplished mimic, with some remarkable individuals having been recorded accurately imitating chainsaws, camera shutters, ambulance sirens, and crying babies, along with a whole repertoire of local bird songs. It is known to imitate (among others) the wonderful whip-cracking sound of Eastern Whipbird, various parrots (such as rosellas), cockatoos, honeyeaters, butcherbirds, and kookaburras. These calls are given in quick succession and intermixed with many of its own bizarre sounds such as rattles, whistles, and thudding noises of its own, everimaginative, creation. Superb Lyrebird is a ground-dwelling bird, which also prefers to run than fly when alarmed, and is also difficult to observe while displaying, when it spreads its tail, lowers it over its head, and uses it like a feathered veil. They are more readily seen when quietly feeding along a forest trail in the early morning or late afternoon. Generally more numerous and less shy than Albert's, and in some areas they have become famously habituated to people (e.g., Lady Carrington Drive, Royal NP, NSW). Where the ranges of both lyrebirds overlap, Superb prefers wet eucalypt forest and lower-altitude rainforest. In the south of its range, however, it can occur in wet eucalypt forest, temperate rainforest, and even dense patches of wet heathland.

A. Spotted Catbird *Ailuroedus melanotis* **26–30 cm/10–12 in.**

The birds on this page are an Australasian family called the **bowerbirds**. Male bowerbirds are famous for building "bowers": stages made from sticks that they often decorate extravagantly to attract females and that they use to call from, display, and mate with multiple females. Nests are often far away from these bowers, and all parenting activities are carried out solely by the females. Bowerbirds often have a particular color preference: for example the Great Bowerbird prefers white-colored items when adorning its bower. Structurally, bowerbirds are chunky birds, with large bodies and strong bills, and are mainly frugivorous. Spotted Catbird is unusual among Australian bowerbirds, being one of only three species that do not construct avenue bowers like the others. It is a large green bowerbird with heavily spotted head and breast, blackish sides to the head, and a conspicuous red eye. Spotted Catbird is very similar to the closely related **Green Catbird** *Ailuroedus crassirostris*, but they are separated in geographic range: Spotted occurs in the tropical rainforests of ne. QLD only, while Green is found to the south in the coastal temperate rainforests of s. QLD and NSW. Although they do not overlap and so can be identified on range, the Green Catbird is less heavily spotted, especially on the head and breast, and has a paler head, lacking the contrasting black head sides of Spotted Catbird. Both Catbirds are inconspicuous rainforest species, usually encountered in pairs, and best located when they give the strange, catlike calls after which they are named, which are reminiscent of cats fighting or in some pain.

B. and C. Regent Bowerbird *Sericulus chrysocephalus* **24–28 cm/9.5–11 in.**

The dashing male Regent Bowerbird (photo C) is one of the most spectacular birds in Australia: all glossy black except for a gaudy golden hood and broad golden flash in the wing, which is most stunning in flight. Females (photo B) are quite different: all grayish brown, mottled and spotted with pale marking on the back, and possessing a bold black cap that constitutes their most prominent feature. Regent Bowerbird is a more traditional bowerbird that does indeed construct a bower. The bower is a fairly simple construction of sticks that forms an avenue (around 23 cm/9 in. long, 20 cm/8 in. wide, and 18 cm/7 in. high) and that is decorated with green or blue items. These can include shiny cicada shells, leaves, snail shells, berries, and human-made plastic items. Unlike some other bowerbirds they do not maintain their bowers for long periods of time (usually 10 days or less), regularly destroying their own or others' bowers when rival males detect them. A new bower takes around 4 hours to build. It is a scarce species restricted to coastal temperate rainforest in s. QLD and n. NSW, where it is often inconspicuous despite its striking appearance. At just a few sites they have become habituated and can be seen with regularity at extremely close quarters (e.g., Lamington NP). An encounter with a golden-hooded male Regent Bowerbird in the rainforests of the east is one of the unquestionable highlights of a trip for any visiting naturalist.

A., B., and C. Satin Bowerbird *Ptilonorhynchus violaceus* **27–33 cm/10.5–13 in.**

Satin Bowerbird favors blue objects when adorning its avenue-style bower, many of which are often plastic items such as bottle tops, straws, and glass, as well as natural objects like parrot feathers (especially Crimson Rosella), snail shells, and flowers (photo C). It is a large and distinctive bowerbird that is familiar to many people in its range, as it can be remarkably approachable and conspicuous in some areas (e.g., Lamington NP). It is strikingly dimorphic: the male (photo A) is all glossy blue with a stout, pale horn–colored bill and legs, and a beautiful soft violet eye; the female (photo B) is equally beautiful: olive on the upperparts, a darker bill, rust-colored wings and tail, boldly scaled underparts, and similarly seductive violet eye. It is common in the mountain forests of ne. QLD, and temperate rainforests and wet eucalypt forests of se. QLD, e. NSW, and VIC. They are most likely to be seen bounding around on the ground in the early morning, foraging for prey such as fruit or insects, or searching for items to ornament their bowers.

D. Great Bowerbird *Chlamydera nuchalis* **32–37.5 cm/12.5–14.5 in.**

The largest bowerbird. A dowdy species, gray-brown with darker markings on the upperparts and a well-concealed violet-pink crest on the nape that is rarely seen outside of courtship displays. Males and females appear the same, unlike many other bowerbird species. Like other bowerbirds though, it constructs large and impressive bowers. It builds a thick-walled bower that can comprise as many as 900 sticks in one single avenue wall and that is decorated just outside either end with white or gray objects such as mammal bones, and snail shells—sometimes, in addition to green or red items like fruits and leaves. This impressive structure averages around 58 cm/23 in. long, 51 cm/20 in. wide, and 41 cm/16 in. high. Many bower sites are used for decades—one site has been used for more than 70 years. The bower is often rebuilt each season, although it can be used over multiple seasons. The bowers are often located in country gardens and outback school yards. Males are polygamous, breeding with multiple females. The female is left alone to build the nest and tend to the young. Great Bowerbird is common in its range, which covers the tropical north of Australia from n. WA eastward to n. QLD. It inhabits dry woodlands, wooded watercourses, and tropical savannas. It is best found at well-known bowers, where the males frequently return to attend their prized possession, although they are generally common and conspicuous birds where they occur that often draw attention to themselves with their quiet, dry hissing calls. They also frequently come to picnic grounds.

B

D

A. Brown Treecreeper *Climacteris picumnus* **14–18 cm/5.5–7 in.**

Treecreepers are known for their distinctive foraging behavior: they crawl upward on trunks and branches picking out invertebrate prey, and also regularly feed on the ground. Australasian Treecreepers are a distinct family from the treecreepers or creepers of Asia, Europe, and North America. Treecreepers are plump, potbellied birds that are highly social and most often found feeding in small parties. They all have powerful feet and claws that enable them to climb. Brown is the most widespread treecreeper, found all across the eastern side of the mainland. They favor areas of dry woods, scrub, and mountain forests where there is a lot of fallen timber and dead wood available for them to feed on. It is largely brown in appearance, dark brown to gray-brown on the back, with paler brown underparts that are streaked with buff on the belly, and checkered buff on the undertail. The bird also displays a fairly prominent pale eyebrow.

B. Rufous Treecreeper *Climacteris rufus* **16.5–18 cm/6.5–7 in.**

A distinctive, rich rufous–colored treecreeper restricted to s. WA and the Eyre Peninsula (SA). Over most of its range it is the only treecreeper present. Although a number of other rufous birds exist in Australia, Rufous Treecreepers can be distinguished from those by the characteristic feeding style described above. They are most likely to be found in small groups feeding either low on tree trunks or on fallen wood in areas with plenty of dead timber, where they frequently forage on the ground. It occurs in a range of wooded habitats, including mallee, jarrah, karri forests, and wandoo woodlands, as well as timbered watercourses, parks, and golf courses. They are especially abundant in Dryandra State Forest and Porongorup National Park (WA), although rare in SA, where they are restricted to remnant mallee areas.

C. Varied Sittella *Daphoenositta chrysoptera* **10–12 cm/4–4.5 in.**

A tiny, dumpy, short-tailed arboreal species similar to the nuthatches of Europe, Asia, and North America, with which is shares a distinctive feeding style: they forage on vertical trunks and branches working their way from the top down in an erratic fashion, sometimes making short upward forays in the process as well. Unlike nuthatches, which are replaced by sittellas in Australasia, **sittellas** are highly social, gregarious species, always observed in small parties. As the name suggests, it is a variable species, gray with streaked upperparts, paler underparts (which can be unstreaked or streaked), and either a black cap or entirely white head (depending on race). They are very active, constantly on the move and regularly flitting from branch to branch, or trunk to trunk, when they display a broad pale bar in the wing (ranging from rufous in some populations to gray in others), a white rump, and extensive white in the tail. Varied Sitella is widespread, occurring across the entire mainland, although absent from TAS, where it can be found in eucalypt forests, mallee, and open woodlands, as well as parks and gardens. It usually prefers rougher-barked trees and areas where there is plentiful dead standing wood.

A. White-winged Fairywren *Malurus leucopterus* 11–13 cm/4.5–5 in.

Fairywrens are a cute Australasian family of tiny plump birds with long, cocked tails. The family comprises both fairywrens and grasswrens. The fairywrens are familiar Australian birds that are often beautifully marked with blue in their plumage—hence, their other name, "bluewrens"—while the larger grasswrens are duller birds with a similar shape, although they lack the bright colors of the fairy-wrens and are often extremely secretive. Some species of fairywrens are delightfully common and amazingly approachable birds, making them firm favorites among visitors to Australia, by virtue of their trusting nature and gorgeous plumage. They are tiny insectivorous birds that are usually dimorphic: the distinctive males are adorned with bright blue colors, while the females, confusingly, are all dull brown. Note, though, that outside the breeding season, male fairywrens have a duller eclipse plumage and then can look quite like females. All fairywrens are most often encountered in small parties, where there are usually males in the group displaying at least some of the vivid breeding colors that can be relied on for ID. White-winged Fairywren is beautiful and striking: all bright cobalt blue with striking white wings. The male is such a conspicuous and striking bird that it is unlikely to be confused with any other. The female is less obvious, being pale brown on the back and plain whitish below with a blue tail. White-winged Fairywrens are birds of dry, semiarid, open, treeless scrubby or grassy country. For example, they are often found in areas of saltbush, spinifex grasslands, canegrass, or bluebush. In areas that were previously forested (e.g., farmlands and wheat fields) they are often encountered perched on farm fences and roadside scrub or seen around farm dams. In inhabited areas such as Alice Springs and Uluru (Ayers Rock) they are most common in scrub around the water treatment plants. It is common in range that covers a huge amount of the interior of mainland Australia, inland of the coastal ranges, but is absent from the tropical north.

B. Splendid Fairywren *Malurus splendens* 11–13.5 cm/4.5–5.5 in.

In a family overloaded with gorgeous birds this is arguably the most beautiful of them all. The male is an extraordinarily stunning, almost entirely cerulean blue wren with striking powder blue crown and cheeks, and just a few narrow black markings breaking up this bright blue coloration. First sightings of the exquisite male often take people's breath away. The female is plain, pale brown on the back with a blue tail, whitish underneath, and has a dull reddish bill and patch around the eye. The bluest of the wrens, the breathtaking male is unlikely to be confused with any other, and is often a highlight of any trip into the interior. Although it occurs in scrubby habitats and bushy areas like White-winged, Splendid tends to be more abundant in wooded habitats such as mulga and mallee. It is common and quite vocal, often drawing attention to groups of them with their high-pitched twit-tering calls. A male appearing suddenly on the top of a bush in the outback is surely to be quickly noticed and never forgotten.

A. Superb Fairywren *Malurus cyaneus* **12–14 cm/4.5–5.5 in.**

This page covers two similar **fairywrens**: a group of tiny birds with long, cocked tails that sport striking blue areas in their plumage, most often seen in vociferous family parties. They are gorgeous birds that from their names clearly do not have enough superlatives to describe them! Superb is a common eastern fairywren, the male of which differs markedly from the other species below in the pattern of its head. Superb is the only one with two well-separated blue areas on the head, delineated by a broad black eye line. It also lacks the bright chestnut shoulder present in the males of Variegated. Females are more challenging if encountered with no males (which rarely occurs), being all brownish with a dark reddish bill and eye ring, although Superb lacks the white tail tips of female Variegated. This common and tame fairywren is found in se. QLD, e. NSW, VIC, se. SA, and TAS. It is the only fairywren represented on TAS. This common blue bird inhabits thickets in a wide variety of habitats that include eucalypt forest, saltmarsh, heathlands, scrubby areas, woodland edges, and even fringes of mallee, where trusting and vocal family groups are usually encountered feeding down low. It is commonly found in suitable habitat in city parks around Sydney, Brisbane, Melbourne, Hobart, and Canberra.

B. Variegated Fairywren *Malurus lamberti* **11–14.5 cm/4.5–5.5 in.**

Australia's most widespread fairywren. Like several other species, male Variegated has a blue and black front end and a white belly, but differs in the pattern of the blue on the head and the presence of rich chestnut shoulders. The male has a bright cerulean blue top to the head that extends down onto the side of the face. The blue markings are not uniform, with a bright shimmering iridescent quality to them. The shade of blue is deeper, more violet toned than on Superb, from which it further differs in the face pattern, lacking two distinct areas of blue like that species. The blue on Variegated is continuous from the crown, and a blue tongue extends down onto the cheeks on either side. Females of both species are similar brown birds with few bold features save for a red bill. Female Superb Fairywrens lack a fine white tip to the tail, which Variegated displays, and as the latter hold their tails cocked and prominently, this can often be seen. However, as most fairywrens are encountered in family groups, the regular presence of males in the group is still often the easiest way to identify them to species when the males are in breeding plumage. Outside the breeding season males go into an eclipse plumage and look much like the females. Variegated is found all over mainland Australia, except the southern and northern extremities. Small groups of this common bird generally favor undergrowth and clearings within habitats like open woodlands, eucalypt forests, mallee, mulga, and even rainforest edges in eastern Australia.

A. and B. Purple-crowned Fairywren *Malurus coronatus* **14–15 cm/5.5–6 in.**

This page illustrates three distinctive fairywrens. The first two are typical fairywrens: small birds with long, cocked tails and bold colors, while the third is a grasswren, a larger, more subtly marked bird that is much more secretive in nature than the typically tame and colorful fairywrens. Purple-crowned Fairywren is a beautiful local species of fairywren that has two tiny, discrete populations: one in the Gulf of Carpentaria (NT), and one in the Kimberley region (WA). The male (photo A) is strikingly marked with a black head and broad lilac ring surrounding a black crown. Otherwise it is brownish with a blue tail and pale whitish underparts. Females (photo B) are also quite distinctive for fairywrens by virtue of their rich chestnut ear patch, which is lacking in all other species. Less gregarious than other fairywrens, more likely to be encountered in pairs rather than large family groups. It is a habitat specialist, inhabiting tall stands of cane grass within thickets of pandanus and paperbarks, often along watercourses. It is a species that is unlikely to be seen unless specifically targeted at one of the few known sites, such as the Victoria River crossing (NT).

C. Red-backed Fairywren *Malurus melanocephalus* **10–13 cm/4–5 in.**

Male Red-backed Fairywrens are distinctively marked: a blackish bird with a striking crimson saddle across the back. Females, in common with many fairywrens, are indistinctive brown birds with reddish pink bill and legs that are usually best identified by checking for some adult-plumaged males in the group, which are usually present, as they are normally found in family parties. Red-backed Fairywren is common across the tropical north from n. WA east through to n. QLD, and in the east from n. QLD south to coastal n. NSW. This attractive bird occurs in tall grasses within open woodland, tropical savanna, rainforest edges, scrubland, lantana thickets, and thickets along the edges of eucalypt forest, as well as town parks and gardens in some areas.

D. Dusky Grasswren *Amytornis purnelli* **15–18 cm/6–7 in.**

Grasswrens are terrestrial birds that are larger and thicker billed than their cousins the fairywrens, but they share the same general shape: plump bodies with long, cocked tails. Grasswrens also differ in their much more secretive nature and subtle plumage markings, which lack any strong, bright colors. Dusky Grasswren is a brown bird with a gray-brown head and breast that are lightly streaked with white flecks. On the back and lower breast it is richer rufous in coloration. It is an uncommon species found in a small area of the outback in central Australia (s. NT, extreme northeast WA, and extreme northwest SA) that inhabits rocky areas with spinifex grass and shrubs. With luck, groups of these highly secretive birds may be seen running around on the ground, scurrying rapidly between spinifex clumps at areas such as Ormiston Gorge in the West MacDonnell Ranges or King's Canyon (NT).

B

D

A. Crimson Chat *Epthianura tricolor* 10–13 cm/4–5 in.

The **chats** are an odd group of small, short-tailed birds with strange taxonomic affinities: traditionally considered a distinct family of their own, the chats have recently been regrouped as a subfamily of honeyeaters. They look very different from much of that family though, with their long necks and short tails, and unlike most other honeyeaters, which are primarily nectar-feeders, chats forage terrestrially for insects. Male Crimson Chats are very striking birds: vivid scarlet below, with a contrasting white throat, black mask through the eye, and a vermilion cap. Females are much more subdued, all grayish brown with a hint of crimson in a wash on the breast and belly. Crimson Chats are wide-ranging, nomadic birds within inland Australia, occurring across the plains, scrub, mallee heathland, and open woodlands across the region, though they are absent from the tropical north and the coastal zone of the east. They are most often encountered in active flocks feeding low to the ground, or on the ground, when they are often identified by their white-tipped tails or vivid red colors in flight as they feed actively within an area.

B. Striated Pardalote *Pardalotus striatus* 9–11.5 cm/3.5–4.5 in.

Pardalotes are a distinctive Australian family of tiny, plump, short-tailed songbirds with thick, blunt-ended bills that all display boldly marked plumage. Indeed, the scientific name *Pardalotus* derives from the Greek word meaning "spotted like a leopard." Striated is a a striking bird, with many races that vary in appearance. It always displays a plain brown mantle, and lacks spotting on the crown and wings, which Spotted Pardalote shows. The crown of Striated varies from solid black to lightly flecked with white. The wings are black with long white flashes of white and a small red mark near the shoulder. It always shows a broad white eyebrow with a warm yellow mark over the bill. Striated is the most widespread pardalote species found in eucalypt forest and woodland throughout the mainland and TAS. It is usually encountered feeding in the crowns of eucalypt trees, where groups of them usually draw attention to themselves by their incessant chipping calls.

C. Spotted Pardalote *Pardalotus punctatus* 8.5–10 cm/3–4 in.

A stunning, tiny songbird with strikingly marked plumage. Like all pardalotes, it is blunt billed and plump bodied, with a short tail. Even more strikingly patterned than the Striated Pardalote, from which it differs in having a boldly spotted crown, a scalloped gray mantle, and conspicuous white spots on the sides of the wings. It also displays a bolder, clean-cut, yellow throat, and rich red upper tail. Spotted also possesses a bold white supercilium, although never shows a bold yellow spot at the front end of it, as Striated does. It is a delightfully common species in the coastal zone from near Cairns (QLD) south around to sw. WA. It is absent from much of northern Australia and from the dry interior, preferring eucalypt forests, woodlands, and parklands in the wetter parts of the continent (including TAS). Groups of them are most usually found, like other pardalotes, feeding in the canopies of eucalyptus trees.

C

A. Eastern Spinebill *Acanthorhynchus tenuirostris* **14–16 cm/5.5–6 in.**

Spinebills are gorgeous, sunbird-shaped honeyeaters: they have long, down-curved bills used for probing for nectar. The two spinebills do not overlap geographically, so they can be identified by location. Eastern displays a bold white throat with a soft rosy patch in its center, bordered below by two broad black braces, and solid cinnamon underparts below that. It has a deep blue–gray crown, black mask, red eyes, and an olive back bordered above by a rich rufous collar. It displays prominent white flashes in its tail, which are often exposed when it is fanned as Eastern flits from one flower to another while foraging in shrubs. It is a common species within rainforests, woodlands, heaths, and gardens in eastern Australia. It has two distinct populations: one centered in the highlands around Cairns (QLD), and another from se. QLD south to VIC and TAS, and west into se. SA. Most often encountered at flowering shrubs in pairs or singles.

B. Western Spinebill *Acanthorhynchus superciliosus* **13–16 cm/5–6 in.**

A stunning, multicolored honeyeater endemic to WA. It has a characteristic long, down-curved bill. Males are arguably the most beautiful of all the honeyeaters, with a vibrant coppery brown throat bordered with two strong crescents below, first white, then black, and a clean white belly below that. It has a deep blue head, which is broken up with a thin but conspicuous white supercilium behind the eye, and separated from the olive upperparts by a prominent orange collar. The plain olive females lack bright markings except for a broad chestnut collar. Large areas of white are exposed in the tail tip, which is evident when fanned in flight, when Western is flitting between flowers. It is a common bird within its restricted range in woodlands and heaths with stands of banksias.

C. Brown Honeyeater *Lichmera indistincta* **12–16 cm/4.5–6 in.**

Brown Honeyeater is an unspectacular bird, uniformly olive-brown with indistinct yellow edging on the wings, and a small yellow triangle behind the eye being the only prominent feature. It inhabits many habitats including rainforest edges, mangroves, parklands, gardens, heaths, vegetated watercourses, and eucalypt forests from n. WA through to QLD, and south to n. NSW. The most numerous honeyeater in its range. These active birds are usually encountered around flowering shrubs in parks or gardens, where they are often vocal, conspicuous, and acrobatic in their pursuit of nectar.

D. Scarlet Myzomela *Myzomela sanguinolenta* **10–13 cm/4–5 in.**

Myzomelas are small, sunbirdlike honeyeaters with longish, down-curved bills. Males are dazzling birds: bright scarlet except for dark, blackish wings and tail, and a white lower belly and vent. Females are inconspicuous: all ruddy brown except for a subtle reddish wash on the chin. Scarlet Myzomela is a blossom nomad in coastal eastern Australia (from around Cairns, QLD, south to e. VIC) and so can be remarkably common at flowering times, and when their distinctive descending calls often ring out from the trees, although they can also be completely absent from these areas at other times. It generally feeds in the canopy, although will descend to feed lower when blossoms allow, such as when urban garden shrubs are flowering.

A. Black Honeyeater *Sugomel niger* **10–13 cm/4–5 in.**
This page covers three species of striking pied honeyeaters. **Honeyeaters** are the largest family in Australia (170 species), which are varied but share a brush-tipped tongue that helps them feed on nectar, although they can also feed on insects and pollen. Black is a small honeyeater with a narrow, down-curved bill that is a blossom nomad, traveling great distances to find flowering trees. Males have an all–jet black body except for a white belly and vent. A black line runs down from the throat onto the belly as well, making for a distinctive pattern not shared with any other Australian bird. Females are indistinctive brown birds, perhaps best identified by their size and shape. Black Honeyeater has a southerly distribution, being found within the interior of Australia from w. WA across the center to w. QLD, NSW, and nw. VIC. This scarce species inhabits drier areas of mulga and mallee and can also occur in open woodland, where it is mostly likely to be encountered in blooming eucalypts or *Eremophila*s. Can sometimes be observed in gardens in tourist resorts in central Australia, (e.g., Alice Springs and Ayers Rock).

B. New Holland Honeyeater *Phylidonyris novaehollandiae* **16–20 cm/6.5–8 in.**
The following species pair comprises large black-and-white honeyeaters with more powerful bills than the above species, and bold yellow flashes in the wings and tail, which need to be identified from each other. New Holland has a piercing whitish eye, a small patch of white on its face, and white markings on the tail tip, unlike White-cheeked. New Holland is a southern species (where in some areas it can overlap with White-cheeked), found from n. NSW, throughout s. VIC, se. SA, and also on TAS. Another western population exists in s. WA. This striking honeyeater is delightfully common on heathlands, and also occurs widely in eucalypt forests, especially where there is a thick understory of shrubbery such as banksias and *Grevillea*s, and are usually found in active groups. On some areas of southern, coastal heathland (e.g., Royal NP near Sydney, and Bruny Island on TAS) it can be the most common bird in the area.

C. White-cheeked Honeyeater *Phylidonyris niger* **16–20 cm/6.5–8 in.**
A striking pied honeyeater with bold orange-yellow markings in the wings and tail that is most similar to New Holland Honeyeater. Unlike that species, White-cheeked has a dark eye and a massive white cheek patch, and lacks white corners to the tip of the tail. It is found patchily in e. QLD, e. NSW, and s. WA in eucalypt forests and heaths. In s. QLD and n. NSW it tends to be restricted to coastal heaths, whereas the Cairns region population tends to have wider habitat preferences, including paperbark and banksia stands in tropical savanna. In WA this common honeyeater can often be found in the same areas as New Holland.

A. Lewin's Honeyeater *Meliphaga lewinii* **19–21 cm/7.5–8.5 in.**

This page covers medium-sized honeyeaters best identified by their head and breast patterns. Lewin's is a common and highly vocal eastern honeyeater, all plain olive with a bold yellow crescent-shaped ear patch, and a strong yellow gape line behind the bill that extends under the eye. Lewin's Honeyeaters are common down the entire eastern coastal strip of Australia from n. QLD south to e. VIC. They are found in wet habitats, mainly rainforest and wet eucalypt forest, but will also wander into densely vegetated gardens. Its loud call, a vibrating, machine gun–like rattle is a characteristic sound of the eastern forests and can be heard at any time of the day. They are inquisitive birds that are especially common in Lamington National Park (QLD).

B. Bridled Honeyeater *Lichenostomus frenatus* **20–22 cm/8–8.5 in.**

A very local and striking species of the wet forests of ne. QLD. The head pattern is distinctive: all blackish with a prominent pinkish yellow line (or bridle) that runs from the base of the bill and curves up to form a border beneath the eye. Just above the eye there is a small white smudge. The base of the black bill is also yellow. Within range this unique combination of facial features distinguishes it from all other honeyeaters. Bridled is fairly common in wet eucalypt forests and mountain rainforests, where it is most likely to be encountered in pairs or small groups around picnic areas where they have become habituated (e.g., Mount Hypipamee NP, QLD).

C. Mangrove Honeyeater *Lichenostomus fasciogularis* **19–21 cm/7.5–8.5 in.**

Mangrove Honeyeater is within a complex of three honeyeaters that are separated geographically and prefer different habitats. They are all gray-brown birds with a black mask, yellow on the face, an indistinct yellow flash in the wing, and brown-streaked underparts. Mangrove Honeyeater can be differentiated from the other two species—**Singing** (*L. virescens*) and **Varied** (*L. versicolor*)—by its all-yellow throat, which is bordered below by a thick gray horizontal smudge across the chest that separates the throat from the heavily streaked underparts below. It is a specialized species, confined to coastal mangroves from Townsville (QLD) south (e.g., in Brisbane) to n. NSW. It is replaced on coasts north of its range (e.g., in Cairns) by the closely related Varied Honeyeater, which differs in having all-yellow underparts with no dark breast band. Singing is a subdued inland sister species, largely similar to the coastal Mangrove Honeyeater, although Singing shows no yellow on the throat; the yellow is restricted to the sides of the face. It is also streaked from the throat down the underside, and lacks the dark breast band that Mangrove exhibits. It is found commonly throughout dry areas of the mainland (but is absent from the eastern coastal areas) and occurs in a variety of habitats, including mallee, mulga, and open woodland, and in southwest Australia also inhabits coastal heaths. Singing is a common garden bird in Perth (WA) and Alice Springs (NT).

C

A. Yellow Honeyeater *Lichenostomus flavus* **17–18 cm/6.5–7 in.**

All the birds on this page are varied species of small honeyeaters, the largest single family of Australian birds. Yellow Honeyeater is well named, being an all–plain yellow honeyeater with no other conspicuous markings that distinguishes it from all other species in this family. Although moderately common, it has a small range, being confined to northeastern QLD, where it can be found in eucalypt forest, the edges of tropical rainforest, mangroves, and parks and gardens. Most likely to be found in pairs or singly in gardens or parks around towns, (e.g., in Cairns or Townsville). It is regular and easily found along the Esplanade in Cairns.

B. White-plumed Honeyeater *Lichenostomus penicillatus* **15–17 cm/6–6.5 in.**

A small, plain, olive honeyeater with bold white plumes on the neck, which enables ID. The head also has a distinct yellow cast to it. White-plumed is found across most of central Australia, though it is absent from the wetter areas of southwestern Australia, the tropical north, and wet parts of eastern Australia. They are associated with watercourses, though they can be found in a variety of habitats including mallee, mulga, and suburban gardens in Sydney and Melbourne. It is a famously pugnacious species, often observed fighting other larger honeyeaters around nectar sources.

C. Macleay's Honeyeater *Xanthotis macleayanus* **17–21 cm/6.5–8 in.**

A distinctive, boldly marked honeyeater confined to the wet forests of ne. QLD. It is an olive bird, heavily streaked with white over much of the body, with a neat black cap and a massive area of coral-colored bare skin around the eye. Common within its small range, centered in the Cairns region, mainly found in rainforests and paperbark swamps, but also in eucalypt forests, mangroves, and flowering gardens. Groups are best looked for around flowering eucalypts or visiting sugar feeders in some areas (e.g., around the town of Paluma). They are acrobatic feeders, often observed feeding upside down.

A. Helmeted Friarbird *Philemon buceroides* 32–36 cm/12.5–14 in.

Friarbirds are strange, large honeyeaters that all possess bare skin on their head, and most of them also have a prominent knob on the top of their bill. They are all grayish brown, and best identified to species by close examination of the head and neck. Nectar forms a large portion of their diet, like that of many other honeyeaters, in addition to insects and fruits. They are noisy, highly visible honeyeaters that are often aggressive around nectar blossoms. Note that the young birds of all species lack the red eyes of adults and lack the prominent knobs, making them all very similar at this age. Helmeted is the largest friarbird (it is the largest honeyeater in Australia) found in the tropical north, in the coastal zone of both QLD and NT. It has a distinctive "hammer-shaped" head, with a square tuft of feathers forming a crest on the nape. Helmeted Friarbird has a stout, long bill with a prominent knob on the top of it that slopes backward toward the eye, a mainly dark face of deep blackish blue facial skin, and a uniform gray tail without a pale tip. It is a common, noisy, and aggressive honeyeater, found in almost all habitats, most likely to be encountered in pairs or small groups fighting over nectar around flowering eucalypts.

B. Silver-crowned Friarbird *Philemon argenticeps* 25–32 cm/10–12.5 in.

A friarbird of the tropical north, occurring only in the north of WA, NT, and ne. QLD. Like a smaller, shorter-billed version of Helmeted Friarbird. However, the knob on the bill top is higher and more prominent in Silver-crowned, the underparts are paler and whiter in color than those of Helmeted, and the large dark blue facial skin comes to a point behind the eye (rounded in Helmeted). Found in open woodlands, gardens, and mangroves in the tropics, where it is best looked for around blossoming trees.

C. Little Friarbird *Philemon citreogularis* 25–29 cm/10–11.5 in.

The smallest and most un-friarbird-like of the friarbirds: it lacks a knob on the bill, has just a limited amount of bare skin on the face below the eye, and lacks the red eye of all the other adult friarbirds (although note that young friarbirds of all species are dark eyed). It also has a narrow pale tip to the tail. In short, a plain friarbird lacking any of the prominent facial features of the others, and one of only two that has a pale tip to the tail (along with Noisy). Found throughout the tropical north of Australia from WA east to QLD, and down the eastern side of Australia from QLD down to n. VIC, in a variety of open wooded habitats, gardens, parks, and mangroves.

D. Noisy Friarbird *Philemon corniculatus* 30–35 cm/12–14 in.

A distinctive friarbird with a complete bald head of dark skin, including the top of the head (which is feathered in all other friarbirds). It also possesses a prominent high knob on the top of the bill that sticks straight up (not sloping backward as in the other two knobbed species: Helmeted and Silver-crowned). The Noisy is also one of only two species (along with Little) that has a narrow pale tip to the tail. Found in a variety of open wooded habitats in the eastern half of QLD, NSW, and VIC. Incredibly noisy and conspicuous, and often seen chasing other honeyeaters or friarbirds away from flowering trees.

A. Rufous-banded Honeyeater *Conopophila albogularis* **12–14 cm/4.5–5.5 in.**
A distinctive honeyeater of the tropical north that has a broad rufous band across the chest, with a bright white throat and chin (which contrasts with the gray head and darker chest band below), and clean white belly. Otherwise, this honeyeater is quite plain. The only other bold markings are a broad yellow flash in the wing and outer tail. Rufous-banded Honeyeater is confined to the tropical north from n. NT east into the extreme north of QLD, where it is a very common bird within tropical savanna, tropical eucalypt forest, monsoon forest, and mangroves, and along vegetated watercourses. It is most often encountered in small, active parties that frequently fight with other honeyeaters over nectar sources. Any visitor to the NT is unlikely to miss this bird.

B. Black-headed Honeyeater *Melithreptus affinis* **13–14.5 cm/5–5.5 in.**
Another honeyeater that shares bright olive upperparts, white underparts, and a black head with a number of other species. However, Black-headed Honeyeater is confined to TAS, where it overlaps with only one other similar species (Strong-billed), which it can be identified from by virtue of its all-black head (lacking any white line on the nape) a solid black throat, and a fine white eyelash. On TAS (the only region in which it occurs) it is a common honeyeater, mainly found in the eastern half of the island, across a range of habitats including dry eucalypt forests, woodlands, temperate rainforest, and coastal heathland. Like all *melithreptus* honeyeaters it is most likely to be encountered in small groups.

C. White-throated Honeyeater *Melithreptus albogularis* **12–14.5 cm/4.5–5.5 in.**
The following two species are from a confusing group of half a dozen or so honeyeaters that all share rich olive-yellow upperparts, bright white underparts, and a black head with varied markings around the eye and throat. Honeyeaters from this group are best identified by checking the color of the bare skin around the eye and studying the color of the throat (as well as on geographic range). White-throated Honeyeater has an all-white throat with no shading or dark areas, a pale blue crescent of bare skin over the eye, and a clear white collar around the nape. The combination of white throat and blue crescent eliminate all other similar species. It is a common honeyeater in the north (n. WA, n. NT, and n. QLD), and east (e. QLD south into ne. NSW), where it occurs in tropical savanna, eucalypt forest, open woodland, and vegetated watercourses, as well as in parks and gardens. Most often found in small active parties around blooming trees.

D. Strong-billed Honeyeater *Melithreptus validirostris* **15–17 cm/6–6.5in**
The Tasmanian version of the White-throated Honeyeater, which differs from the only other similar sympatric species, Black-headed Honeyeater, in showing a clear white band across the nape and possessing a white throat. Within this group it is also unique in its feeding habits, in that it searches for insects among strips of bark much in the manner of a sittella or nuthatch (found in Eurasian and North American). It is an uncommon species that is confined to TAS and is found mainly in small groups within wet eucalypt forest throughout the island.

A. Blue-faced Honeyeater *Entomyzon cyanotis* **26–32 cm/10–12.5 in.**

A large, distinctive honeyeater with a bold patch of royal blue skin on the face, a black head with a prominent white stripe down the side of the throat, and a thin white band on the nape. The upperparts are all bright olive green, and below the prominent black throat the underparts are crisp white. It is like no other and easily recognized, being equally distinctive in flight, when this large golden olive honeyeater flies with a deep undulating flight and shows broad patches of white or green on the wing. It is common in the tropical north of Australia and down the east side of the mainland from n. QLD south to nw. VIC and se. SA. They occur in a variety of habitats, including open woodlands, eucalypt forest, tropical savanna, farmlands, wooded watercourses, golf courses, and gardens. It forages for insects, fruits, and nectar. They are gregarious and usually encountered in pairs or small flocks, most likely to be found around flowering trees where they can often aggressively defend this rich nectar source from all comers. They also scavenge picnic grounds such as Adelaide River (SA), and Mount Malloy and Canungra (QLD).

B. Noisy Miner *Manorina melanocephala* **24–28 cm/9.5–11 in.**

Miners are a subgroup of noisy, gregarious, gray-brown honeyeaters with bright yellow bare parts and facial skin. A very familiar bird in eastern Australia, where rabbles of these miners frequent many urban areas. Most similar to Yellow-throated Miner of inland Australia. However, Noisy Miner has a black face and crown, which contrasts with a clean white forehead. It is uniformly gray down the back including the rump, unlike Yellow-throated, which has a white rump. Noisy Miners are common in the east from n. QLD south to VIC and around to Adelaide. They also occur on TAS. Noisy Miners occur in a variety of open habitats (e.g., open woodland, eucalypt forest, gardens, and parks) but are absent from closed forests and densely covered areas. Generally, found in wetter habitats to the east of Yellow-throated Miner. They are most likely to be found in groups in urban parks, where they are often seen noisily and vigorously defending their territories from other groups.

C. Yellow-throated Miner *Manorina flavigula* **22–28 cm/8.5–11 in.**

An inland miner similar in appearance to the common Noisy Miner of the east. However, Yellow-throated shows a bright white rump and has a gray-brown crown (similar in coloration to the rest of the upperparts) and forehead. Although Noisy is a familiar and common bird in the east, Yellow-throated Miner is far more widespread over the rest of the continent, occupying a range of drier habitats west of the core of Noisy Miner's range. It occurs from WA eastward across central Australia into e. QLD, e. NSW, and VIC. It is largely absent from the eastern coastal belt that is occupied by Noisy Miner, and tends to avoid well-populated urban centers. It is also a generalist, found in a variety of drier inland habitats (relative to Noisy Miner), from open woodlands (including mulga, mallee, and brigalow) to gum-lined watercourses to gardens and golf courses. It is usually observed in noisy family parties.

C

A. Spiny-cheeked Honeyeater *Acanthagenys rufogularis* **22–27 cm/8.5–10.5 in.**
The birds on this page are all large brown-streaked honeyeaters. Spiny-cheeked is a distinctive honeyeater with a rich peachy breast, and bold black-and-white stripes down the side of the face. The white stripe contains the spines that give it its name. Furthermore, the bird has a salmon pink eye ring and base to the bill. This head pattern makes it unlike any other honeyeater. It is widespread across much of the dry interior of the mainland from WA to w. NSW and QLD, and is absent from the wetter coastal regions of the east and the tropical north. It is common in mulga, mallee, open woodland, and farmlands with scattered trees or scrub, and also turns up in outback gardens. Most likely to be encountered in flowering shrubs within inland gardens (e.g., Alice Springs and Ayers Rock).

B. Red Wattlebird *Anthochaera carunculata* **33–37 cm/13–14.5 in.**
Wattlebirds are brown, heavily streaked honeyeaters that are some of the largest species in the family. They are aggressive and territorial around nectar sources. The first two species exhibit strange pendulous wattles of skin that protrude from the ears. The combination of dull fleshy pink ear wattles, red eye, pale whitish cheeks, and yellow belly ID this honeyeater from all others. It occurs in eucalypt forests, mallee, open woodlands, and heathlands in southern Australia from s. WA eastward to VIC and ne. NSW. Often noticed around cities and towns (e.g., in native gardens in Sydney and Perth) when flying between flowering gardens, as its large size and deep undulating flight draw attention (when the lack of rufous in the wing displayed by Little Wattlebird can be noted). Indeed, this is where they are most likely to be encountered: foraging nectar in gardens, where groups of this common species often aggressively defend their blossoms from other honeyeaters.

C. Yellow Wattlebird *Anthochaera paradoxa* **43–50 cm/17–19.5 in.**
This massive honeyeater replaces the similar Red Wattlebird on TAS and is confined to eastern TAS. It is the largest honeyeater species. Another brown, heavily streaked bird but with unique fleshy yellow wattles that hang down from the ears, a whitish face, and lemon yellow wash on the belly. It occurs in a broad range of habitats including coastal heaths, dry eucalypt forests, open woodlands, parks, and native gardens. Yellow Wattlebirds are common and easily seen, most often observed foraging for nectar in banksias in towns, which they also defend vigorously.

D. Little Wattlebird *Anthochaera chrysoptera* **27–35 cm/10.5–13.5 in.**
Also known as Brush Wattlebird. A small wattlebird that lacks wattles, with fine white streaking and a prominent rufous wing flash and white tail tip, best viewed in flight. It is a coastal honeyeater found from se. QLD south through e. NSW into coastal VIC and se. SA. It also occurs on TAS. Little Wattlebirds are most abundant in coastal heaths but also occur in eucalypt forests, scrubby thickets, and parks and gardens. Like other wattlebirds they frequent nectar blossoms (especially banksias), often in town gardens, where they are most likely to be encountered, foraging for nectar and fighting conspicuously with other honeyeaters in defense of these. It is regular in gardens in the suburbs of Sydney.

A. Yellow-throated Scrubwren *Sericornis citreogularis* 12–15 cm/4.5–6 in.

Scrubwrens are small, warbler-like birds that are closely related to gerygones and thornbills, which occupy the same family. They are gregarious birds with powerful voices, and regularly chatter to one another as they forage within the forest. Both scrubwrens are parasitized by cuckoos, such as the Fan-tailed Cuckoo. Scrubwrens are forest-dwelling birds that generally forage and are encountered on the shady forest floor. There are two common species in eastern Australia: this species and the White-browed Scrubwren, both of which are largely brown birds with a bold eyebrow/supercilium, and contrastingly pale underparts. However, they differ significantly in the color of the eye, and the color of the underparts: Yellow-throated Scrubwren is washed yellow below, most strongly on the throat, and has a dull reddish brown eye. Yellow-throated is a common species in tropical and temperate rainforests, and woodlands in coastal eastern Australia, found in two isolated populations, one in n. QLD, and another from s. QLD south down much of the coast of NSW. Although they often occur together, Yellow-throated tends to prefer the denser interior forest areas, while White-browed generally favors the edges and more sparsely covered parts. The nesting habit of the Yellow-throated Scrubwren is quite different from that of White-browed, as the former constructs a large domed nest of vegetation that is suspended from a branch or vine some 10 m/30 ft or more up, and often overhanging rivers or creeks.

B. White-browed Scrubwren *Sericornis frontalis* 11–13 cm/4–5 in.

A small brown bird similar in appearance and behavior to the Yellow-throated Scrubwren. However, the White-browed Scrubwren differs in looking a little smaller in direct comparison and in having a dull whitish throat and chest, and a prominent, beady pale eye. Like the Yellow-throated, it is also most often seen hopping along the dimly lit forest leaf litter, when it can be quite approachable in some areas (e.g., O'Reilly's sector of Lamington NP, QLD). White-browed Scrubwren is a widespread, coastal species, occurring across the entire south coast, stretching north up the coast to ne. QLD. Although it frequents some habitats similar to those of Yellow-throated, like rainforests and woodlands, where they can often be seen in the same areas, White-browed is more adaptable and also occurs in thickets, heaths, mallee, saltmarshes, mangroves, and even gardens. White-browed Scrubwren builds a domed nest that is typically on or near the ground, and not significantly elevated like that of Yellow-throated.

A. Brown Thornbill *Acanthiza pusilla* **10 cm/4 in.**
Thornbills are an Australasian group of tiny, active, kinglet-like birds with thin bills
that occur in small parties. They are among the most challenging Australian birds
to identify, as they are dull colored and hyperactive, making it difficult to see their
key features. Brown is a red-eyed, brown bird with pale off-white underparts, rich
buffy flanks, fine blackish streaking from the throat down to the chest, pale whitish
wing edgings, and a rufous forehead. It has a rusty rump and upper tail that contrasts with a broad black subterminal tail band and pale tip. Brown is the common
thornbill of its type in the eastern forests of s. QLD, NSW, and TAS. **Inland Thornbill** (*A. apicalis*) occurs to the west of Brown Thornbill, from the western side of
eastern Australia (QLD and NSW) through to the west coast of WA, which differs
in lacking a rufous forehead, is generally whiter below, and has a brighter, rusty
rump, but is best identified by range. **Tasmanian Thornbill** (*A. ewingii*) occurs
with Brown on TAS, and can be distinguished from Brown by its rufous wing edgings (not white), mottling (not streaking) on the throat and breast, and white (not
buffy) flanks. All these thornbills are likely to be seen in flocks, sometimes mixing
with other thornbills and gerygones. Brown and Tasmanian are found in the
understory of woodland and rainforest, while Inland occurs in a variety of scrubby
habitats and open inland woodlands.

B. Yellow-rumped Thornbill *Acanthiza chrysorrhoa* **10–12 cm/4–4.5 in.**
Yellow-rumped Thornbill is found over much of Australia, except for the tropical
north. It is rather like another species with which it can be confused, the similarly
sized **Buff-rumped Thornbill** (*A. reguloides*), with which it overlaps in coastal
eastern Australia: they are both pale-eyed thornbills with contrastingly pale rumps
that stand out in flight against the dark tail. Yellow-rumped has an even brighter,
lemon yellow rump, and also has distinctive white spotting on its black forehead.
The combination of rump color, eye color, and the forehead pattern aid ID. Yellow-
rumped is not a fussy species, being found in open woodlands, scrubby areas, gardens, and farms, and in common with most thornbills, is often encountered in
small flocks, although this species tends to forage mostly on the ground and moves
away slowly when approached. While other thornbills may be encountered on the
ground, Yellow-rumped is noticeably more terrestrial.

C. Weebill *Smicrornis brevirostris* **8–9 cm/3–3.5 in.**
The smallest Australian bird, this tiny yellow thornbill is similar to the closely
related thornbills and gerygones from which it can be differentiated by its short,
stubby, horn-colored bill. The bill and small size give it a shape rather like the more
intricately patterned pardalotes. Weebill also shows a creamy iris and a pale supercilium, and also has a white tip to the tail, which is very evident when Weebills are
fluttering around foliage, as they typically do when foraging for insects. A gregarious bird, most often encountered in pairs or small groups, occurring in drier
woodlands throughout the mainland, but absent from the driest desert areas. It's
"weebill" or "mini-me" call is a common sound of inland Australia.

A. Rockwarbler *Origma solitaria* 13–14 cm/5–5.5 in.

Formerly known as Origma, derived from a term meaning mine or tunnel. This name presumably refers to its habit of feeding and nesting within rocky outcrops. An extremely localized, warbler-like bird (although actually in the same family as thornbills), confined to Hawkesbury Sandstone of se. NSW. The entire population occurs within a radius of approximately 250 km/155 mi around Sydney. A plain, reddish bird with a whitish throat, and a relatively long tail (compared with that of thornbills). It is locally common in its limited range, where it occurs on outcrops and is most often seen hopping over them, where it blends in well with these tan-colored, arkosic sandstones and often disappears into crevices between them. Generally not active until after the sun hits the rocks in the morning.

B. Large-billed Gerygone *Gerygone magnirostris* 13–14 cm/5–5.5 in.

Gerygones, also known as Australian Warblers, occupy the same family as thornbills. They comprise tiny, confusing, nondescript, insectivorous birds with strident, repetitive songs. Many of these are beautiful, although Large-billed has a less melodious song than the others. It is these robust songs that lend them their name, gerygone, which derives from a term meaning "born of song." Large-billed Gerygone is not noticeably large billed, and so this does not aid ID. It is generally plain gray-brown with off-white underparts, indistinct white crescents around the eye, and no bold features aside from its loud song. It lacks an obvious supercilium and the white markings on the upper tail that most of the other sympatric gerygones possess. It is a water-loving species, found around streams and mangroves in the tropical north of Australia, from n. WA east to n. QLD, occurring only as far south as Mackay. It is a common species perhaps best found on a cruise through mangrove areas in its range, where they make conspicuous hanging mossy nests that are typically located over the water.

C. Brown Gerygone *Gerygone mouki* 9.5–11 cm/3.5–4.5 in.

A tiny brown warbler that is not strikingly different from the other gerygones, which are similarly nondescript, lacking any obvious bold features. However, Brown Gerygone can be differentiated from the sympatric Large-billed Gerygone by its bold white mark between the bill and the eye. It also displays white markings near the tip of the tail, although these are not usually evident unless the tail is spread, or if viewed from below. Although they do overlap in some areas—they both occur in mangroves in n. QLD—they can often be separated by range and habitat: Brown does not occur across the north coast of Australia, being confined to the east from n. QLD south to e. VIC. Thus much of its range is south and east of that of Large-billed Gerygone. Brown also inhabits rainforests, where it is a common and vocal bird its distinctive "what-is-it" song repeated constantly. Brown Gerygones are most often come across in pairs or small parties feeding in the forest understory. Another very similar species, **Western Gerygone** (*G. fusca*) occurs to the west of Brown's range, looks remarkably similar, differing mainly in song, (it has arguably the most melodious song of all the gerygones), and range.

C

A. Apostlebird *Struthidea cinerea* 29–32 cm/11.5–12.5 in.

Apostlebird is a large songbird with no obvious close relations: it shares a two-species family with the very different White-winged Chough. It is all grayish brown with few markings, save for light white flecks all over the body, and darker brown wings. It is a stout bird reminiscent of Old World Babblers *Timaliidae* (the only Australian bird that is like these), with a heavy, short, thick bill. It is highly social and almost always seen in large boisterous groups that forage mainly on the ground and make lots of harsh scratchy calls to one another. It is a bird of open dry country, including open woodlands (e.g., mulga), scrubby country, and farmlands. There is hardly a golf course within its range that does not have a resident group. Apostlebird is common in c. NT, the southern two thirds of QLD, and much of NSW except the coastal strip. It also occurs in se. SA and nw. VIC. It is a conspicuous bird wherever it occurs, groups of which are most likely to be encountered feeding along the verges of inland roads fringed with open woodlands and scrubland.

B. Gray-crowned Babbler *Pomatostomus temporalis* 25–29 cm/10–11.5 in.

The following two entries are from a family called **Pseudo-babblers**, or **Australian Babblers**, highly social, vocal songbirds that are characterized by long, down-curved beaks and long tails, and exhibit colonial nesting and communal foraging behavior. They construct massive separate stick nests as a group for roosting and breeding and are cooperative breeders: many group members and multiple generations assist in raising the young. Mobs of babblers are usually encountered foraging on the ground. Gray-crowned can be differentiated from Hall's and White-browed by its bold yellow eye and pale gray crown. In parts of its range the breast is reddish brown, unlike that of White-browed and Hall's. It occurs in northern and eastern Australia, from c. WA eastward to e. QLD, and south to VIC. It is a common and trusting species (unlike all other babblers), found in open woodlands, tropical savanna, scrubland, grasslands, and farmlands with scattered trees, where noisy bands are most likely to be found scampering across the ground or flushing from roadside verges.

C. Hall's Babbler *Pomatostomus halli* 22–24 cm/8.5–9.5 in.

Hall's Babbler is a rare bird, confined to the interior of QLD and n. NSW. Very similar in appearance to the more widely seen **White-browed Babbler** (*P. superciliosus*), *not illustrated*. Both can be differentiated from the similar Gray-crowned in having dark eyes, and a solid chocolate brown crown. Hall's differs from the very similar White-browed in displaying a broader supercilium and having a smaller, better-defined white bib. White-browed is found across much of the southern half of the mainland, although it is absent from coastal areas at the east of the range. Although uncommon, it is far more regularly seen than the restricted-range Hall's Babbler, and occurs in dry open habitats like mulga, open woodlands, brigalow, and mallee. Likely to be encountered in large groups foraging on the ground or moving low through the understory. Both of these similar babblers are more secretive than Gray-crowned, and more likely to flush and move off rapidly.

A. Australian Logrunner *Orthonyx temminckii* 17–20 cm/6.5–8 in.

The two species on this page are from a bizarre Australasian bird family, the **logrunners** (one other species occurs on the island of New Guinea). They are plump, ground-dwelling songbirds that use their powerful feet to scratch in forest leaf litter for insect prey. All logrunner species can use their strong tails to prop themselves while sweeping the leaves sideways from underneath their plump breasts to get at prey buried below. They are weak fliers, often scampering away on the ground (when they can suggest a mammal instead of a bird), rather than flying when alarmed, and can even hide underneath the leaf litter. All species of logrunner are usually encountered in pairs, and are quite vocal birds, calling loudly and often. The two Australian species do not overlap geographically: Chowchilla being the northern species, and Australian Logrunner occurring to the south in the coastal region of southern QLD down into southern NSW. Although they are similar behaviorally and in general shape (potbellied in appearance), they are markedly different in coloration. The Logrunner is barklike mottled brown on the back with several bold pale gray bands on the wing, a paler gray face and bold underparts that are different in the males and females. The female Logrunner has a rich–burnt orange throat and white underparts, while the male is all white from the throat down to the vent. As the name suggests, they do feed around logs and are often seen running onto fallen logs, which they also use as calling posts. Although they are sometimes elusive rainforest birds, they rely on their camouflage and can be approached very close when feeding by walking rainforest trails quietly, when they can often be detected by the sound of rustling in the leaf litter. However, when they are calling, their nature changes markedly, and they can become quite furtive. They are forest-floor dwellers of temperate rainforest.

B. Chowchilla *Orthonyx spaldingii* 26–28 cm/10–11 in.

Chowchilla is the larger northern version of logrunner, a localized species in the mountain rainforests of ne. QLD. It behaves and is shaped much like its southern cousin: a potbellied terrestrial bird most often encountered scratching in the shady forest leaf litter for prey. It is a plainer species lacking Logrunner's intricately patterned upperparts, instead being plain uniform blackish or dull rufous above, with a variably colored underside. Female Chowchillas have an orange throat and clean white underparts, while males have a white throat and underparts. Both males and females possess a bold cerulean blue eye ring. The Chowchilla is named after its loud and very strange call, "chowchilla!" The call is very distinctive, carrying far and wide when given, and once learned, is never forgotten and is usually the best indication of the presence of this often elusive denizen of the rainforest floor. Unlike their southern cousin, the Logrunner, they are best approached as this is when they are often oblivious to human presence and at their most confiding. Best found in the early mornings when they are their most vocal.

A. Spotted Quail-Thrush *Cinclosoma punctatum* **25–28 cm/10–11in.**

Quail-thrushes are odd songbirds with plump, quail-like bodies but long tails and thrush-like bills that, as the name suggests, look like a cross between the features of these families. They are not related to either quails or thrushes but occupy a different family, called **Quail-Thrushes and Jewel-Babblers**. Only quail-thrushes occur in Australia (jewel-babblers only in New Guinea). They are scarce and furtive terrestrial songbirds that are skulking in their habits, usually foraging on the ground (often in thick cover), making them difficult to observe; they are infrequently encountered. They are strikingly patterned, dimorphic birds most often encountered in pairs that are highly territorial, with high-pitched songs. Spotted is no different; the male is a gorgeous bird with a bold head pattern: brown on the crown with a prominent white eyebrow, pale blue-gray face, and a black throat patch that contrasts strongly with a large white teardrop below the eye. The underside is blue-gray on the breast, which changes into a boldly spotted white underbelly. On the top the bird is brownish with bold black streaks all the way from the nape to the upper tail. The female is similar, although with a plainer head that lacks the bold markings of the male, still possessing a white supercilium but having a pale peach throat instead. It is found locally within eucalypt forest with a grassy understory, often within rocky areas, from se. QLD down the coastal zone of Australia through NSW and into TAS, where it is always scarce, sparsely distributed, and hard to find. Even a fleeting glimpse of this beautiful bird is considered fortunate!

B. Eastern Whipbird *Psophodes olivaceus* **25–30 cm/10–12 in.**

Eastern Whipbird is in a family called **Whipbirds and Wedgebills**. Whipbirds are famous for their loud and distinctive calls and are strikingly patterned, crested birds. It is found in the coastal zone of eastern Australia from ne. QLD down to e. VIC. It is a bird of rainforests and woodlands with dense undergrowth, and is common throughout its range. A skulking bird, most often seen on or near the ground, that is more often heard than seen. The bird has a remarkable and strident call that literally sounds like the loud cracking of a whip and always draws attention when heard for the first time. The male is a large songbird with a black head and breast, and a broad white mustachial stripe down the side of the face that is its most striking feature. A brief view may yield nothing more than this flash of white as it scampers away. The back is dull greenish. It is a long-tailed bird with a prominent crest on the top of the head. The female has the same general shape, although with a less pronounced crest, and is dull greenish all over. These handsome birds are most often found alone or in pairs scratching in the leaf litter along the edges of forest trails in the early morning. They are often shy and furtive, and are weak fliers that tend to bounce away on the ground when disturbed rather than take flight. The incredible and loud call of the Eastern Whipbird is one of the great sounds of the Australian rainforests.

A. White-breasted Woodswallow *Artamus leucorynchus* **17 cm/6.5 in.**
Woodswallows are swallow-like birds with broader wings and longer, prominent bills. Although they are aerial feeders (mainly insectivorous), some will also feed on nectar blossoms when they occur, and all species perch more frequently than do the true swallows. They are gregarious birds and are often encountered in flocks. Woodswallows are a discrete family found sparsely in Asia but reach their greatest diversity in Australasia. White-breasted Woodswallow is the most familiar and frequently encountered species in northern Australia. It is easily recognized by its uniform gray upperparts, except for a bold white rump patch, an all-gray hood, and pure ghostly white underparts. When it is in flight, the dark-hooded appearance is obvious and a good ID feature, along with the white rump patch, and, from the underside, a plain, all-black tail. As it is a generalist, it can be found in many habitats throughout its range (the tropical north of Australia and throughout most of eastern Australia) and is commonly present in towns, where flocks are often found perched on overhead wires.

B. Masked Woodswallow *Artamus personatus* **19 cm/7.5 in.**
A nomadic woodswallow of inland Australia, and only very rarely around the coasts. Although it can be found over much of the mainland, it is a scarce species that wanders widely and is generally not easy to find. A distinctive woodswallow by virtue of its bold black mask and throat, which contrast strongly with the pale gray crown and nape. Superficially similar to White-breasted, although that species has an all–dark gray hood that is uniform in color on the throat, crown, and nape, unlike the Masked. In flight the Masked Woodswallow has no pale rump and has a white undertail, different from the superficially similar White-breasted. Like all woodswallows it is likely to be found in flocks, although Masked is one of the most aerial of this group, often seen flying high overhead. This species also regularly mixes in with flocks of White-browed Woodswallows. It is found in a variety of dry, open habitats.

C. White-browed Woodswallow *Artamus superciliosus* **18–19 cm/7–7.5 in.**
Arguably the most handsome and most distinctive of all the woodswallows. A gorgeous, striking, blue-gray bird with deep chestnut underparts and a bold white eyebrow, unlike any other woodswallow species. In flight it shows a clean ivory white underwing with a contrasting chestnut underside to the body quite different from that of any other species. White-browed Woodswallow is highly nomadic over its range, which is much of eastern Australia, and is often found in high-flying flocks, often with Masked Woodswallows. It inhabits a range of habitats, including open forests, woodlands, farmlands, mallee, and mulga. This striking woodswallow may feed on nectar when blossoms occur, although also regularly hawks insects on the wing, like all woodswallows.

A. Black-faced Woodswallow *Artamus cinereus* 18 cm/7 in.

This page depicts three more woodswallow species. Woodswallows occupy a different family from that of true swallows, although they have a similar style of feeding: they are aerial feeders that pick up insect prey on the wing. In contrast with swallows, Woodswallows, have longer bills and broader-based, triangular, sharply pointed wings. A pale ash gray woodswallow with a small, inconspicuous, dusky gray mask around the eye and the base of the bill. This face mask is not as extensive or as bold as that of Masked, which has a larger, jet black mask. This grayish swallow is also duller colored below. In flight Masked looks largely white below, while Black-faced appears pale gray bodied with a striking tail pattern: black on the underside with two bold white marks at the tip of the tail (Masked has an all whitish tail). This open-country species is found throughout large areas of the mainland from the west side of WA east to NSW and QLD, although it is absent from extreme southeastern NSW and TAS. One of the more abundant woodswallows that forage widely within their range but are less nomadic than Masked and White-browed.

B. Dusky Woodswallow *Artamus cyanopterus* 18 cm/7 in.

Dusky and Little Woodswallow form a similar-species pair of dark chocolate brown woodswallows; however, they differ in range, habitat, size, and wing color. Dusky Woodswallow shows pure white underwings in flight that contrast strongly with the chocolate brown body. The underwings of Little are dusky brown in flight and so do not contrast so strongly with the body color. When perched, Dusky Woodswallow also displays a thin white leading edge to the closed wing, absent in Little. Both show a black tail in flight with bold white tail spots. These are the only two dark brown woodswallows and so are likely to be confused only for each other if seen well. These two similar birds are separated geographically: Dusky is the southern species, a breeding migrant to TAS, and occurring year-round over most of NSW, s. WA, and se. QLD. Can be seen in both open woodlands and closed forests. Dusky Woodswallow often perches, sallying regularly from its chosen perch (usually a dead snag), which is how it is most likely to be encountered.

C. Little Woodswallow *Artamus minor* 12 cm/4.5 in.

The smaller, northern cousin of Dusky Woodswallow. Also chocolate colored, although it lacks the distinct white line on the closed wing that Dusky exhibits; Little has entirely dark brown wings when closed. In flight the underwings contrast less, as they are washed with brown, unlike the clean white underwings of Dusky. Little occurs across the northern half of the mainland: n. WA, across the entire NT, and most of QLD. Although Little Woodswallows have large and varied feeding habitats that include grassy wooded areas, tropical savanna, scrubland, and vast areas of spinifex grasslands, they are most likely to be encountered around gorges, where they nest and tend to rest more regularly.

A. Black Butcherbird *Cracticus quoyi* **33–44 cm/13–17 in.**

Butcherbirds are predatory species that share the family **Bellmagpies** (*Cracticidae*) with the larger **currawongs** and Australian Magpie. The birds in this family are large black or pied birds, with powerful bills and strident songs that are a conspicuous feature of the dawn chorus wherever they occur. Butcherbirds are so named because they often wedge their prey—baby birds to reptiles to small rodents—within the fork of a tree while tearing the prey apart. Butcherbirds hunt from a raised perch and then suddenly pounce on their prey on the ground. All four butcherbirds possess strong grayish bills that are deep based, and hooked at the tip, which is black. Black Butcherbird is the only butcherbird that has an all-black body. Thus it may be more likely to be confused with the crows or currawongs, which are all also largely black. Examination of the bill, however, should render ID straightforward: this butcherbird has a large, pale gray bill with a black tip; all currawongs and crows show unhooked, all-blackish bills. There are several very similar forms of Black Butcherbird; the immatures of one such form are all rufous, and the bill again provides the ultimate indication of species. Black Butcherbird is a tropical species, found in mangroves, monsoon forests, and rainforests in the Wet Tropics of ne. QLD and in the tropical north of the NT. It is not uncommon and can be seen most easily in tropical town parks such as within Cairns and Darwin.

B. Gray Butcherbird *Cracticus torquatus* **28–32 cm/11–12.5 in.**

Gray Butcherbird is a common and widespread black, white, and gray bird, which overlaps throughout much of its range with the similar Pied Butcherbird, another common species from which it must be distinguished. Compared with adult Pied Butcherbird, Gray has a white throat, lacking the black throat and hooded appearance of Pied. As the name suggests, Gray Butcherbird is gray, on the mantle, where adult Pied arc jct black. The black hood of Pied Butcherbird is bordered conspicuously on the nape by a broad white collar, lacking in Gray, where the dark head fades into the gray mantle. Particular care needs to be taken with immature butcherbirds, when Gray and Pied can be very similar in appearance. However, young Pied usually still shows a shadow of a hood, while Gray always shows a pale throat, distinct from the darker head coloration. Gray Butcherbird occurs through much of the continent, except in the driest desert areas, being found in a range of habitats including eucalypt forest, rainforest, monsoon forest, scrubby country, and open woodland. It is a common bird of Australian country towns.

A. Pied Butcherbird *Cracticus nigrogularis* 32–35 cm/12.5–13.5 in.

The two birds on this page are from the same family, **Bellmagpies**, an Australasian family comprising butcherbirds, currawongs, and Australian Magpie, characterized by powerful, melodic songs, strong beaks, and black or pied plumage. Butcherbirds typically perch in trees, dropping to the ground only to snatch prey. Both species on this page are pied birds that need to be differentiated from each other, while Pied Butcherbird also needs to be distinguished from the similar Gray Butcherbird, with which it overlaps over much of the continent. A familiar, boldly marked pied butcherbird, found over much of mainland Australia. Adult Pied Butcherbird shows a complete black hood, solid black back, a complete white collar, and extensive white wing markings, unlike the sympatric Gray Butcherbird. It can always be differentiated from the similarly pied Australian Magpie, as that species, while highly variable, always displays a black underside—where Pied Butcherbird is always white, and the magpie always shows a large pale nape—where the butcherbird is black. Pied Butcherbird is a common species throughout the mainland but is absent from deserts and rainforests, and does not occur in the southeast and TAS. They inhabit open country, including farmlands, open woodlands, scrubby areas and grasslands, and are most easily seen perched prominently, while hunting, from roadside trees or wires.

B. Australian Magpie *Gymnorhina tibicen* 36–44 cm/14–17.5 in.

A common, large bellmagpie that is unrelated to "true" magpies (which occupy the crow family). Unlike the smaller butcherbirds, this long-legged bird walks on the ground rather than hops, pacing the ground for long periods in search of insect prey. Butcherbirds generally hunt from raised perches, dropping to the ground only to pounce on prey. Like most butcherbirds, magpies have strong hooked bills, strident and conspicuous calls, and are pied. While highly variable in its large range, the magpie always has a solid black underside and a large pale to white nape patch, which differentiates magpies from all the butcherbirds. It is a widespread and common species found widely throughout the mainland and TAS. However, it is generally much rarer in humid tropical areas and is absent from both the driest deserts and sw. TAS. It is adaptable, occupying most habitats where there are trees, including many urban areas and cities: it can commonly be found in most cities south of Cairns (QLD), and often frequents parks and gardens. Male Australian Magpies are famously aggressive in defense of their traditional territories and have been known to attack pets and even people, especially cyclists who pass through their territories during the June-to-December breeding season. Although regular, this behavior is generally still limited to certain aggressive individuals, and mostly involves harmless swooping at the intruder. However, they have been known to attack more vigorously on occasion, driving some children to wear bicycle helmets or to take other bizarre protective measures at such times, such as wearing discarded ice cream containers!

A. Pied Currawong *Strepera graculina* 41–51 cm/16–20 in.

All the birds on this page are large black species with white in their plumage. The first three are **currawongs** that belong in the Bellmagpie family. They are predatory, eating nestlings, lizards, insects, and also berries. All currawongs have a yellow eye and a bold white tail tip. They are best identified by geographic range and the patterning of the white. Pied is the only currawong with a broad white base to the tail, a bold white crescent on the upperwing (which forms a white speculum on the closed wing, visible in flight), and a white vent. The most frequently encountered currawong, common throughout eastern mainland Australia, although absent from TAS. It is the only currawong in QLD. It can be found in woodlands, rainforest, scrubland, farms, parks, and gardens, and is a familiar bird, as it occurs in many urban areas.

B. Gray Currawong *Strepera versicolor* 45–53 cm/17.5–21 in.

A southern species found across the mainland from s. WA to se. NSW, and TAS. It overlaps with Pied in s. NSW and with Black on TAS, and so must be differentiated from each of these species. There are several forms with varying amounts of black on the upperwing, although all forms have a black rump that separates this species from Pied, and on TAS the white vent of Gray differentiates it from Black Currawong. In TAS it also has a white flash on the upperwing in flight and as a speculum on the closed wing, unlike Black. Occurs in a range of habitats: open woodland, farms, scrub, heath, and very rarely in urban areas.

C. Black Currawong *Strepera fuliginosa* 46–48 cm/18–19 in.

Occurs only on TAS, where Gray is also present. This species is unique in lacking a white vent, being all black below. Gray Currawong on TAS (the only place they overlap) has large white flashes in the wing, visible in flight, unlike the inconspicuous crescent on the upperwing of Black. It may also be confused with **Forest Raven** (another large black bird on TAS), although currawongs have longer, different-shaped bills, and display a white tail tip (the raven is all black). It is found in a variety of humid habitats over most of TAS.

D. White-winged Chough *Corcorax melanorhamphos* 45 cm/17.5 in.

Another crow-like bird with white in its plumage, but is in a different family from Currawongs. Sits within a two-species family that it shares with the very different brown Apostlebird. Despite the name, it is unrelated to the Eurasian choughs, which belong to the true crows. Choughs are highly social, cooperative nesters with conspicuous large mud nests. They are also terrestrial, almost always seen in groups feeding on the ground, and display massive white wing flashes in flight. It is red eyed with a slim, down-curved bill that along with the white wing markings separates it from the currawongs. Choughs are dry-country birds (mallee, scrubland, and open woods such as brigalow), found in the southeast corner of SA, VIC, much of NSW, and se. QLD. Conspicuous groups of them are most likely to be encountered foraging on the ground or flushing from roadside verges when their most prominent feature, the large white wing markings is easily seen.

B

D

A. Australian Raven *Corvus coronoides* 52 cm/20.5 in.

The three crow species on this page are all large black birds that are very difficult to ID to species, despite often being common and widespread in their ranges. They are most safely identified with an intimate knowledge of their calls, and sometimes by range. All are entirely black with a pale eye. Australian Raven is common in southern and eastern Australia, widely present in sw. WA, s. SA, most of NSW, and the southern half of QLD. All ravens have shaggy throat shackles, most evident when calling, and have inconspicuous gray downy bases to the head and neck feathers, apparent only when the wind ruffles these feathers. Torresian Crows have white downy bases in comparison. The throat shackles are most prominent in Australian Raven than in the other crows here. The Aussie Raven has one of the more memorable calls: "aah-aah-aah-faaaarck," with the last note elongated and descending, with a wailing quality. This is the common city crow of southern Australia found in many habitats.

B. Forest Raven *Corvus tasmanicus* 52 cm/20.5 in.

A localized crow found only on TAS and very locally in ne. NSW and coastal VIC. It is the only crow on TAS. On the mainland its range overlaps with that of several species, including Australian Raven, so ID requires more care. Forest Raven is the largest billed and shortest tailed of the crows. The gray downy bases to the neck and head feathers, if seen, indicate a raven species and not a crow, although this can be seen only rarely, when wind ruffles these feathers. It is best identified with knowledge of its distinctive deep, gravelly call ("kaar-kaar-kaar"), much deeper than that of the other crows. On TAS it is common and frequently seen; on the mainland it is rare and local, much less commonly encountered than the more abundant Australian Raven.

C. Torresian Crow *Corvus orru* 50 cm/19.5 in.

An abundant, widespread crow in north Australia, and the only crow in ne. QLD. It is the common crow of Brisbane and Townsville. Torresian Crow occurs over the entire NT, all of QLD, n. WA, and n. NSW. Unlike on the ravens the downy base of the head and neck feathers is white, although this can be very difficult to judge. It also has a conspicuous behavioral trait: when it lands, it shuffles its wings awkwardly before closing them. In flight it has a square-tipped tail, while ravens have rounder-tipped tails, although again, this is subtle and not often easy to judge accurately. This crow does not possess the extensive throat shackles of Australian Raven, although it can display a slight shackle if calling. Torresian Crow call is high and nasal (unlike the deep, gravelly call of the Forest Raven, and lacks the descending nature and wailing quality of Aussie Raven): "uk-uk-uk-uk" or "aarr-aarr-aarr-aarr." It is a common crow, and anyone visiting Brisbane or n. QLD should expect to see it multiple times. The closely related **Little Crow** *Corvus bennetti* also occurs in central Australia, is almost identical in appearance, and is especially common in the Alice Springs/Ayers Rock area.

C

A. Ground Cuckoo-shrike *Coracina maxima* **33–37 cm/13–14.5 in.**

Cuckoo-shrikes are a family of dull gray, mainly insectivorous birds that have short thick bills similar to those of shrikes, and cuckoo-like bodies, although are completely unrelated to either shrikes or cuckoos. Ground Cuckoo-shrike is a distinctive species of dry habitats within inland Australia. It is the largest cuckoo-shrike and the only one that possesses a forked tail. It also has a piercing yellow eye and a distinctive white rump that is barred black, and has this same pattern on the breast. It is terrestrial in its habits, more so than the other cuckoo-shrikes, and is most likely to be encountered in small groups foraging on the ground in cow paddocks. It can be found over much of the interior of mainland Australia in dry woodlands, away from the coastal zones, although is nomadic over vast distances and thinly distributed, making it rarely encountered.

B. Black-faced Cuckoo-shrike *Coracina novaehollandiae* **33 cm/13 in.**

A widespread, large, powdery gray bird with a bold black face and throat, which is its most prominent feature. It has a square tail, like White-bellied, but quite unlike that of the fork-tailed Ground Cuckoo-shrike. It has a noticeable and distinctive habit of shuffling its wings awkwardly when it lands. The all-black throat and pale gray crown separates adult Black-faced from the smaller White-bellied. Immatures of both species are similar, as Black-faced lacks a black throat at this age, although the black mask of immature Black-faced is longer, extending behind the eye onto the ear coverts. Their flight styles are also quite different: Black-faced has a sweeping, undulating flight, while White-bellied is quite direct. It is a common species of open woodland and forest all over Australia and TAS, where it is most readily found around parks and gardens or hunting prey from exposed overhead wires (e.g., within the city of Brisbane). It is the only cuckoo-shrike on TAS.

C. White-bellied Cuckoo-shrike *Coracina papuensis* **26–28 cm/10–11 in.**

A small, pale, plain-colored bird, similar to Black-faced Cuckoo-shrike. All pale gray with a white underside, a contrasting small black face mask from the bill to the eye, and an inconspicuous white eye ring (lacking in other cuckoo-shrikes). Immature Black-faced, which has a reduced mask at this time, can be very similar, although White-bellied is markedly smaller, and its black mask does not extend onto the ear coverts, as it does in young Black-faced. Furthermore, White-bellied is always markedly smaller than Black-faced. White-bellied is found in the north of WA, n. NT, and all along the east side of QLD, NSW, and VIC. It is the common bird of tropical savanna in northern Australia, where it greatly outnumbers Black-faced. In eastern Australia it occurs in open dry woodlands, where they are often singly or in pairs perched up prominently.

A. White-winged Triller *Lalage sueurii* 18 cm/7 in.

Trillers are cuckoo-shrikes that are dimorphic: the males of the two Australian triller species are strikingly patterned black-and-white birds, while the females are duller, brownish birds. Like all cuckoo-shrikes, they are largely insectivorous, although this species will also take both nectar and fruits. White-winged Triller is unusual in the cuckoo-shrike family in that the male has a nonbreeding plumage, while all others look the same year-round. Breeding males are striking black-and-white birds with black upperparts and white underparts and a large white patch in the wing. Note that both Trillers have wing patches. Breeding male White-winged Trillers can be differentiated from Varied by their lack of supercilium and crisp all-white underparts and vent. The females and nonbreeding males are duller, brownish in comparison, and can show a supercilium and therefore appear closer to Varied in appearance, although both White-winged plumages lack barring on the underparts and have a pale vent that is concolorous with the rest of the underparts. White-winged Triller is a widespread species found commonly throughout the mainland and in northern TAS. It inhabits a vast array of dry habitats, where it may be encountered foraging in the trees or on the ground. In the breeding season male White-winged Trillers make conspicuous display flights, in which they sally slowly over their territories much in the manner of Bobolink of North America or Skylark of Europe.

B. and C. Varied Triller *Lalage leucomela* 19 cm/7.5 in.

One of two triller species in Australia, the males of which are striking black-and-white cuckoo-shrikes. Male Varied (photo B) differs from White-winged in having duller, faintly barred underparts and a rich buff vent (White-winged has clean, bright white underparts and vent). Male Varied also has a pale supercilium, unlike breeding male White-winged, which lacks an eyebrow. Furthermore, the white on the wing of Varied forms two distinct wing bars (unlike in White-winged). The female Varied (photo C) is rather like a subdued grayer brown version of the male. Although male White-winged has a nonbreeding brown plumage that sports a supercilium, as Varied does in all plumages, the underparts of the White-winged at this time are uniform clean whitish, whereas Varied always displays duller underparts with faint bars and a buff vent. Varied is a bird of the coastal zone in n. WA, n. NT, and the east coast of QLD and NSW. It is a triller of dense, wet coastal habitats including forests (monsoon, temperate, tropical, eucalypt) and thicker woodlands. It is usually encountered in singles, pairs, or trios and does not feed on the ground as frequently as White-winged Triller. They forage mainly for invertebrates, but may also feed on fruit.

A. Sandstone Shrike-Thrush *Colluricincla woodwardi* **23–26 cm/9–10 in.**
Shrike-Thrushes are a distinct subgroup of large Whistlers, that, like most whistlers, have stout, thick bills and complex, loud songs that penetrate the dawn chorus. However, unlike many other "traditional" whistlers, the males and females are alike, not strikingly dimorphic. Shrike-thrushes are also generally dull and plain colored, lacking the bright coloration of many males in the whistler family. They feed predominantly on insects, but unlike many other whistlers, shrike-thrushes are more terrestrial, frequently foraging on the ground. A large (it is the largest species) and specialized shrike-thrush confined to sandstone escarpments in northern Australia. It is like a large, long-tailed version of the Rufous Shrike-Thrush: brown on the upperparts with rich rufous underparts and light mottling or streaks on the breast. It is very restricted in its range and is found on sandstone escarpments only in n. WA and the north of the NT. Rufous Shrike-Thrush is distinctly more arboreal and is regularly observed foraging within trees. Sandstone Shrike-Thrush is fairly common within its restricted habitat, where it is usually encountered singly or in pairs, hopping across the rich red rocks under the first rays of sunlight, poking within crevices to search for insects and other prey items. They give their loud territorial calls from these scenic rocks, and never from trees.

B. Rufous Shrike-Thrush *Colluricincla megarhyncha* **19 cm/7.5 in.**
Also known as Little Shrike-Thrush. Rufous is the smallest shrike-thrush and is a brown bird with rich rufous underparts, and light streaking sometimes evident on the breast. In the northeast Rufous Shrike-Thrushes have pale horn-colored bills, while in the rest of their range the bills are dark. It looks very similar to Sandstone Shrike-Thrush, which is significantly larger (Sandstone is the largest shrike-thrush) and longer tailed, and is a local species confined to sandstone escarpments, where Rufous Shrike-Thrush does not occur. Rufous is also much more arboreal and is regularly found within trees. It occurs in the coastal zone of northern and northeastern Australia from the north of WA, through n. NT and QLD and along the coastal region down the QLD coast into n. NSW. Rufous Shrike-Thrush inhabits rainforests, coastal forests, thickets (e.g., lantana), paperbark stands, and mangroves. Like many other whistlers it is often best located by following their loud and strident calls. They are usually found foraging alone or in pairs.

C. Gray Shrike-Thrush *Colluricincla harmonica* **24 cm/9.5 in.**
The most widespread shrike-thrush in Australia and, unlike the other species on this page, largely plain gray, with pale off-white underparts. Some birds have a rufous cast to the mantle (there are several different races; some have plain gray mantles like the rest of the upperparts and head). Gray Shrike-Thrush is common and widespread, found throughout the mainland and TAS, and absent only from a small section of c. WA. It occurs in all habitats and is therefore the most likely shrike-thrush to be encountered. Gray Shrike-Thrush is also famed for its huge repertoire of songs.

A. Golden Whistler *Pachycephala pectoralis* **15–17 cm/6–6.5 in.**
Whistlers, or thickheads, are a family of stout, sparrow-sized songbirds with large heads and thick bills that are very vocal, with resonant, complex songs. The striking males and dull females often look very different. Golden Whistler is a forest bird found in wet habitats throughout eastern and southern Australia. Male Golden is gorgeous, with a black hood bordered with a bright canary yellow collar, bold white throat, and vivid golden yellow underparts. Females are subdued: olive toned with an indistinct wash of yellow on the belly, and few bold markings, best identified as a whistler first by structure, and from other whistlers by an accompanying male or by the yellow wash below. Calls of Golden Whistler are loud and often draw considerable attention. It inhabits the understory and midcanopy within rainforests, and dense, wet woodlands.

B. Rufous Whistler *Pachycephala rufiventris* **16–18 cm/6.5–7 in.**
Rufous Whistler is the common dry-country whistler. Males are boldly marked vocal birds that look very different from the inconspicuous females. Males are grayish with a striking white throat patch surrounded by a thick black border, and rufous underparts. Female are also grayish but lack the conspicuous head pattern; their most useful feature is faint streaks on the upper breast and a pale rufous-washed belly. Rufous Whistler is commonly found throughout Australia in most habitats, except the driest parts of the interior, and is absent from TAS.

C. Green Oriole *Oriolus flavocinctus* **25–30 cm/10–11.5 in.**
Also known as Yellow Oriole. **Orioles** are medium-sized, canopy-dwelling, songbirds with thick bills and a stocky build, that are known for their distinctive, liquid songs. Green Oriole has a warm olive–toned body, a rich yellow wash to the belly, and dark flecks all over the body. It has a prominent reddish eye and a conspicuous reddish bill. It is a canopy bird usually found singly by tracking down its loud song. Green Oriole is a tropical species found in rainforests, mangroves, woodlands, parks, and gardens from n. WA eastward into n. QLD. Although it is common, it generally perches high in the trees, making it hard to see. Their loud, far-carrying, rollicking calls are a distinctive backdrop to the tropical dawn chorus, and they are more often heard than seen.

D. Australasian Figbird *Sphecotheres vieilloti* **27–29.5 cm/10.5–11.5 in.**
Figbirds are colorful orioles, with two races: males in the south ("Green Figbird") have a green underside, while northern races have lemon yellow underparts ("Yellow Figbird"). Males of both races have olive upperparts, a black head with bright red facial skin, and a stout, black bill. The bright yellow or green unstreaked underparts and vivid facial skin help distinguish figbirds from other orioles. Females are similar to orioles but lack rich yellowish olive tones, and display blue bare facial skin. "Yellow Figbird" is found coastally in the tropical north from n. WA around to n. QLD; "Green Figbird" occurs from the c. QLD coast south into s. NSW. Figbirds are found in tropical rainforest, parks and gardens, and eucalypt woodlands. Atypically for orioles, figbirds are flocking species. They are fruit-eating birds that gather noisily in trees such as figs and laurels in cities like Cairns, Brisbane, and Sydney, and are a major disperser of introduced fruit-bearing trees.

A. Spangled Drongo *Dicrurus bracteatus* **28–32 cm/11–12.5 in.**
Drongos are a tropical family of large black insectivorous birds with long, distinctively shaped tails that sit bolt upright on open perches in search of airborne insect prey. Spangled Drongo exhibits a deeply forked tail, with slightly upturned tips. They are acrobatic birds and agile in their pursuit of insects on the wing, when they often draw attention to themselves. They are also highly territorial, often detected when fighting with other drongos or other birds. Drongos are usually found alone or in pairs, normally sitting high on an open branch. They are partially migratory and found in n. WA, n. NT, e. QLD, and e. NSW in rainforest, woodlands, gardens, mangroves, and densely wooded watercourses.

B. Shining Flycatcher *Myiagra alecto* **15–18 cm/6–7 in.**
The male is a small, all-glossy blue-black bird from the **Monarch-Flycatcher** family. Its most striking feature though is a bright orange gape, evident only when its bill is open. The female is strikingly different: rich rufous above, with a white underside and a glossy blue hood. As they are often encountered in pairs, the female can often aid with ID. Otherwise, the male is much smaller than any alternative blackish bird and forages much lower down. Shining Flycatchers are coastal species of the tropical north of Australia (WA, NT, and QLD only), usually found along watercourses in rainforest and mangroves, where they often forage low, very close to the water's surface. They are most likely to be encountered on boat cruises along river channels in their range (e.g., Daintree River cruises, and boat trips in Kakadu NP).

C. Victoria's Riflebird *Ptiloris victoriae* **23–25 cm/9–10 in.**
A **bird-of-paradise**, famed like many others from this extraordinary family for its extravagant displays. Riflebirds have a distinctive shape: plump, short-tailed, with powerful, long, down-curved bills. Thus riflebirds can be distinguished from other black birds by their characteristic body and bill shape. Additionally, the male has a subtle glistening green gorget, and olive-glossed belly that is apparent only in strong sunlight. Females are similarly shaped but gray-brown above, with a conspicuous whitish eyebrow, and lightly scalloped buff underparts. Victoria's Riflebird has an extraordinary display: the male uses a large snag to dance for females, by fanning his wings over the top of his head and opening his bill to reveal a vivid yellow gape. He then jerks his head from side to side and fluffs out his iridescent throat, making this catch the sunlight, and puffs up his breast feathers, accentuating the gloss on his belly also. Often, this is done while circling the female, or alone on a stump to attract the female, when he emits a loud, far-carrying rasping call to draw attention to himself. If the female approaches, then the males often perform all these amazing actions while hanging beneath her. Victoria's are confined to rainforest, mangroves, and wet eucalypt forest in tropical ne. QLD. They are frugivorous and are most likely to be seen in a fruiting tree, or probing the bark of a forest tree in the manner of a treecreeper, or by visiting one of the well-known display sites.

B

A. Willie-Wagtail *Rhipidura leucophrys* 19–21.5 cm/7.5–8.5 in.

All birds on this page are in the **Fantail** family, which comprises small insectivorous birds with short, slim bills, and are characterized by longish tails that are sometimes fanned. Willie-Wagtail is a fantail and not related to wagtails, and is one of Australia's commonest birds. Full of character, it is energetic, friendly, and approachable and is familiar to most Australians, as it is bold and conspicuous by nature. It is the only black-and-white fantail: all black except for a clean white belly and a narrow white line above the eye. It is very widespread and adaptable and is found all over Australia (absent only from southern TAS) in almost every habitat except rainforest. They are often encountered in gardens and parks, and on lawns, where they often hop around on the ground, chattering frequently and wagging their tail conspicuously. They are sometimes seen chasing domestic cats.

B. Northern Fantail *Rhipidura rufiventris* 16–18.5 cm/6.5–7 in.

One of two common gray fantails that are very similar in appearance: gray upperparts with a white-sided tail; pale off-white underparts and a broad horizontal band across the chest, and thin white spot above the eye. Both species share these features, but Northern shows thin white streaks running vertically down the dark gray breast band. Structurally it is larger billed and shorter tailed than Gray and behaves quite differently: it is relatively inactive, sallying after insects from exposed perches. Usually sits quietly and upright (in the manner of a monarch flycatcher), fanning its tail much less than the hyperactive Gray Fantail. It is confined to the tropical north (n. WA, NT, and QLD only), where it occurs in open eucalypt forests and woodlands, mangroves, monsoon forests, and on the edges of tropical rainforest. Although it is common, it is inconspicuous, and less often encountered than Gray Fantail.

C. Gray Fantail *Rhipidura albiscapa* 15–17 cm/6–6.5 in.

A widespread species similar to Northern Fantail but with markedly different behavior: a hyperactive fantail that regularly flares its tail and actively chases insects around, rarely sitting still for long periods. It also lacks the light streaking within the chest band of Northern, and shows bolder white wing bars. Furthermore, the tail is thinly tipped white, and not merely edged white on the sides, as in Northern. Gray Fantail occurs throughout the continent (including TAS), except for the eastern interior of WA. It is a generalist, found in most habitats types both on the coast and inland. They often join mixed feeding flocks, when they often are at their most visible.

D. Rufous Fantail *Rhipidura rufifrons* 15–16 cm/6–6.5 in.

A distinctively colored fantail: a brownish bird with a rich rufous rump and upper tail, small rufous smudge above the eye, and a bold black band across the breast. Like Gray Fantail it is also a hyperactive bird, always fanning its distinctive tail. It is fairly common in wet forests (e.g., tropical and temperate rainforest and eucalypt woodland) of eastern Australia (QLD, NSW, and VIC), where it is usually encountered low in the shady understory.

B

A. Pied Monarch *Arses kaupi* **14–15 cm/5.5–6 in.**

This page shows three black-and-white **Monarch-Flycatcher** species, a family of boldly marked, long-tailed, flycatcher-like songbirds that have wide bills with bristles around them. The first two are both typically arboreal monarch species, usually found in trees. It is a dazzling monarch, black above except for a prominent white collar and a bold white crescent across the back, and white below with a broad black band across the chest, and boasts a beautiful cerulean blue eye ring. This eye-catching rainforest bird has the strange habit of feeding in treecreeper-like fashion by hopping up and down trunks to search for insect prey, flicking its tail and opening its wings conspicuously when it does so. Although it is found only in a small area of the Wet Tropics of ne. QLD, its range does include some very popular tropical rainforest tourist sites (e.g., Curtain Fig), where it may be found with luck.

B. Restless Flycatcher *Myiagra inquieta* **19–21.5 cm/7.5–8.5 in.**

Another black-and-white bird that is distinctly plainer than Pied. Restless has all-black upperparts and head and is solidly pale below, mostly white except for a subtle buff wash sometimes present on the throat. It has no white markings on the upperparts. Restless is found throughout the mainland, and is absent only from the desert areas of central and western Australia. It prefers open wooded habitats, and often occurs along eucalypt-lined, wooded watercourses (especially in Red Gums), but is also found in wooded parks and even golf courses. It is a fairly common species that often draws attention to itself with its scissor-grinder calls.

C. Magpie-Lark *Grallina cyanoleuca* **27 cm/10.5 in.**

An odd, giant, long-legged monarch, usually seen on the ground. It has black upperparts and largely white underparts apart from a black-bordered white throat (females) or a solid black throat patch (males). Magpie-Lark also has a horn-colored bill and a piercing yellow eye. They are extremely common wherever there are trees but like to forage in many open habitats, including lawns around airports and towns. They are also very vocal birds, nicknamed "Peewit" after their loud calls. Although now considered an odd monarch, it was formerly considered in another family, the "mud-nest builders," as it constructs a large bowl-like nest from dried mud, which gives it its other name: "Mudlark." Magpie-Larks tend to nest near Willie-Wagtails, and, oddly, each species helps the other defend their nests. They are incredibly aggressive in defense of their nests and, rarely, have been known to rip hair off people's heads who approached too close! Also known to regularly tussle with the much larger Australian Magpie. When pairs are mated, they often display conspicuously to each other, duetting and both opening their rounded wings and spreading their tails at regular intervals. A strange and very familiar species quite unlike any other Australian bird. Its common and conspicuous nature ensures that any visitor will encounter this wonderful bird shortly after arrival, most likely feeding on a well-trimmed town lawn.

A. Spectacled Monarch *Symposiachrus trivirgatus* **14–16 cm/5.5–6.5 in.**
This page contains three blue-gray species from the Monarch-Flycatcher family: a group of large, active, flycatcher-like, insectivorous birds that have wide gapes and strong bristles around the base of the bill, which aid them in capturing insects in flight. Spectacled Monarchs are grayish in color with a black face mask (that passes through the eye, unlike any other species on this plate), black throat, and rich deep orange breast. It has a boldly marked white-tipped black tail that becomes noticeable when it is actively sallying for insects when foraging, when it fans it habitually. It is a fairly common bird of coastal eastern Australia, occurring from Cape York in extreme n. QLD south to the c. NSW coastal zone, where it inhabits the understory and gullies within rainforests and along densely vegetated watercourses.

B. Leaden Flycatcher *Myiagra rubecula* **15–17 cm/6–6.5 in**
The following species pair are similar, closely related monarch-flycatchers that can be extremely difficult to differentiate. Behaviorally, Leaden Flycatchers have a distinctive and easily noticeable habit of regularly quivering their tail. Leaden Flycatcher is strikingly dimorphic: males are bicolored birds with deep powder blue upperparts and head, and a striking clean white underside; females are similar above but have a peach-colored chin and throat. The males are distinctive, while females are remarkably similar to Broad-billed Flycatchers and need to be told apart with some caution. Where these two species overlap in range (in the tropical north), Broad-billed shows a broader bill with the outer edges of the bill curved outward. Note though this is often hard to discern in the field. Broad-billed generally has darker, deeper blue upperparts relative to female Leaden, and deeper and brighter colored orange throat and chest. Leaden Flycatcher is a common species found across the tropical north of Australia from WA east to QLD, and in eastern Australia from n. QLD south into s. and e. VIC. It also occurs seasonally on TAS. Leaden occurs in eucalypt forests, open woodlands, mangroves, and tropical savanna, and along the banks of vegetated rivers, but generally avoids dense forest.

C. Broad-billed Flycatcher *Myiagra ruficollis* **15–17 cm/6–6.5 in .**
A monarch of the tropical north (confined to n. WA, NT, and QLD). Adults are not sexually dimorphic like the Leaden Flycatcher. It is very similar in appearance to the female of the more common and widespread Leaden Flycatcher, with blue-gray upperparts, rich orange throat and chest, and white underparts. However, on close inspection this species has a slightly broader bill, which bows outward along the outer edges; darker blue upperparts; and deeper orange coloration on the throat and chest. Broad-billed also do not habitually quiver their tail, which Leaden does with extreme regularity. Note, though, that these are all subtle plumage differences that usually require much field experience to use effectively. Broad-billed Flycatchers inhabit monsoon forests, mangroves, tropical savanna, and gallery forest, where they are fairly common.

A. Hooded Robin *Melanodryas cucullata* **16 cm/6.5 in.**

Australasian Robins are a group of small insectivorous birds with relatively large heads that hunt from perches and often drop to the ground to pick up prey. Some hunt by perching on the sides of vertical tree trunks. They are not related to robins in either Europe or America but are a family that is confined to the Australasian region. Although many are brightly colored, this page shows less colorful species. Although they may not be brightly colored, male Hooded Robins are striking pied birds with jet black hoods and crisp white underparts, and are all black above save for a white flash in the wing and a white line on the shoulder. The males are therefore unlike any other robin. Females are less distinctive: they are pale gray all over but with darker wings, and still show long white bars in the wing. These bars show as a distinct bar on the upperwing in flight, when the sides to the upper tail also flash white. It is the only plain gray bird with this bold wing pattern and can therefore be identified by that feature alone. Although it occurs over much of the mainland, Hooded Robin is absent from stony deserts and the Cape York Peninsula of QLD, and is very scarce in the areas of the tropical north where it occurs. They are uncommon and often missed, but are more abundant in the south of their range. Hooded Robins occur in dry-country habitats such as mulga, mallee, eucalypt forest, tropical savanna, and open woodland, but avoid wetter areas such as rainforest. They are often found sitting on exposed perches (such as dead snags), watching for prey.

B. White-breasted Robin *Eopsaltria Georgiana* **15–16 cm/6–6.5 in.**

A plain gray robin confined to the coastal strip of southwest WA. All gray above with indistinct white tail corners, and whitish below, with the only bold marking a horizontal white bar on the wing visible only in flight. It is most similar to female Hooded Robin but does not show the broad wing bar when perched that Hooded does. However, in flight they are remarkably similar but White-breasted lacks the white upper tail sides of Hooded. White-breasted Robins are an uncommon species found in wet eucalypt forests and thickets, and along vegetated creeks. Most likely to be encountered perched low in the understory or clinging to the sides of a vertical trunk. They can be found in Porongorup National Park and also in forests on the edges of Perth (e.g., Wungong Dam Reserve).

C. Gray-headed Robin *Heteromyias cinereifrons* **17–18 cm/6.5–7 in.**

A gray robin that is confined to highland rainforests in ne. QLD. Although largely gray, it is a striking species, with a bold white bar in the wing (visible when perched), jet black lores, and a pale gray head with a warm wash to the ear coverts. The back is rufous and becomes bright rust colored on the rump and tail. Underneath, it is contrastingly white. They are a trusting terrestrial robin in their tiny range (it is fairly common within range), where they are usually encountered hopping around on the ground or on tables, or perched on small posts within picnic areas (e.g., Mount Hypipamee NP and Curtain Fig, QLD), when they can often allow very close approach. Like many of the Australasian Robins, Gray-headed may also be observed perching low on the side of vertical tree trunks.

C

A. Red-capped Robin *Petroica goodenovii* **12 cm/4.5 in.**

Australasian Robins are unrelated to Robins of North America and Europe, constituting a separate Australasian family. They are large-headed, insectivorous birds that capture their prey on the ground, by flying down from a perch above. They are usually dimorphic; the boldly patterned males look very different from the browner females. This page depicts a group of beautiful robins that all exhibit red in their plumage. Red-capped is a dazzling dry-country robin similar to Scarlet Robin. However, Red-capped possesses a bright red cap and is the only robin in Australia with this feature. The duller female still has a hint of red on the forehead, if only as a subtle wash, that is lacking in all other similar robins. Red-capped Robins are widespread over the southern half of mainland Australia in dry habitats such as open woodland, mulga, brigelow, and mallee, in more arid regions than the other "red robins." They are mostly likely to be encountered sitting on a low open branch, from where they launch regular forays onto the ground to capture insects. It is delightfully abundant in some inland areas, where their distinctive grasshopper-like trills are often heard, and they often allow close approach. One of the highlights of any day in inland Australia is catching sight of a jaw-dropping male Red-capped Robin.

B. Scarlet Robin *Petroica boodang* **13cm/5in**

Scarlet Robin is a very striking robin, with a black mantle and wings, a bold white wing flash, and a shocking scarlet breast. It is remarkably similar to Red-capped Robin, that doesn't normally overlap in range, Scarlet preferring wetter habitats. However, Scarlet displays a black crown with a bright white forehead (the forehead and crown are both scarlet in male Red-capped). The brown female Scarlet is more colorful and contrasting than other similar female robins, with a distinct red wash on the breast, and a prominent white forehead spot, lacking in all other similar species. Scarlet Robin occurs in forests and woodlands in the southeast mainland and s. WA, as well as TAS. Both Scarlet and Flame can also be found in more open country when not breeding (e.g., farmlands and paddocks). Scarlet Robins are most likely to be seen perched on prominent low fence lines or open branches.

C. Flame Robin *Petroica phoenicea* **14 cm/5.5 in.**

Another beautiful southern robin that occurs in the southeast corner of mainland Australia and TAS, and therefore often overlaps with the similar Scarlet Robin. Flame Robin, although still an undeniably striking bird, is a little more subdued than the Scarlet with sooty gray (not black) upperparts, a reduced white forehead spot, and a crimson, not scarlet, breast. Flame is also found within woodland, forest, and scrub from sea level into the mountains (up to nearly 1800 m/6000 ft), although it also occupies open habitats (e.g., farmlands) when not nesting. They are most easily seen when they emerge onto the tops of low scrub in the early morning sunlight to sing, when their rich and colorful plumage is shown to full effect.

A. Eastern Yellow Robin *Eopsaltria australis* **15 cm/6 in.**

All three species on this plate are yellow robins. Australasian Robins are a family of small, large-headed, insectivorous songbirds that are not related to either European or American Robins but are instead in a separate family confined to Australasia. They often pounce onto insects on the ground, and all three species on this page have the distinctive habit of perching on the sides of vertical trunks while searching for prey. All three robins on this page have yellow on the underparts. Eastern Yellow is a bright yellow robin of the east, with dull ashy gray head and upperparts and bright canary yellow underparts (from the throat down). This robin has two different forms: in the northeast, Eastern Yellow Robin shows a vivid canary yellow rump, which is olive in the southeastern form. It is most similar to the Western Yellow Robin (which is found only west of the range of Eastern Yellow) but differs in having an extensive gray throat and upper breast, unlike its western cousin. In range it is most easily confused with Pale Yellow Robin, which possesses a pale face (between the bill and the eye), while Eastern Yellow Robin has a uniform all-gray head and face. Furthermore, Pale Yellow lacks the vivid yellow rump of the northeastern Eastern Yellow Robin. It is a common bird in eastern rainforests, woodlands, and thickets from ne. QLD south to VIC. It behaves much like Pale Yellow Robin and is most often observed perched low in trees or on the side of trunks, from which it frequently hops down onto the ground to snatch insects.

B. Western Yellow Robin *Eopsaltria griseogularis* **15 cm/6 in.**

The western cousin of Eastern Yellow Robin that is very similar in appearance, but occurs only in the west. There are two races in Western Yellow Robin: the eastern form displays an olive green rump, while the western race shows a bright yellow rump. It differs from Eastern Yellow in having a pale gray throat and chest but is otherwise similar. These two species do not overlap: Western Yellow Robin is found only in the south (extreme southern SA) and west of Australia (sw. WA). It occurs in open forest and woodland, mallee, and other scrubland, where it is fairly common. Western Yellow often forages higher in trees than the other species pictured here. It is most likely found perched high in the trees, unlike the other, understory robins on this page.

C. Pale Yellow Robin *Tregellasia capito* **13 cm/5 in.**

Pale Yellow Robin is the most subdued of the group on this page, with dull yellow underparts, and shows a pale white (or sometimes yellow) face, while the other two yellow robins have gray faces with no conspicuous pale markings around the eye. Pale Yellow Robin is also uniform olive on the head and upperparts, and lacks the smoky gray coloration on the head that the others possess. It is a rainforest robin found only locally in the fragmented rainforest of the east, where it is fairly common in its small range: in the tropical and temperate rainforests of ne. QLD, s. QLD, and northern NSW. It is frequently found perched below eye level on vertical trunks, from where it often flits down to the ground to capture prey.

C

A. White-throated Needletail *Hirundapus caudacutus* 20cm/8in

All birds on this page are aerial feeders, spending much of their life on the wing hawking insects. Swifts and swallows are different families of aerial birds. **Swifts** have narrow, scythelike, pointed wings, with tiny feet that prevent them from perching on anything but vertical surfaces. Swifts mate, drink and feed in flight. The Needletail is a huge migrant swift from Asia, occurring between October and April. It is the fastest bird in flapping flight: up to 170 km/h (105 mph), when they catch insects on the wing by opening their wide gapes to capture prey. Long thought to never perch in Australia, they have recently been found to roost in trees. This boldly patterned swift is unlikely to be confused with any other aerial bird: larger than the rest, dark brown with a striking bright white horseshoe shape on the undertail, and clean white throat. The needles on the tail are fine and unlikely to be seen. The Needletail is found in open skies above a variety of habitats all over eastern Australia. Two other smaller swifts also occur in Australia: **Fork-tailed Swift** *Apus pacificus* (a migrant that occurs throughout the continent in October to April) and **Australian Swiftlet** *Aerodromus terraereginae,* a resident species confined to e. QLD. These species are much smaller than needletails, and all dark in coloration, except for a white rump. They can be told apart by tail shape: the larger Fork-tailed has a long, forked tail, while the swiftlet has a short, squarish tail.

B. Welcome Swallow *Hirundo neoxena* 14–15 cm/5.5–6 in.

Swallows and Martins are broader-winged aerial feeders than swifts that, unlike them, regularly land and are able to perch on the ground. Swallows usually construct nests of dried mud under bridges and eves of houses, making them familiar to many people. Welcome is the common Australian swallow and one of its commonest birds over all of southern and eastern Australia (including TAS), and absent only from n. WA and almost all the NT. It is distinctive, similar to the familiar Barn Swallow of Europe and Asia: glossy blue above, with a rusty face, but lacks the dark chest band of Barn. It has a deep forked tail and a scattering of pale spots on the upper tail that usually are visible only at close range. Other Australian swallows or martins do not share the deeply forked tail of this species. Commonly encountered over urban areas and many different habitats, where it is numerous and common, and very likely to be seen by any visitor.

C. Fairy Martin *Petrochelidon ariel* 12 cm/4.5 in.

Martins are swallows that differ in their square tails, which have only a shallow notch. Fairy Martin can be identified from the combination of white rump and rusty top to the head. **Tree Martin** *P. nigricans* is very similar overall (it also has a white rump and squarish tail), except it has a dark head concolorous with the upperparts. Both are common over all of mainland Australia, although Fairy is absent from TAS, where Tree is the only martin present. Fairy Martins are known as "Bottle Swallows" owing to their bottle-shaped nests constructed from mud, while Tree Martins nest within cavities in trees. Fairy Martins are often found around nesting or roosting colonies near culverts. Both martins are social species, usually encountered in large groups.

A. Brown Songlark *Cincloramphus cruralis* 18–25 cm/7–10 in.

Songlarks are not true larks but are instead in a family called **Grassbirds**, which comprise a group of streaked brown birds with slim bills, long legs, and long tails. They lack the pronounced hind claw that both bushlarks and pipits characteristically possess. Songlarks, especially Rufous, are generally more arboreal than true larks and pipits. All the species on this plate have fluttering spring display flights, which make them more visible in this season. Adult male Brown Songlarks are distinctive: plain dark brown all over, unlike the other species pictured on this page. However, females and nonbreeding males are brown streaky birds quite similar to Rufous Songlark, although lacking the rich rufous rump patch of that species and having more extensive dark markings on the upperparts as well. Both songlarks can be differentiated from pipits by virtue of their plain, unstreaked underparts. Brown Songlark is widely distributed in open country habitats on the southern mainland, but is absent from northern Australia. It is found in open country such as farmlands and scrubby country, where the males are most likely to be seen in spring singing from the tops of fences or posts with conspicuously cocked tails.

B. Rufous Songlark *Cincloramphus mathewsi* 16–19 cm/6.5–7.5 in.

A pale songlark with a bold rusty rump. The upperparts are plain, lacking the extensive dark centers to the feathers that Brown exhibits. Rufous Songlark also possesses unstreaked underparts, unlike Australasian Pipit and bushlarks. It is widespread on mainland Australia, and absent only from the Cape York Peninsula (QLD) and the interior of e. WA. Tends to prefer habitats with more trees than Brown. Occurs in open woodlands, and croplands with scattered trees. It is most often encountered in spring when the males perch high on open branches and call frequently while in conspicuous sallying display flights.

C. Australasian Pipit *Anthus novaeseelandiae* 17–18 cm/6.5–7 in.

Formerly called Richard's Pipit, from which it is now generally considered a different species. **Pipits** are slim billed, streaked, brown, long-tailed songbirds that walk on the ground with a distinctive bobbing gait, when they regularly wag their tails up and down, between regular spurts of running. This is the only regularly occurring pipit in Australia and is widespread over the entire continent (including TAS). The pipit can be identified from the songlarks by virtue of its heavily streaked chest and white outer tail feathers, which are clearly visible in flight. Another brown, streaky bird, the **Australasian Bushlark** *Mirafra javanica,* is the only native true lark in Australia, which may also be confused with this species and with the songlarks, although it is a stouter bird, with a stubbier, thicker bill and shorter tail than the pipit, and shows white outer tail feathers and a heavily streaked breast, which differentiate bushlarks from songlarks. Australasian Pipit is found in open country, often in areas where the other "little brown jobs" pictured on this page also can occur. Small groups of them are most likely to be encountered feeding on areas of short turf such as cricket fields and well-manicured grassy roadside verges.

C

A. Mistletoebird *Dicaeum hirundinaceum* **10–11 cm/4–4.5 in.**
Mistletoebird is the sole member of the **flowerpecker** family in Australia: tiny, dumpy, short-tailed birds with stubby bills. In shape rather similar to pardalotes, though lacking their intricate markings. Males are unmistakable, with striking red throats, a broad black line running down the breast, a soft rose-colored vent, and deep blue upperparts. Females are less colorful, gray birds, though they still show the distinctive rose vent that aids ID. They feed on mistletoe, wherever it occurs, across a broad range of habitats. This beautiful bird is widespread, and absent only from TAS and the driest desert regions.

B. Olive-backed Sunbird *Cinnyris jugularis* **11–12 cm/4.5–5 in.**
Also known as Yellow-bellied Sunbird. The only **sunbird** in Australia, a group of characteristically shaped birds with long, down-curved bills used to forage for nectar. Both sexes are bright lemon yellow below and olive above, although males have striking metallic blue throats. The bill shape alone makes them recognizable, and they are familiar to many people in their range, as they often feed on garden flowers, which they defend vigorously, and frequently nest under the eaves of houses. It is restricted to the coast of QLD from Rockhampton north to Cape York, where it occurs in rainforests, mangroves, and gardens.

C. Australian Yellow White-eye *Zosterops luteus* **10–12.5 cm/4–5 in.**
White-eyes comprise small, gregarious, warblerlike birds that possess bold white eye rings, which are the defining feature of the family. In Australia there are two regular species: Australian Yellow is a coastal species in the north (from the c. WA coast around to the sw. side of Cape York QLD), and **Silvereye** *Z. lateralis* is a widespread species throughout eastern and southern Australia, including TAS. The distinctive ring around the eye easily identifies either of these species to family, and they are also easily told apart: Yellow is solidly bright lemon yellow below, and bright yellow-green above, while Silvereye is less colorful—gray-olive above, and the yellow on the underside is confined to the throat. The head may also be washed yellow. Some Silvereye races, of which there are many, also show a rufous or gray wash along the flanks.

D. Crested Shrike-Tit *Falcunculus frontatus* **15–19 cm/6–7.5 in.**
An oddly structured member of the whistler family. Like many whistlers, boldly patterned, with a striking black-and-white head, and bright lemon yellow underparts. However, it has a crested head and strongly hooked bill. There are three distinct populations: in n. WA and the n. NT ("Northern Shrike-Tit"); in the east in s. QLD, e. NSW, VIC, and e. SA ("Eastern Shrike-Tit"); and in s. WA ("Western Shrike-Tit"). These forms do not differ greatly in their appearance (they vary subtly in the color of the upperparts and extent of yellow on the underparts) but have sometimes been proposed as distinct species. "Eastern Shrike-Tit" is the most abundant form, while Northern is rare. They inhabit rainforest, eucalypt forest, woodland, and heaths (in the west), and are generally inconspicuous birds that feed high in the trees. They are sometimes located by the sound of stripping bark, when they use their powerful hooked bills to extract insects from beneath.

A. Red-eared Firetail *Stagonopleura oculata* 11–12 cm/4–4.5 in.

This page depicts three handsome species of **waxbills**, which are small, finchlike birds with red bills, bright red upper tails, and often striking plumage features. Waxbills forage low for seeds and insects, and are therefore most likely to be seen near ground level. Red-eared Firetail is a restricted-range species found only in the extreme south of WA. This largely brown finch with a finely vermiculated back has a thickly scalloped black-and-white belly and undertail, the characteristic scarlet rump and upper tail of all firetails, a small black face mask, and red patch on the ears. It is found in wet areas with substantial undergrowth within its restricted west Australian range, such as heaths, well-vegetated watercourses, and eucalypt forests with a thick understory. It is an uncommon, furtive, and reclusive finch that often feeds low in thick cover (usually singly or in pairs) and therefore can be difficult to find. The similar looking **Beautiful Firetail** *S. bella* occurs in heaths in southeastern Australia and TAS but lacks the red patch behind the eye, and also lacks the black-and-white scalloping on the lower belly that Red-eared possesses. As there is no overlap, they can also be identified on range alone.

B. Red-browed Firetail *Neochmia temporalis* 11–12 cm/4–4.5 in.

Also known as Red-browed Finch. The well-named Red-browed Firetail has a fiery red eyebrow and bright scarlet upper tail and rump, which form its most prominent features. The eyebrow alone serves to ID this species. It is a common eastern finch from the Cape York Peninsula in n. QLD south along the coastal strip to VIC, and se. SA. These firetails are found in a range of habitats, including gardens, golf courses, woodland and forest clearings, grasslands, and croplands, where their bright red rumps in flight often draw attention to attractive flocks of these birds. This species is often around human habitations in their range and sometimes visits feeders (e.g., O' Reilly's, Lamington NP, QLD), where they can be very approachable and photogenic. It is the only firetail known to frequent feeders.

C. Diamond Firetail *Stagonopleura guttata* 12 cm/4.5 in.

A stunningly beautiful and scarce finch. Like the others, it, too, has a bright vermilion red rump and upper tail, but unlike the others, it has a pale dove gray head and white underparts with a contrasting broad black breast band and black flanks that are dotted with bold white spots. Found in open woodland, riverside Red Gums, eucalypt forest and mulga in eastern Australia from se. QLD, to e. NSW, VIC, and far southeastern SA. This breathtaking finch is most likely to be found in pairs, perched low in the understory, or on a barbed wire fence on the edge of forest.

C

A. Crimson Finch *Neochmia phaeton* **12–14 cm/4.5–5.5 in.**
This page depicts three striking species from the waxbill family. Waxbills and finches are small sparrowlike birds that often possess bold colors and have small conical bills for foraging on seeds and insects. Finches are social birds, often nesting in colonies and foraging in flocks, and rarely encountered alone. Male Crimson Finches are gorgeous long-tailed finches with a red bill and rich crimson face (surrounded by a powdery gray hood) and breast, with light white spotting on the flanks. The tail is similarly colored red, although the mantle is brown. No other finch has this much red in its plumage. The female is more subdued, with mostly brown coloration and a bold red face and bill, so is similar to Star Finch but lacks the white breast spots of that species. However, they are usually found in flocks, where the presence of males aids ID. Crimson is a tropical species found in n. WA, n. NT, and n. and ne. QLD only, where it inhabits tropical grasslands, areas of sparse paperbark trees, croplands, pandanus groves, and even gardens and grassy roadside verges.

B. Gouldian Finch *Erythrura gouldiae* **14 cm/5.5 in.**
A scarce and dazzling multicolored finch of the tropical north. An unmistakable bird with vivid bright colors throughout the plumage: bright emerald green on the back, with an electric blue rump and black tail with thin wispy central feathers that extend into a point, which makes it a very distinctively shaped finch. The breast is lilac, and the rest of the underparts are washed lemon yellow. It always possesses a pale ivory-colored bill, although the head pattern, while always striking, is variable, with several different color morphs. Some have rich scarlet faces, others have solid black faces, and others show yellow-orange on the face. Several color morphs can be found within the same flock. They are patchily distributed in n. WA, NT, and n. QLD (very rare in QLD), and occur in tropical savannas, grasslands, and other wooded areas with nearby water. Like all the finches, it is most likely to be encountered in flocks frequenting waterholes in the drier parts of its range, where they frequently gather to drink in the late afternoon, making for a wonderful and colorful end to any day. This is the prize bird for most birders visiting the NT.

C. Double-barred Finch *Taeniopygia bichenovii* **10–11 cm/4–4.5 in.**
Although lacking in color compared with the other species on this plate, still a very strikingly patterned and handsome finch. A brownish bird with bright white underparts and two bold black horizontal bars across the chest (the upper bar circles up and borders the white face). The black eye is conspicuous, standing out boldly from the white face. The wings are black and dotted boldly with white. It has a small conical, all-blackish bill. Quite unlike any other finch. It is a common species of the tropical north (WA, NT, and QLD) and eastern Australia (QLD, NSW, and barely into the extreme north of VIC). Double-barred Finches are the most trusting of the northern finches and can be found in flocks in open woodlands, tropical grasslands, grassy roadside verges, and croplands.

C

A. Zebra Finch *Taeniopygia guttata* 10 cm/4 in.

Also known as Chestnut-eared Finch. Males are strikingly patterned: bright red bills, bold chestnut ear patch, finely barred black-and-white breast, and rufous flanks dotted with white spots. It is the most wide-ranging finch in Australia, absent only from the coastal extremities of the mainland and TAS. Zebra Finch is most often detected when a flock is disturbed from a roadside, when they expose their white rumps and bold "zebra" patterned tail, or when a group visits a water hole. Females are dull grayish birds lacking most bold markings but still displaying the distinctive tail pattern. It occurs over much of the drier parts of the country, in a variety of habitats, including grasslands, croplands, saltbush scrub, and other open country.

B. Chestnut-breasted Munia *Lonchura castaneothorax* 11–12 cm/4.5 in.

Also known as Chestnut-breasted Mannikin. A handsome, strikingly marked finch displaying a black face and rich orange breast with a thick black border that separates the vibrant breast from a clean white belly. It is gregarious; flocks inhabit grasslands, croplands, and rank grasslands bordering wetlands all across northern Australia, and down eastern Australia to s. NSW. It is most often found when a large flock is inadvertently disturbed from foraging low in tall grasses, and they emerge to perch conspicuously on the tops of the fine stems, which sway prominently under their weight.

C. Long-tailed Finch *Poephila acuticauda* 15–16 cm/6 in.

The following pair are similar brown finches, found only in northern Australia. Both display long, sharply pointed black tails and prominent white rumps. However, Long-tailed differs from the closely related Masked Finch in having a powder blue head, peach-washed underparts, and a large black throat patch. The bill is relatively smaller than that of Masked Finch, and varies in color from yellow in the west, to coral-red at the eastern end of its range. Therefore, eastern birds can be differentiated from Masked by the color of the bill. Long-tailed is a common finch confined to northern Australia from Broome (WA) eastward to nw. QLD (Mount Isa), where it inhabits grassy woodlands and pandanus, usually near water. They are social birds, most often encountered in pairs or groups, and most easily found visiting water holes when coming into drink, when their tail patterns are often conspicuous.

D. Masked Finch *Poephila personata* 12–14 cm/4.5–5.5 in

Very similar in appearance to Long-tailed Finch: both are largely brown in color and display a distinctive long, pointed black tail and a white rump. However, the smaller Masked lacks the powder blue hood of Long-tailed and shows a continuous black mask around the face, not just a clean black throat bib. The body of Masked Finch is also uniformly brown, lacking the warm peach flush to the underside of Long-tailed. In the east of its range Masked further differs in bill color: its relatively heavier bill is yellow, while in this area Long-tailed Finch shows a wax red bill. Masked is a common finch within grassy woodlands in northern Australia from Broome (WA) to just west of the Atherton Tablelands (QLD).

B

A. Eurasian Blackbird *Turdus merula* 25 cm/10 in.

An introduced thrush species from Europe (originally introduced into Melbourne in the 1860s) that has a beautiful melodic song. Found in southeastern Australia (e. SA, se. NSW, and TAS). The male is distinctive, being all glossy black with a prominent yellow bill and eye ring. The female is all brown with a duller yellow bill. Within their range they are strongly associated with urban areas. It is fairly common in the suburbs of Sydney and Melbourne.

B. Common Myna *Acridotheres tristis* 23–25 cm/9–10 in.

An introduced Asian starling that is found extensively in eastern Australia. It was introduced to both VIC and QLD to control pests. Since then it has had a devastating effect on native wildlife, aggressively competing with them for cavity nesting sites and also destroying cash crops in many areas, leading to the development of programs to capture them and control their numbers. Note that Common Myna is unrelated to Noisy and Yellow-throated Miners, which are actually honeyeaters. It is found patchily in ne. QLD, se. QLD, and e. NSW and VIC. A very distinctive brownish bird with bold yellow facial skin behind the eye and a bright yellow bill and legs. In flight it also displays broad white flashes in the wing. It is familiar to many people in their range, as they are an urban species found around towns and cities, and along highways, where they are most likely to be found foraging in groups on the ground. It is common around Cairns, Brisbane, and Sydney.

C. European Starling *Sturnus vulgaris* 20–22 cm/8–8.5 in.

A familiar starling species introduced from Europe to Sydney and Melbourne in the 1800s, and now commonly present in southeast Australia from se. QLD through all of NSW and VIC into e. SA and TAS. Originally introduced to control crop pests, this aggressive species has now come to be a pest itself, consuming valuable farmed fruits and crops, and also adversely affecting cavity-nesting native birds, which it outcompetes for nesting sites. A plain, glossy black bird with a bright yellow bill and reddish legs in breeding plumage. In winter dress the body is boldly spotted buff, and the bill is dark. Young birds are all brown. An aggressive, adaptive, and familiar bird found in a range of habitats, although most likely to be found either in urban areas or in croplands, where they are usually encountered in groups feeding on the ground or perched prominently on overhead wires.

D. House Sparrow *Passer domesticus* 15 cm/6 in.

A familiar Old World species now found widely across eastern Australia (QLD, NSW, VIC, and SA). Males are streaked brown birds with gray caps, rufous napes, black throats, and chunky black bills. Females lack the male's bold head pattern, are brown and streaky on the upperparts, and have a brownish head with an obvious pale supercilium. A generalist species that is most likely to be encountered in noisy, boisterous flocks within urban areas, although it also occurs widely in farmlands and scrublands outside of these. It is found around almost every town and most farmhouses throughout eastern Australia. It is the introduced species that has had the greatest penetration into native habitats, as many of the other introduced species are largely restricted to urban or heavily human-modified environments.

AMPHIBIANS

A. Red Tree Frog *Litoria rubella* **3–4.5 cm/1.2–1.8 in.**
Also known as Desert Tree Frog. The coloration of this rotund frog varies from cream to reddish brown above, finely flecked with black, and exhibits a broad dark band running along the side from the tip of the snout to the hind limbs. It is smooth in texture and possesses the broad toe pads typical of tree frogs. It occurs across the north of Australia (c. WA east to n. NSW), where it is found both coastally and inland, and often takes shelter under buildings and stones.

B. Peron's Tree Frog *Litoria peronei* **4.5–6.5 cm/1.8–2.6 in.**
Peron's, Roth's, and Tyler's are closely related and share a similar structure and general coloration: long hind limbs, broad toe pads, extensive webbing between the digits, and extensive markings on the hidden surfaces (armpits, groin, posterior surface to the hind limbs), which aid ID. Peron's exhibits a uniformly colored eye, with an odd, *cross-shaped* pupil, a feature shared with Tyler's. It possesses a clear black line over the tympanum (circular pad around the ear opening), which is lacking in Tyler's. Peron's tends to sit high and occurs near water in open woods and eucalypt woodlands in southeastern Australia.

C. Roth's Tree Frog *Litoria rothi* **3.7–5.7 cm/1.5–2.2 in.**
Roth's is the most strikingly patterned of these three similar species (which includes Tyler's and Peron's), exhibiting black armpits and groin, and bold black-and-yellow patterning across the back of the thighs. The upper half of the eye is red, and there is a clear black line above the tympanum, both of which further aid ID. Roth's is a northern species found in waterside vegetation.

D. Tyler's Tree Frog *Litoria tyleri* **4.3–5 cm/1.7–2 in.**
Tyler's differs from Roth's in showing less extensive black-and-yellow markings on the posterior of the thighs, and has a uniform gold iris, lacking the red upper half displayed by Roth's. Tyler's also lacks the black line around the tympanum that both Peron's and Roth's possess. A coastal eastern species found in eucalypt forest around permanent waters, from se. QLD south to s. NSW.

E. Lesueur's Frog *Litoria lesueuri* **3–7 cm/1.2–1.8 in.**
Very similar e. QLD and n. NSW form is sometimes split as **Wilcox's Frog** (*L. wilcoxii*). Similar in structure to Jungguy Frog (long hind limbs and extensively webbed toes, but *unwebbed* fingers) and similarly colored (brownish with a dark line running from the snout through the eye down to the hind limbs), with which it is also sometimes considered the same species. However, Lesueur's differs in the pattern on the posterior surface of the thighs: black, spotted with blue.

F. Jungguy Frog *Litoria jungguy* **3.1–7.1 cm/1.2–2.8 in.**
Patterned similarly to closely related Lesueur's Frog, with a dark line running from the eye down the flanks, although differing in the pattern on the rear of the hind limbs: in Jungguy the black is peppered with cream, not blue, spots. Lacks webbing on the fingers, although it is present on the toes. A rainforest species confined to ne. QLD, from the Atherton Tablelands to Tully.

A. Green Tree Frog *Litoria caerulea* **7–11 cm/2.8–4.3 in.**
A distinctive, large, pudgy, bright green frog. Brown to bright green above, some-times with sporadic white spotting; a white underside; and the characteristic large circular pads at the end of the digits common to arboreal frogs. Has distinctive horizontal black iris slits. It is found across all of northern Australia and in the east south to c. NSW, where it favors canopies and damp cool areas, and is famed for turning up in outback toilets and showers.

B. Eastern Dwarf Tree Frog *Litoria fallax* **25–30 cm/9.5–11.5 in.**
A slender tree frog that ranges from bronzy to bright green in coloration on the upperparts, with a white underside, a black line running from the snout through the eye to the shoulder, and vivid orange coloration on the rear of the thighs. It is a slim and long-legged tree frog, with lengthy hind limbs, broad toe pads, and exten-sive webbing between the toes. An eastern, coastal species, found in vegetation around permanent waters (e.g., reeds), from Cairns (QLD) south to c. NSW.

C. Striped Marsh Frog *Limnodynastes peronii* **5–7 cm/2–3 in.**
A distinctively patterned wetland species: brown above with bold black longitudi-nal stripes running down the back, usually broken up by a contrastingly white midline. A large black mask covers the eye and is usually bordered beneath by a paler yellow line. It is a terrestrial species and therefore lacks any noticeable web-bing between the digits, and possesses shorter hind limbs than arboreal frogs. Commonly found around permanent wetlands, such as suburban ponds and town parks, along most of the east coast.

D. Rocket Frog *Litoria nasuta* **3.5–6.5 cm/1.5–2.5 in.**
Although variably colored, from yellowish brown to dull brown, it can usually be readily identified by its structure: Rocket Frog has extremely long hind legs (and toes), giving it a triangular shape from above, and has a distinctive line of dark warts down the back. Generally also displays a broad dark line running from the snout through the eye, which breaks up into blotches on the flanks. Found within open forest and woodland in northern and coastal eastern Australia.

E. Great Barred Frog *Mixophyes fasciolatus* **6–9 cm/2.5–3.5 in.**
A brownish forest frog, with scattered dark markings, distinctly barred legs, and a solid black line running from the snout through the eye and curling around behind the tympanum. There are distinctive black triangular markings on the posterior surface of the thighs. The feet are webbed, though the hands are not, with only small pads. It also possesses large eyes that are set high on the head. Occurs along creeks within rainforest, beech forest, and eucalypt forest, in montane areas of the central coast of eastern Australia (e.g., Lamington NP).

F. Cane Toad *Bufo marinus* **10–23 cm/4–9 in.**
A familiar frog and pest species, disastrously introduced from Hawaii to control the Cane Beetle from affecting the sugarcane crop. Its presence has been devastat-ing for native wildlife, as venomous glands on the toad have poisoned predatory animals that preyed on it, and it has also ferociously outcompeted other native amphibians. The size and warty nature of the adult make it unmistakable in its range, which is currently from NT south around to Brisbane, although it is contin-uously expanding its range.

REPTILES

A. Northern Snapping Turtle *Elseya dentate* **27–35 cm/10.5–13.5 in.**
A large-headed freshwater turtle (unrelated to snapping turtles of the Americas) with distinctive bumps known as *tubercles* along the head and neck. The carapace is often significantly wider at the rear than at the front. Generally herbivorous, this species occurs in rivers across the tropical north of Australia, where they sometimes bask on logs above the water, often revealing their presence only when they are disturbed, and a loud splash is heard as they flee.

B. Snake-necked Turtle *Chelodina longicollis* **30–35 cm/12–13.5 in.**
Within a group of eight long-necked turtles, from which it differs in the striking coloration of the underside of the shell: the segments are outlined with a thick black border that contrasts strongly with the pale background color. An eastern species found in inland and coastal lakes, rivers, and billabongs from se. QLD around to se. SA. When alarmed can emit a powerful-smelling liquid.

C. Gould's Goanna *Varanus gouldii* **1.2–1.6 m/4–5 ft**
Also known as Sand Monitor. **Monitors** are a group of huge carnivorous lizards that walk with a distinctive swagger and regularly flick out their thick, distinctly forked tongues. Gould's is variably colored from pale to dark, and boldly patterned with extensive dark and pale spotting. The tail is similarly patterned, although it is unmarked and pale on the final third. There is a clearly defined black line behind the eye. Gould's is a widespread terrestrial monitor inhabiting gorges and open sandy environments across most of the continent except for the wet coastal regions.

D. Lace Monitor *Varanus varius* **1.2–2.1 m/4–6.5 ft**
A massive arboreal monitor. Variably gray to bluish with pale spots over the upperparts, often arranged in rows. The tail is banded blackish and cream, and the bands become broader toward its tip. A distinct "Bell's" form occurs in dry areas of QLD and NSW that displays broad blackish and cream bands across the whole body. All forms show distinct black and yellow bands under the chin. Lace Monitor occurs in wooded and forested habitats in eastern Australia, from e. QLD around to se. SA.

E. Black-headed Monitor *Varanus tristis*
Also called Freckled Monitor. An arboreal monitor that ranges in color from reddish brown to blackish, and shows distinctive pale rings with dark centers scattered across the body. In some populations the head and neck are dark and unmarked, as is the tail (except for pale rings around the base), while other populations show freckled patterning continuing onto both the tail and head. In all individuals there are enlarged scales on the top of the head that are noticeably larger than the scales above the eyes. It occurs in wooded areas with rocky outcrops, widely throughout all of northern and central Australia.

A. Northern Knob-tailed Gecko *Nephurus sheai* 8.9–12.5 cm/3.5–5 in.

Knob-tailed Geckos are a group of nocturnal geckos readily identified by their odd shape: large headed with short, broad-based tails that taper suddenly at the tip into a circular knob, quite unlike any that of other Australian reptile. Northern has rose-shaped white patches scattered across its limbs, banded digits, and a very short, stunted tail. It is found in rocky areas of northern Australia, (nw. NT and ne. WA only).

B. Asian House Gecko *Hemidactylus frenatus* 7.5–15 cm/3–6 in.

An introduced Asian species that inhabits houses, where it can be found foraging on walls, and draws attention to itself by its regular, loud "chack-chak-chak" call. A small, flattened gecko, with widely padded feet, and a tail that displays a series of spiny projections. House Geckos are currently found patchily in northern and eastern Australia (including within Darwin).

C. Fat-tailed Gecko *Diptodactylus conspicillatus* 7.5–10.5 cm/3–4 in.

A gecko with a strange, swollen tail that is roundish and distinctly flattened, with a bumpy upper surface covered with coils of enlarged scales. The digits are especially long, lacking the wide padded toes of many geckos. It can further be identified by close inspection of the snout: the rostral scale is not connected to the nostrils. Variably colored, generally pale bodied with scattered dark markings across the entire body. A dry-country species, absent from the wet coastal areas, found from w. WA around the top of the continent to n. NSW. Hunts termites and rests in spider holes, where it uses its bloated tail to block the entrance.

D. Marbled Velvet Gecko *Oedura marmorata* 13–18 cm/5–7 in.

Velvet geckos are a group of species with strikingly patterned bodies that are covered with many smooth tiny scales, giving them a velvety textured appearance. Marbled is variably patterned darkish purple/brownish and marbled with various white markings that often take the form of five to six bands across the body between the neck and the thighs. The tail shape is variable: thick and flat in some populations, and round and slim in others, making coloration the best means of ID. It is arboreal, found in wooded environments, and prefers rocky areas, in inland Australia (NT and w. QLD and NSW), but is absent from wet coastal regions.

E. Thorny Devil *Moloch horridus* 15-20 cm/6-8 in.

One of the most spectacularly odd reptiles in Australia: covered all over with prominent thorns or spines, and displays a particularly large hump on the nape. The unique shape of this extraordinary reptile makes it easy to ID. Strikingly patterned over its entire body with bold reddish brown, tan, and white markings. Thorny Devil is a dry-country dragon species found in sandy desert regions of central Australia that feeds only on ants, often taking thousands in a single meal.

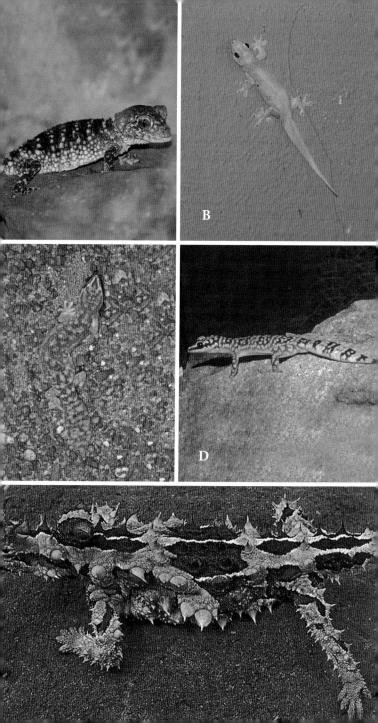

A. Water Dragon *Physignathus lesueurii* 60–90 cm/23.5–35.5 in.
Dragons are diurnal lizards with an upright posture, many of which are decorated with spines, which form spectacular crests or beards in some species. Water Dragon is a large lizard that is the only riparian dragon and therefore is the only one likely to be seen swimming. It possesses a crest of spines that runs from the nape down the back. A coastal eastern species found from Cooktown (QLD) south to e. VIC, with two isolated populations in c. QLD and e. SA.

B. Eastern Bearded Dragon *Pogona barbata* 35–60 cm/14–23.5 in.
A large lizard with a distinctive beard of spines, a further row of spines running down the flanks, and a prominent, arc-shaped set of spines across the nape. It has a conspicuous yellow gape. Found within eucalypt forests and woodlands in coastal eastern and southern Australia, to around Adelaide (SA).

C. Frilled Lizard *Chlamydosaurus kingii* 75–92 cm/29.5–36 in.
One of the most dramatic Australian lizards, with a spectacular neck frill that it raises in display while opening its gape and hissing impressively. This huge frill (up to 30 cm/12 in. wide) encircles the entire head and neck, and is so large that it is evident even when folded, extending noticeably behind the head. It is generally arboreal, though comical if disturbed on the ground, when it runs upright on its hind limbs, fleeing for the sanctuary of the nearest tree. Frilled Lizard is found in northern and eastern Australia, from n. WA east to n. QLD, and south to below Brisbane, where it inhabits eucalypt forest, woodlands, and tropical savanna.

D. Northern Water Dragon *Amphibolurus temporalis* 35–45 cm/14–17.5 in.
Two extremely similar dragons confined to the tropical north of Australia, this species and **Gilbert's Dragon** (*A. gilberti*) are both diurnal, arboreal species with long tails, long limbs, a single prominent ridge of nuchal spines, and a broad white band running from the snout to the flanks. These species may be inseparable in the field, without examining fine, near-microscopic features. However, Northern Water Dragon favors pandanus and paperbark swamps, while Gilbert's is more variable in its habitat preferences but often prefers eucalypt woodland and rocky areas. Gilbert's also has the distinctive habit of raising its forelimbs, the origin of the name "Ta-ta Lizard".

E. Burn's Dragon *Amphibolurus burnsi* 50 cm/19.5 in.
Together with Gilbert's and Northern Water Dragons in a complex of similar, long-tailed, long-limbed lizards that possess a keel of spines on the nape and along the midline of the back, and rows of spines running parallel to the vertebral crest. They all also show a variable pale band running along the side of the face that extends conspicuously down the flanks. Burn's differs from Gilbert's and Northern Water Dragons, though, in exhibiting sporadic spines on the thighs, with a distinct line of these on the back end of the thighs. Burn's is an inland species, found in open woodlands and along waterways in sw. QLD and nw. NSW.

C

E

A. Ring-tailed Dragon *Ctenophorus caudicinctus* **25–32 cm/9.5–12.5 in.**
Ring-tailed Dragon is from a group of small dragons characterized by a line of spines that curve beneath the eyes. Ring-tailed possesses a short crest of nuchal spines and is variably colored, generally pale with a variety of dark spotting and banding. The tail is usually boldly marked with broad bands. A dry-country species, found in rocky, arid areas of north and central Australia.

B. Pink-tongued Skink *Cyclodomorphus gerrardii* **35–45 cm/14–17.5 in.**
A large, pale (pinkish brown to gray), big-headed skink that usually has bold black bands across the body and its long prehensile tail. Adults display a black patch on the tip of the snout. Only adults have pink tongues; juveniles have blue tongues and a pale snout. Most likely to be confused with blue-tongued skinks, which have shorter tails and stunted legs, are thicker bodied and have proportionally larger heads, and blue tongues. Furthermore, Pink-tongued Skink's head is more clearly delineated from the body. An eastern species found in wet coastal areas of eastern Australia that is most frequently observed after heavy rains when it emerges to hunt slugs and snails.

C. Eastern Blue-tongue *Tiliqua scincoides* **45–60 cm/17.5–23.5 in.**
A large, thick-headed skink, with a variably colored body, though generally pale colored, with prominent darker broad bands across the entire body. Compared with Pink-tongued Skink, it is bulkier and thicker set, with a larger head, and shows a shorter, broader tail, stunted legs, and a deep blue tongue that is often displayed when threatened. The head is also less distinct from the neck in this species than in Pink-tongued Skink. It is widespread in northern and eastern Australia, and occurs in most habitats.

D. Shingleback *Tiliqua rugosa* **30.5–45.5 cm/12–18 in.**
A robust, large-headed skink that displays a distinctive stumpy tail that imitates the head end. It is heavily armored, with large, ridged scales. Although variably colored, from pale and heavily banded to plain uniform brownish, and possessing a blue tongue, Shinglebacks (or "Stumpy-tails") are always identifiable by their unique tail. It is found in arid or semiarid open areas, mallee, scrub, and eucalypt woodland, in the south, from s. WA around to sw. QLD.

A. Estuarine Crocodile *Crocodylus porosus*

The largest reptile in Australia, a fearsome predator that is DANGEROUS to humans. Two crocodile species occur in Australia: Estuarine or Saltwater and **Freshwater Crocodile** *C. johnstoni*. Estuarine is larger, with a broad snout that displays an uneven upper surface with bumps and ridges, while Freshwater is much smaller (up to 3 m/10 ft) with a smooth, narrow snout. Both species are confined to tropical Australia. Estuarine inhabits coastal and tidal rivers and estuaries, but does also occur in freshwater areas; Freshwater is found around permanent freshwater lakes and rivers, and only rarely occurs in tidal areas.

B. Burton's Snake Lizard *Lialis burtonis* 30–60 cm/12–23.5 in.

An odd, legless lizard that looks like a snake, with a long, sinuous body, long, attenuated snout, and no visible limbs. It differs from snakes in having movable eyelids, ear openings, and an unforked tongue, and shows indistinct flaps where the hindlimbs formerly were. It is very widespread, occurring in most habitats, and is absent only from the far south coast of the mainland and TAS.

C. Jacky Lizard *Amphibolurus muricatus* 25–35 cm/9.5–13.5 in.

A dragon characterized by five spiny crests, especially prominent on the nape, and down the midline of the back. Ranges from gray to dark brown, with variable black markings along the vertebral region, usually broken up with pale markings that often form two distinct lines on either side of the midline. There are scattered spines across the thighs, too. The gape is conspicuously yellow. Found coastally, from se. QLD to se. SA, where it inhabits eucalypt forest, woodland, and heathland.

D. Eastern Striped Skink *Ctenotus robustus* 22–30 cm/8.5–11.5 in.

Skinks are the most diverse group of Australian reptiles, with this species coming from a group called **Striped Skinks** that comprise over a hundred species of small, long-tailed skinks that show boldly striped bodies and conspicuous ear openings, and have microscopic features like raised scales at the rim of the ear, which define them. It is strikingly marked, displaying a prominent black stripe along the midline from nape to tail, outlined with thinner white stripes on both sides, and pale white flank lines run from the eye to the tail. Widespread in eastern and northern Australia, in a range of habitats.

E. Common Dwarf Skink *Menetia greyii* 6–9 cm/2.5–3.5 in.

A tiny skink from a group characterized by the structure of the digits: four on the forelimbs and five on the hindlimbs. Dwarf skinks lack obvious ear openings and lobules. Heavily striped, usually showing a bold black stripe along the flank from the head to the tail, which is often bordered below with a shorter white stripe running from the head to the tail. Very wide ranging across most of the continent except for the wetter coastal regions east of the Great Dividing Range. A terrestrial species that inhabits many dry habitats.

A. Common Tree Snake *Dendrelaphis punctulata* **1–1.5 m/3.5–5 ft**

Long and thin, with a small head, big eyes, and a ridge running down either side. The color varies from green (eastern Australia) to brownish, black, or blue (c. QLD) to golden yellow with a dark head (northern Australia), and is usually yellow on the underside. It is arboreal and NONVENOMOUS, and is regularly found around habitations. When threatened, it can produce a strong odor and raise its scales to reveal blue skin beneath. Common coastally in many habitats from n. WA around to n. NSW.

B. Brown Tree Snake *Boiga irregularis* **1–2m/3.5–6.5ft**

A distinctive, long, thin, arboreal snake with a bulbous head that is much broader than the slender neck and body behind. It has massive eyes with distinctive pupils that form narrow black vertical slits. There are two distinct forms: the northern form, known as "Night Tiger" (n. WA, n. NT, and w. QLD), is extremely boldly patterned with a creamy body and reddish bands along the entire length; the eastern form (coastally from e. QLD south to NSW) is brownish, with darker bands across the body, and a pale pinkish underside. Mildly VENOMOUS, although not dangerous.

C. Bandy-bandy *Vermicella annulata* **50–75 cm/19.5–29.5 in.**

A slim snake, boldly banded black and white across the entire body, unlikely to be confused with any other. A nocturnal, burrowing species that hunts blind snakes. Bandy-bandy occurs in nearly all habitats in northern and eastern Australia. VENOMOUS, although not dangerous.

D. Orange-naped Snake *Furina ornate* **60–70 cm/23.5–27.5 in.**

A slender, boldly patterned snake. Reddish brown to dull orange in color, with a reticulated body and contrastingly patterned head: black with a broad orange nuchal band segregating the black head from the black nape. Similarly-patterned Red-naped Snake-bold (*F. diadema*) is smaller with a less extensive, red-colored band on the nape. Orange-naped occurs in woodlands, shrubs and grasslands in northern Australia, while Red-naped is confined to the east, where it occurs in many habitats. Both are VENOMOUS, although not dangerous.

E. Carpet Python *Morelia spilota* **2–4 m/6.5–13 ft**

A large, boldly patterned, NONVENOMOUS constrictor that is the only widespread python species in Australia, and the most often encountered. Coloration is variable with a number of forms recognized, although all are strikingly marked: central forms are reddish brown, patterned with paler, irregular blotches; in the southeast it is olive colored with a regular pattern of pale diamond-shaped blotches across the body, known as "Diamond Python"; in the west (sw. WA) it is dark blackish/greenish brown with long, stretched-out pale areas, outlined in black, which give it a very contrasting look.

F. Black-headed Python *Aspidites melanocephalus* **1.5–2.5 m/5–8.5 ft**

A very distinctive nocturnal constrictor (NONVENOMOUS), easily identified by the unique combination of boldly banded body (varying from cream to brownish with dark banding) and a solid black head and neck. A northern species, occurring from n. WA eastward to n. QLD, where it occurs in woodlands, heathlands, and shrubby areas.

A. Taipan *Oxyuranus scutellatus* 2–3 m/6.5–10 ft

The first four species are very similar large, plain snakes that are all DANGEROUS, aggressive, and VENOMOUS, and should *never* be approached. Taipan's head is long and narrow, but distinct from the neck, with large eyes, and an angular brow that gives it a stern expression. Ranges from plain and pale to dark brownish with a paler, creamy ventral surface and snout. Taipan occurs coastally in woodlands, monsoon forests, and eucalypt forests in the north.

B. Eastern Brown Snake *Pseudonaja textilis* 1.5–2.5 m/5–8 ft

A large, DANGEROUS, VENOMOUS, plain-colored snake that varies from fawn to dark brown or blackish. The head is narrow with relatively large eyes, although the head of this species is slimmer still than Taipan's and is barely distinct from the neck. Juveniles can be patterned with a black head and a black band behind the neck, and are sometimes banded over the entire body. An aggressive, much-feared species that when threatened, forms an upright S and can strike swiftly and repeatedly. It is common in eucalypt forest, heath, tropical savanna, agricultural lands, and suburban areas of the east.

C. King Brown Snake *Pseudechis australis* 1.5–2.5 m/5–8 ft

Also known as Mulga Snake, it is a massive DANGEROUS and VENOMOUS snake, similar in appearance to Taipan and Eastern Brown: generally plain, varying from pale brown to dark brown to blackish. Unlike those species it has a broader, more distinct head and relatively small eyes. King Brown occurs across much of the continent, in a variety of habitats from monsoon forests to deserts and open woodlands, and is absent only from the far south.

D. Eastern Tiger Snake *Notechis scutatus* 1.2–1.7 m/4–5.5 ft

A large VENOMOUS, DANGEROUS snake, variably colored from pale olive to blackish, that sometimes has a series of bold, creamy yellow tiger stripes, while other individuals are uniformly patterned. A broad-bodied and thick-headed species, with a barely discernible neck between the broad head and wide body. Tiger Snake is a southern species. It also occurs on TAS. Tiger Snake generally prefers wet environments such as swamps and alongside waterways, but also occurs in grasslands in some areas.

E. Common Death Adder *Acanthophis antarcticus* 70–100 cm/27.5–39.5 in.

Death Adders are a group of DANGEROUS VENOMOUS distinctively shaped snakes with short stout bodies; large heads; and *a strange, short tail that ends when it suddenly tapers into a thin spine*. They vary in coloration from reddish to grayish. Species can largely be identified by range: **Common** (*antarcticus*) occurs in rainforests, shrubby areas, and heaths in e. Australia from QLD to coastal NSW, with another southern population (s. WA and s. SA); Northern-bold (*A. Praelongus*) occurs in north; Desert-bold (*A. pyrrhus*) in the western deserts; and Pilbarra-bold (*A. wellsi*) in the Pilbarra of WA.

F. Red-bellied Black Snake *Pseudechis porphyriacus* 1.5–2 m/5–6.5 ft

A familiar DANGEROUS, VENOMOUS snake with a unique coloration: blackish above, with a pale reddish pinkish underside, most strongly marked on the side, making it easily recognized. Found within wet coastal areas of eastern and southern Australia, from Cape York (QLD), to se. SA. Most often observed sunning itself around the edges of pools and marshes.

B

ABBREVIATIONS

c. central

cm centimeter

e. east, eastern

F female

ft foot

H height

ID identify, identifying, identification

in. inch

kg kilogram

L length

lb pound

m meter

M male

mm millimeter

n. north, northern

ne. northeast, northeastern

NSW Australian state of New South Wales

NP National Park

NT Australia's Northern Territory

nw. northwest, northwestern

QLD Australian state of Queensland

s. south, southern

SA Australian state of South Australia

se. southeast, southeastern

sw. southwest, southwestern

TAS the island of Tasmania

VIC Victoria

w. west, western

WA Australian state of Western Australia

GLOSSARY

Australasia A geographic region comprising Australia, New Zealand, New Guinea, and associated islands.

Banksia A genus of native Australian plants with characteristic brightly colored conelike inflorescences. Many of these are important food sources for nectar-eating birds such as White-cheeked Honeyeater, and seeds are important for some parrot species. The dominant genus in heathlands.

Brigalow An Australian habitat and type of open woodland with a good mix of acacia, cypress pine, and eucalypt trees. Typically has a number of "malleeform" trees, which are multistemmed; each grows out from the base.

Carapace The shell of a turtle.

Conspecific Considered part of the same species.

Constrictor A group of snakes that kill their prey by coiling their body around it and suffocating it by continually tightening their grip.

Cryptic As in cryptically colored, i.e., an animal camouflaged with colors that blend in well with its surroundings.

Dewlap Flap of loose skin under the throat, e.g., displayed by Brolgas (a crane species).

Dihedral The V shape formed by the wings of a bird.

Dimorphic Having two distinct forms; e.g., some birds have sexually dimorphic color forms: males and females are differently colored.

Diurnal Active by day.

Dorsal Pertaining to the back; e.g., the dorsal surface of a skink refers to the upper surface, *including* the back.

Eclipse A dull-colored plumage acquired by males of some birds after the breeding season. Especially notable in ducks and fairywrens.

Endemic Confined to a certain area (e.g., Australian endemic means confined to Australia).

Eremophila A genus of native Australian trees that includes Fuchsia Bush, many of which are pollinated by birds, most notably honeyeaters and woodswallows.

Frugivorous Fruit-eating, e.g., frugivorous birds indicates birds that eats fruit.

Frontal shield A hardened or fleshy area of a bird's forehead that extends down to the bill, such as in some gallinules, like coots and moorhens.

Gallery Forest Thicker forest that lines watercourses in an otherwise more open habitat.

Gape The opening of the mouth, e.g., the inside of a bird's mouth.

Gorget An area of shining feathers on the chin or throat of a bird, such as displayed by Victoria's Riflebird.

Gregarious Living in groups.

Grevillea A genus of native Australasian flowers, important to nectar-eating birds; mainly small bushes, although some occur as large trees, such as the Silky-Oak.

Jarrah A type of eucalyptus tree, or woodland dominated by this WA species.

Karri A form of wet sclerophyll forest in WA, dominated by this massive species of eucalypt tree.

Lobules Lobelike protrusions often found in reptiles.

Local Confined to certain areas.

Mallee A southern Australian habitat made up of specific Eucalypt species that have a distinctive multistemmed structure; the trunks separate near ground level.

Mandible Section of a bird's bill (beak); can refer to either the upper or lower section.

Mangrove An intertidal wooded habitat with a muddy substrate, found around the north and east coasts of Australia.

Mantle The area on the upper surface of a bird between the nape and the back.

Monsoon Forest Humid tropical forest found in the extreme north of Australia that occurs where there are marked wet and dry seasons; leaves drop during the dry season.

Mulga An Australian habitat; an open form of semiarid scrubland and woods associated with certain acacia species, notably Gray Mulga; an important habitat within inland Australia for birds such as Mulga Parrot and Hall's Babbler.

Nape The back of the neck of an animal.

Nocturnal Active by night.

Nuchal crest A crest on the nape, often observed in reptiles such as dragons.

Old World Geographic region comprising Africa, Asia, and Europe.

Pandanus A genus of palmlike plants that are actually unrelated to them.

Paperbark A group of untidy-looking, conspicuously tattered, native Australian trees within the genus *Melaleuca* that display characteristic flaky bark that appears to have been partially peeled off.

Pelagic Ocean dwelling, e.g., albatrosses are pelagic birds that spend most of their lives at sea.

Pied Colored black-and-white.

Plumage Entire covering of feathers over a bird's body.

Rostrum The jaw of a whale.

Rump Area on an animal between the tail and the back.

Scapulars An area of feathers located around the shoulders of a bird.

Sclerophyll Eucalypt woodland.

Shorebird Species of long-legged waterbirds from the following families: Oyster-catchers, Plovers, Sandpipers, and Stilts and Avocets. In Europe these are alternatively called "waders."

Subterminal The penultimate, e.g., the subterminal band near but not at the very tip of the tail

Sympatric Occupying the same geographic range, as when two species occur together.

Talon Sharp claws possessed by raptors and owls.

Tassie A term used for the island of Tasmania.

Terrestrial Ground-dwelling.

Tropical Savanna A sparsely wooded area comprising eucalypt trees and with an extensive grassy understory.

Tubercle Projection seen on the bodies of reptiles or amphibians.

Tympanum Ear opening visible as a pad on the head of amphibians and reptiles.

Underwing coverts The underside of a bird's wing extending from the armpit to the bend of the underwing.

Vent The area below the belly, toward the underside of the tail base, that surrounds the anus of a bird.

Ventral Referring to the lower surface, e.g., the ventral surface of a skink is the belly.

Vertebral Around the spinal column.

Wandoo A type of eucalyptus tree or woodland dominated by this species in WA.

Wing linings The underwing coverts of a bird.

FURTHER READING

Cogger, H. G. *Reptiles and Amphibians of Australia*. New Holland.

Menkhorst, P., & Knight, F. *A Field Guide to the Mammals of Australia. Third Edition*. Oxford University Press.

Morcombe, M. *Field Guide to Australian Birds*. Steve Parish Publishing.

Onley, D., & Scofield, P. *Albatrosses, Petrels, & Shearwaters of the World*. Princeton University Press.

Pizzey, G., & Knight, F. *The Field Guide to the Birds of Australia. Eighth Edition*. Harper Collins.

Shirihai, H., & Jarrett, B. *Whales, Dolphins, and Other Marine Mammals of the World*. Princeton University Press.

Simpson, K., & Day, N. *Birds of Australia. Eighth Edition*. Princeton University Press.

Slater, Peter, Slater, Pat, & Slater, Raoul. *The Slater Field Guide to Australian Birds. Second Edition*. New Holland.

Swan, G. *A Photographic Guide to Snakes and Other Reptiles of Australia*. New Holland.

Thomas, R., Thomas, S., Andrew, D., & McBride, A. *The Complete Guide to Finding the Birds of Australia*. Csiro Publishing.

Tyler, M. J., & Knight, F. *Field Guide to the Frogs of Australia*. Csiro Publishing.

Wilson, S., & Swan, G. *A Complete Guide to Reptiles of Australia. Third Edition*. New Holland.

ABOUT THE AUTHORS

Iain Campbell
Iain grew up in Evans Head in New South Wales and spent his youth chasing wildlife all over the continent, and quickly became an obsessive birder. In 1999 after an extended sojourn living in West Africa he moved to Ecuador and opened Tandayapa Bird Lodge. Since then he has established Tropical Birding, an international, global tour company, which has brought him back regularly to guide tours through his native Australia. Iain now resides in Quito with his wife, Cristina, and children, Gabriel and Amy.

Sam Woods
Sam grew up in Surrey, England, where the influences of David Attenborough and schoolboy friends soon nurtured an avid interest in nature and birds in particular, after a chance encounter with a pair of Blue Tits in a London park. Since graduating in Environmental Science he turned his interests toward global birding and wildlife watching, which led to a career working as a tour leader with Tropical Birding. He now resides in Ecuador, although spends his professional and personal life crisscrossing the globe in search of wildlife, which has led him to Australia on numerous occasions over the last six years.

PHOTO CREDITS

All photos in the book were by the authors, except the following:
Steve Arlow 54D, 68A, 88C, 94A, 102D, 112C, 130A, 174A, 200B, 224A, 240C
Nick Athanas 20A, 136C, 168C
Keith Barnes 9B, 102C, 126B, 128D, 182A, 202A, 226C, 228B, 242B
Ken Behrens 42B, 64A
Adrian Boyle 38B, 186C, 202C, 254C
Simon Buckell 100B, 100C, 104A
Rohan Clarke 26A, 46A, 96D, 124A, 156A, 182C, 220A, 254D, 254E, 262C, 264B
Lee Dingain 42A
Hugh Harrop 42D
Geoff Jones 192D
Nick Lesberg 36B, 36D, 66A, 68C, 90A, 96B, 96C, 112A, 114B, 184B, 196B, 214A, 244D, 248A, 248C, 248D, 248E, 248F, 250B, 250C, 250D, 250E, 250F, 252B, 256C
Alan McBride 60D, 72B, 72C, 88A, 136B
Brett Taylor 252D, 252E, 262F, 264F
Steve Wilson 262D, 264A, 264E

INDEX

Boldface indicates plates

282